LANSING'S YOUNG ARCHITECTS

WILLIAM APPLEYARD

R. ARTHUR BAILEY

AND FREDERICK THOMAN

JAMES MACLEAN

SOLOVERSO PRESS

PUBLISHER

❧DEDICATION❧

Solo MacBreed 2005-2016

I know it is customary to dedicate a book to a loved one or a group of people, but this book is dedicated to our Siberian Husky, Solo, the namesake of SoloVerso. She was named Solo, not for Hans Solo as many people believed, but because she was the only one of her litter to survive childbirth, hence the name Solo. She had a difficult life, before she came to us, her vocal cords were cut and she lived outdoors in a kennel with little human contact. Given her history you would have expected a difficult dog, but she wasn't; she was tender with everyone she met, especially children. The image above was one I took the day she had her stitches out after her first surgery, she was so happy. Unfortunately, Solo's small intestine was racked with cancer, so on the day of the first big snowfall in Lansing in December of 2016, Solo passed away. She so loved the snow.

❧CONTENTS❧

❧PREFACE❧

I started this book with some apprehension as my previous book brought unsolicited comments from family, friends and colleagues that were interesting. Many felt that my next book should be on a topic that had more popular interest. I have to tell you that I thought long and hard about this, but I enjoy writing on topics that no one else has. There is something to be said about being first. As Finley A. Hooper, a wise old professor, and my advisor, told me a long time ago, 'you need to write on subjects that are available to you'. Therefore, I have concentrated on topics concerning Lansing, Michigan, which are somewhat obscure but available to me. One of the interesting aspects of Lansing history that I have found is the relationships between many of the early settlers of the area. I was particularly struck by the role James Appleyard played in mentoring his son William and his daughter-in-law's brother, R. Arthur Bailey, as architects and contractors. It is also intriguing that the 1896 Lansing City Directory listed Fred Thoman as boarding at 113 N. Walnut, the home of James Appleyard. Fred would have been about 27 in 1896 and may have been working with James before 1896; the sources are unclear. This book is an attempt to discover the influence of James Appleyard on these three men; William Appleyard, R. Arthur Bailey and Fred Thoman and to chart the history of their works.

❧ACKNOWLEDGEMENTS❧

So now you are going to be hit with a long list of people I need to thank for their assistance in the research of this book. You may find this boring, but I do not. Writing a book is a long and difficult task, however it is made easier because the people and organizations listed below have a commitment to history, which makes the task of the researcher easier. Simply said they all have been fantastic! I have worked on a variety of projects with Craig Whitford, 'Mr. Lansing' as he is known in some circles, and have bounced questions and ideas off him for years. Timothy Bowman who as always was willing to help me whatever the question. The Historical Society of Greater Lansing, led by Bill Castanier, has been a fantastic support. Valerie R. Marvin, the State Capitol Historian, has been patient with my inquiries especially with the bizarre questions I would ask. Special thanks to Matt Pacer at the Library of Michigan and Whitney Miller archivist at Michigan State University Archives for responding to my requests by email no matter the time of day. Susan Wineberg, co-author of Historic Ann Arbor: An Architectural Guide, graciously answered questions regarding Ann Arbor history. Courtney Beattie, of the Ypsilanti Historical Society, Steve Wejroch, Archivist for the Archdiocese of Detroit, Tom Vajdik, Local History Librarian at Winsor Public Library, Elaine Shilstut, librarian at the Presbyterian Historical Society, Angela Kindig, Assistant

Archivist University of Notre Dame Archives, Pamela Spoor, Head of Reference Services Manistee County Library, Lisa Conathan, Head of Special Collections Williams College Libraries, Keith Kerr, Archives Specialist National Archives and Records Administration and Linda Moore, Public Services Librarian, Hillsdale College all answered my inquiries regarding specific individuals or structures with great speed and accuracy. This demonstrates the fact that if you seek exactness and unbiased information speak to a librarian or archivist. Special thanks to Darla Baron, Perry, Michigan, Josh Rouan, Baldwin Public Library Birmingham, and Anne Rapp, Director McKay Library Augusta, Michigan, for their assistance on specific properties. They saved me a lot of travel time. Brad & Donna Pruden graciously allowed me to use their image of Lieutenant Colonel Augustus Sherwin Bement. When I had a question concerning the history of Delhi Township, Michigan, Inge Logenburg Kyler was always kind enough to provide an answer. The same can be said for Rodney Jewett and Ed Busch. Rodney possesses knowledge of certain aspects of the history of Ingham County and Ed answered queries regarding the history of the Universalist Church of Lansing. Finally, Win Stebbins answered questions on a variety of topics with a grace that few individuals have. Doug Johnson for his help on Usa Forrester. A huge thank you goes out to Michael Walter for his help in acquiring photographs of structures in Detroit. There were several other libraries and organizations who assisted in my research or provided the images in the book. The Department of Special Collections and University Archives, W.E.B. Du Bois Library, University of Massachusetts Amherst; Historic Preservation Commission of South Bend & St. Joseph County, Indiana; Grand Rapids Public Library; Colorado State University Archives; South Dakota State University; Multnomah County Library Oregon; Special Collections and University Archives, University of Massachusetts Amherst Libraries of the use of the Fred Chester Kenney image; and the Michigan State University Archives. If I have inadvertently missed anyone the fault is mine and I apologize.

A big smile to Liz Breed, who loves me for no reason that I can discern.

There is one being not to be thanked, well one that was difficult, that is Harold our Standard Poodle, Great Pyrenees, Newfoundland puppy mixed. Harold always found the most inconvenient time to need a bone, be petted, go outside or start randomly barking. Have you ever heard a dog like this bark? But we love him, I just wish he was more like the namesake of the company.

❧AN IMPORTANT NOTE ABOUT THE SOURCES❧

When I began my research into the architectural works of William Appleyard, R. Arthur Bailey and Fred Thoman, I quickly discovered that none of the architects had left their personal or professional papers to a library or archive. That compelled me to restrict my research to the published sources, i.e. contemporary newspapers, industry publications and secondary sources. Undoubtedly Appleyard, Bailey and Thoman designed more structures than are presented in this work. Unfortunately there is no way to know what they were or where they were, there simply are no sources. So, in many ways this work can be considered a starting point for the lives of these men, with the hope that this book will generate interest in their architectural works and possibly discover other sources of information. One of the most confusing aspects of conducting research regarding Bailey's Detroit works is that the street addresses in the city changed in 1921 when Detroit adopted the Chicago Grid system, i.e. 150 Van Dyke became 650 Van Dyke. Couple these revisions with the fact that the street names in Detroit changed often and you get the perfect mix to drive a researcher over the edge. For instance, Champlain Street became East Lafayette Street. People may also wonder about the lack of street suffix's, which is easily answered because they changed over time from avenue or boulevard to street. It seemed easier to list the street name under the image and exclude the suffix. When listing the address, the modern street number is given first with the older street number listed in parentheses.

There also is the challenge that no property tax rolls for Wayne County survived. I have been unable to locate any of the property tax records for any of the Wayne County municipalities that are referenced in this work. Hopefully they are moldering away in some storage facility yet to be discovered. A list of the abbreviations of the newspaper citations are located in the bibliography. The earliest image of a structure is used in this book, no matter what the quality; current photographs are displayed when no earlier image of a structure exists. In many ways, the city of Lansing is fortunate to have the Stebbins and other real estate collections that provide images of many of the structures in the area. Unfortunately that is not that case in Detroit, where no extensive survey of homes and buildings exists. Where credit is due for an image it is noted under the image. Many of the images have been provided by private collectors who wish to remain anonymous.

Eustace Hall on the campus Michigan State University, in East Lansing, Michigan is my favorite structure designed by William Appleyard

❧INTRODUCTION❧

For a time in the late Nineteenth Century, Lansing, Michigan was the home of several young and dynamic architects. There was Earl Mead, who designed many of the vacation homes in Northwest Michigan, Edwyn Bowd who was the architect of the Michigan Agricultural College, Darius Moon who rose from obscurity to become a Lansing legend and three young architects, William Appleyard, Rufus Arthur Bailey and Fredrick Thoman. The lives of the three young architects will be examined in this work. What makes the careers of these three architects fascinating was that they were all in a sense mentored by James Appleyard a well-known contractor, and in his own right, a practical architect. In Michigan in the 19th Century, architects did not have to be licensed by the state; architects could practice their profession without regulation. The majority of the architects during this time period learned their craft by practical experience, by attending at an institute of higher education or by an apprenticeship, guided by a practicing architect. This all changed in 1915 with the enactment of Public Act of 1915, No. 120 when architects needed to be registered by the state. Of the three fledgling Lansing architects, only one continued to practice architecture, one died unexpectedly and the other choose not to continue as an architect. What follows is an account of their work as architects. There is something that needs to be stated in regard to this work. There are no papers in any archives or elsewhere that outlines the architectural work that William Appleyard, R. Arthur Bailey and Fred Thoman completed. This book is based upon citations and references. culled from a variety of sources. There is no doubt that there were more works completed by these three architects, but at this time they are yet unknown.

❧CHAPTER ONE❧

JAMES APPLEYARD

James Appleyard 1834-1896

James Appleyard, a name that is often associated with the building of the Michigan State Capitol, was also a key figure in the lives of three young Lansing architects: William Appleyard, R. Arthur Bailey and Frederick J. Thoman. James Appleyard was born in Yorkshire, England on February 24, 1834 to George and Anne (née Lynfoot) Appleyard. In 1851, James immigrated to the United States with his parents and settled in Rochester, New York. James worked as a master builder with his father, a trade James learned in England under George's guidance. In 1856, James took a position with the Nehemiah Osborn & Company of Rochester, New York where he served as Superintendent of Construction and directed the building of the Milwaukee Post Office and the Chicago Post Office. After James became a partner in the firm in 1860, he directed the construction of Baltimore's Customs House, Post Office and later Detroit City Hall.

The Capitol of the State of Michigan for which James Appleyard served as the Superintendent of Construction. (LOC)

In July 1871 James was selected as the Superintendent of Construction for the Iowa State Capitol Building, a position he relinquished in December of 1871 to focus on the Michigan State Capitol bid. Nehemiah Osborn & Company was awarded the contract for the construction of the State Capitol in Lansing, Michigan in July of 1872 and James moved to Lansing to oversee the construction. With the completion of the Capitol, the firm of Nehemiah Osborn & Company was disbanded and James decided to stay in Lansing and helped to build his adopted city.

Union Depot located at Third Avenue and Fort Street in Detroit, Michigan. The building was designed in the Romanesque Revival style by James Stewart & Company of St. Louis, Missouri. James Appleyard served as the Superintendent of Construction.

After settling in Lansing, James was Superintendent of Construction for the University of Michigan Library, the Hoyt Library in Saginaw, the Union Depot on Fort Street in Detroit and several buildings in the Lansing area. In 1884, James was asked by John V. Farwell, a Chicago millionaire and head of the Capitol Syndicate, to oversee the construction of the Texas State Capitol which was designed by Elijah E. Myers and who also was the architect for the Michigan State Capitol. James declined, due in part to Myers, with whom he was a notoriously difficult man to work. With a reputation for excellence, James also served as an expert witness for a tragedy that occurred on May 11, 1877 when the dome of the Winnebago County Courthouse collapsed killing nine men. At a coroner's inquest in Rockford, Illinois, James testified in regard to the plans of the courthouse and the methods used in its construction. (*Chicago Daily Tribune 5/18, 1877*)

Designed by architect James Anderson, with James Appleyard supervising the construction. The Detroit City Hall was considered one of the finest public buildings in the United States. The building was torn down in 1961. (LOC)

James married Miss Johanna Lysaght in 1856, the couple had three children, William P., George T., and Elizabeth Appleyard. Johanna Appleyard passed away in September 1873. Several years later James married Miss Augusta Sanborn, the couple had three children Johanna, Frances and Louis L. Appleyard. Augusta Sanborn was born in Ohio, and trained to be a teacher at Appleton College, Wisconsin. She came to Lansing in 1871 to teach at the Franklin Avenue School. After her marriage to James, Augusta became a member of the Lansing Woman's Club, President of the Hospital Association and was active in St. Mary's Church. Augusta passed away at the family home on March 19, 1921.[1]

---

[1] For Johanna see the *LRW* 9/19/1873 for Augusta see *LSJ* 3/19/1921.

The Lansing Woman's Club Building at 118 W. Ottawa, Lansing, Michigan was the last building that James Appleyard designed. In 1911 Edwyn A. Bowd was engaged by the club to design the third-floor addition.

Three of James' sons trained under him, William and George followed their father into the building business and became architects. William worked in the Lansing area and George was in Grand Rapids, Michigan, while Louis worked for the Glidden Company in Cleveland, Ohio. The last building that James designed in Lansing was the Lansing Woman's Club Building at 118 W. Ottawa in 1889, which still stands today. While supervising the construction of the Club House, James suffered a serious injury to his hip when several tons of earth pinned James against a scaffold. (*SR* 9/20/1889) This was just the start of James' medical problems. It seems the supervision of the Union Depot in Detroit took a heavy toll on James' health and in January 1893 he suffered a physical breakdown and entered St. Joseph's Retreat. In 1894 he returned to Lansing and seemed fully recovered. Just five months later James' 'mind gave away' and he returned to St. Joseph's Retreat. James Appleyard passed away at St. Joseph's Retreat in Dearborn on June 29, 1896.[2]

---

[2] *LRW* 7/2/1896, *SR* 6/30/1896, *Detroit Evening News* 6/30/1896 and *Past and Present* 222

During his life James acted as a mentor to three young architects, William P. Appleyard, Rufus Arthur Bailey and Frederick Thoman.[3] On August 17, 1876 James' son William, married Miss Mary J. Bailey who was the sister of Rufus Arthur Bailey. Through this connection Rufus Arthur Bailey came into contact with James Appleyard with whom he learned the building and architectural business. Rufus served as the Superintendent of Construction of the Lansing Post Office in 1893 after the original superintendent, James Skinner, was struck down by illness. Two years later Rufus designed his first documented building for John W. Edmonds and Charles Cannell. Frederick Thoman's relationship with James Appleyard is a bit of a mystery. Frederick junior was born in 1869 and would have started to train as a contractor/architect under James in the early 1890s. He may have worked on the construction of the Lansing Woman's Club Building on Ottawa Street in 1889. What we do know is that in the 1896 *Lansing City Directory* Frederick junior is listed as living with the Appleyard family and since the data for city directories was compiled in the previous year it is safe to say that Frederick junior was living with the Appleyard family in late 1895. Since there was no 1895 Lansing City Directory it is possible he was living with the family in 1894. Interestingly, 1894-1896 was the period that James Appleyard was at St. Joseph's Retreat receiving treatment. Neither William Appleyard or R. Arthur Bailey were in Lansing in 1894-1896, meaning that Frederick junior must have been considered a trusted family friend and colleague to assist James and his family during this difficult period.

[3] At this point it is important to remember that architects did not require a state license, in most cases their training was by apprenticeship.

✎CHAPTER TWO✎

WILLIAM P. APPLEYARD

William P. Appleyard 1857-1905

William P. Appleyard has long been forgotten in Lansing and that is tragic because at one point he had the potential to become the premier architect in Mid-Michigan. William was a mentor to young Edwyn A. Bowd, who later became the foremost Lansing architect. James Appleyard along with William also guided the early careers of Rufus Arthur Bailey and to a certain degree, Frederick Thoman. William was born in Canandaigua, New York on March 17, 1857 the son of James and Johanna (née Lysaght) Appleyard. In 1872, James moved his family to Lansing, Michigan where he served as contractor for the Michigan State Capitol. William went to public schools in New York and Detroit, then attended Notre Dame University from September 1873 to February 1874. While at Notre Dame, William studied Geography, Physiology, German, Drawing, and Piano and he left the university without a degree.[4] William's first responsibility after leaving Notre Dame University was to design the flag walks at the Michigan Capitol, undoubtedly a commission awarded by his father. After the Capitol's completion, William worked as an engineer and architect in the Lansing area.

---

[4] This little ditty about William Appleyard appeared in the Notre Dame Student paper *The Scholastic*. "It has been asked what luxury does the Collegiate Study-hall enjoy more than the others? Why, it has an Appleyard." *The Notre Dame Scholastic* 77.

William did not stay in Lansing for long. In July of 1879, he traveled to Leadville, Colorado to oversee his father's investment in a mine, which may or may not have resulted in a windfall for the family. The *Jackson Citizen Patriot* reported that James was offered $1,000,000 for his mine and it is unknown whether James accepted the bid. (*JCP* 11/13/1879) In 1880 William obtained a position in the architectural office of Milton Earl Beebe in Buffalo, New York, Beebe was an eminent architect whose early works included the Cambria County Courthouse in Ebensburg, Pennsylvania, 1880-1881 and the McKean County Courthouse in Smethport, Pennsylvania, 1880-1881.[5] Later in October of 1881, William returned to Michigan and assisted his father who was overseeing the construction of the new library at the University of Michigan. After his return to Lansing, William received several important commissions and his career as the leading architect in Lansing seemed assured. However, by 1888, William decided to leave Lansing for Minneapolis, Minnesota and sold his architectural business to Edwyn A. Bowd. (*LJ* 4/3/1888) After arriving in Minneapolis William formed a partnership with Adam Lansing Dorr, and the firm of Appleyard & Dorr was established.

"About April First Architect Wm. P. Appleyard will move to Minneapolis where he will enter into business with A. [Adam] L. Dorr, a popular architect of that city, under the firm name of Appleyard & Dorr. Mr. Appleyard is confident that he has a good thing. Already Mr. Dorr has $100,000 in unfinished work in his office and plans have been submitted by both gentlemen for the court house and city hall of that place, which if accepted will put them in a way to make a nice little bundle.[6] Edwin A. Bowd who has been in Mr. Appleyard's office for a year and who is a very competent young man will conduct the Lansing office. Mr. Appleyard's numberless friends will greatly regret his removal from Lansing" (*LJ* 3/3/1888).

Just six months after he arrived in Minneapolis, in October of 1888, William accepted a position with the McElroy Car-Heating Company while still retaining his position in the Appleyard & Dorr architectural firm. William then relocated to Chicago in 1890 and it is possible that Adam L. Dorr agreed to this change in the hope of landing architectural commissions from Chicago clients.[7] It is interesting that James F. McElroy, the owner of the McElroy Car-Heating Company, had been the superintendent of the Michigan School

---

[5] Beebe left Buffalo in 1898 and settled in Fargo, North Dakota, where he designed the Eddy County Courthouse, New Rockford, North Dakota and many other structures. Milton Earl Beebe passed away in 1922.

[6] The design contract for the Minneapolis City Hall and Hennepin County Courthouse building was awarded to Franklin B. Long and Frederick Kees, who designed an iconic building and is still in use today.

[7] James McElroy founded the McElroy Car Heating Company in 1887. In 1889 McElroy Car Heating Company merged with the Sewell Car Heating Company creating the Consolidated Car Heating Company, known today as CMP Industries. James McElroy passed away in Laconia, New Hampshire on February 10, 1915. See also *LJ* 10/5/1888 and *LJ* 10/8/1888.

for the Blind when William was hired as the architect to enlarge the Main building and design the Superintendent's Cottage for the facility. It seems that William recognized the potential of the railroad and began to ignore his architectural practice. The firm of Appleyard & Dorr existed until 1890 and undoubtedly dissolved over William's decision to accept a position with the McElroy Company.[8] William's work history between 1890 and 1904 is bewildering and at times unclear; he was employed in a variety of positions with the Pullman Company and the New York, New Haven & Hartford Railroad. It is unknown if William was still practicing as an architect during this period. On February 1, 1904 William left the New York, New Haven & Hartford Railroad to become the Superintendent of Equipment for the Pullman Company, a position he held until his death.

On August 17, 1876 William married Miss Mary J. Bailey, the daughter of prominent Lansing resident Rufus Alonzo Bailey; the couple had no children. William passed away on September 19, 1905 and his death was peculiar. William was waiting at the Sixty-Third Street Station in Chicago for his wife Mary who was returning home after a trip to Lansing. "The accident occurred at 10:30 o'clock, and there were few witnesses. Mr. Appleyard had been waiting several minutes for the arrival of the Michigan Central train bearing his wife, and as it came in sight he ran forward ready to board it. It is supposed he stumbled and fell in front of the engine. His body was badly mutilated and thrown to one side. Employees of the Illinois Central found that life was extinct." Mary Appleyard was seated at the rear of the train and was unaware that the delay was a result of the death of her husband. She left the train at Thirty-Ninth Street Station, where she expected to meet her husband. It wasn't until she arrived at her home was she made aware that her husband was struck by the train that she had been riding on (*SR* 9/20/1905).

It is quite possible that William sought to surprise his wife and travel the remainder of the journey with her, which could explain why William rushed to board the train at the Sixty-Third Street Station. The couple normally met at the Thirty-Ninth Street Station which was near their residence. William's body was returned to Lansing for burial at Mt. Hope Cemetery. Funeral services were conducted at the home of Charles W. Gilkey at 909 Jerome Street. The service was led by Reverend George B. Stocking and the pallbearers were Clarence E. Bement, John F. Crotty, Fred Shubel Jr., James P. Edmonds, Dr. Frank Shumway and J. Edward Roe, a who's who of Lansing's up and coming businessmen.[9] One other odd factor is that William's funeral was not held at the family home at 123 N. Walnut, which the family still owned.

---

[8] Dorr had a successful career as an architect designing several significant buildings in Minneapolis. Adam Lansing Dorr died in Los Angeles, California, on October 14, 1928.
[9] *LJ* 9/20/1905, *SR* 9/20/1905, *LJ* 9/21/1906, *LJ* 9/22/1905, *Chicago Daily Tribune* 9/20/1905 and the *Chicago Daily Tribune* 9/21/1905

UNIVERSITY OF MICHIGAN LIBRARY

University of Michigan Library In Ann Arbor, Michigan.

"Will Appleyard has returned from Philadelphia, and will assist his father at Ann Arbor, who has the contract for building a new library building, and other work connected with the university" (*LR* 10/4/1881).

The original plans for the library at the University of Michigan were created by the architectural firm of Ware & Van Brunt. Before the designs were approved the partnership between William R. Ware and Henry Van Brunt was dissolved. The final plans for the building was completed by the firm Van Brunt & Howe, for which they were $2,896. James Appleyard was awarded the contract for the construction of the building when his bid of $85,375 was accepted by the Board of Regents. Construction of the first library building at the University of Michigan began in 1881. The library was completed on November 22, 1883. The structure can only be described as magnificent. There were two towers, the east tower held the University clock with five bells while the west tower was ornamental. The curved reading room was built of red brick with the book delivery desk at the base of the semicircle next to the book stacks. The University's Art Collection was housed on the second floor above the book stacks, while above the reading room a semicircular gallery of paintings and sculpture was displayed. (Donnelly 1674)

Notice the circular reading room for the library with the multiple windows on two levels to allow as much natural light as possible to enter the library. (LOC)

Frank M. Howe and Henry Van Brunt were the architects for the University of Michigan Library. This was the first commission for the firm of Van Brunt & Howe. The architects went on to design the Cheyenne Union Depot in Wyoming, the Hoyt Library in Saginaw, Michigan and many other structures across the United States. The final cost of the building was in excess of $100,000. In 1898 the building was enlarged when a new book stack area was added, which allowed an increase on the size of the book collection to 200,000 volumes.

Front Elevation of the library at the University of Michigan. (LOC)

The building was of red brick with two towers, the reading room was a semi-circular structure, and the second floor housed the university's art collection. In 1915, a plan to renovate the structure was rejected because beams in the main reading room, the staircases, the roof and the framed structure of the structure were all made of wood and presented a fire hazard. The building was declared unsafe and torn down in 1918, only the 1898 fireproof stacks survived. This formed the basis for the new Central Library designed by architect Albert Kahn, known today as the Harlan Hatcher Graduate Library. What is important about William's work with his father on the library at the University of Michigan was the experience he gained in helping to manage such a large project.

MICHIGAN AGRICULTRAL COLLEGE LIBRARY

Michigan Agricultural College Library and Museum Building. (CADL/FPLA)

On May 3, 1881, the Office of the Board of Trustees and the President of the Michigan Agricultural College reviewed the plans of several architects for the new library: Lemuel D. Grosvenor, Jackson, Michigan; Scott & Company, Bay City, Michigan; John H. Fisher, Lansing, Michigan; Watkins & Arnold of Bay City, Michigan; Julius Hess and Charles H. Marsh both from Detroit. The contract was awarded to Charles H. Marsh who was paid $800 for the plans and specifications and to act as superintendent during the construction of the building.[10] He was also awarded the contract for the Chemical Laboratory addition. Charles H. Marsh died suddenly at his office in Detroit on October 8, 1881. (*DFP* 10/9/1881) Marsh was 31 years old at the time of his death due to heart disease. He passed away just after the completion of what was considered his finest work, the Church of Our Father in Detroit.[11]

---

[10] Offices of the Board of Trustees and President of the MAC, Meeting Minutes, May 3, 1881.
[11] Marsh also designed the First Congregational Church, Charlotte, Michigan and the First Congregational Church, Romeo, Michigan.

Church of our Father, Detroit, MI., designed by Charles H. Marsh.

On October 10, 1881, Mr. Appleyard was appointed to complete the construction of the library due to the death of Charles H. Marsh.[12] This may explain why W. J. Beal's *History of the Michigan Agricultural College* attributed the design of the building to both James and William Appleyard, who undoubtedly were crucial in the completion of the building. "The building for library, museum, offices of president and secretary, was designed by Messrs. Appleyard and erected in 1881" (*Beal*, 270). It is unknown to what extent James or William modified Marsh's original design.

The *Lansing Republican* published a lengthy article in February of 1882 describing the new Library and Museum at the Michigan Agricultural College; sections of the article are reproduced below.

---

[12] Offices of Board of Trustees and President, MAC, Meeting Minutes, October 10, 1881 and *LR* 2/9/1882

New College Buildings

"At the session of the legislature of 1880-81, appropriations were made for an addition to the chemical laboratory at the Agricultural college [designed by Dr. Frank S. Kedzie], and also for the erection of a building for the library and museum. Early in the spring of 1881 the state board of agriculture advertised for plans and accepted those of Charles H. Marsh of Detroit (recently deceased) for the library and museum building. The contracts for the chemical laboratory and the library and museum were let to Fuller & Wheeler of Lansing, the first for $5,800 and the second for about $22,000. They commenced work July 1, 1881 and both buildings were completed Feb. 1, 1882. On Tuesday last the board of agriculture met to inspect and accept the library and museum building. In company with Mr. Fuller the scribe also "inspected" those buildings on Tuesday afternoon. The library and museum is located on the level plat about 20 rods east of the main building, and about 15 rods northeast of the new boarding hall. The building is in the shape of a T, the one arm running north and south being 37 feet by 82 feet, and the other one 42 by 62 feet, running east and west. It consists of a basement 8 feet deep, a main story 16 feet in height, and a second story 14 feet in height, and over the main entrance a tower, the extreme point of which is 92 feet from the ground.

"The building is of red brick, with water tables, window and door caps, and sills and trimmings of cut stone. The main entrance is on the west side, by double doors, over which is a stone cap bearing the inscription, in Gothic letters "library and museum". Entering here one finds himself in a vestibule, 6½ by 13 feet in size, communicating with the interior by double doors. On the other side of these doors is a window of cathedral glass 2 by 8 feet in size, set in small squares, and over the doors a large transom. Beyond these doors is the main hall, 13 feet wide by 22 feet in length, on the north side of which rises a wide staircase, leading to the second floor. The floor in the hall tiled with white marble, bordered and dotted with red slate. At the right, and opening from the hall are two rooms, ensuite [bathroom], each 16 by 17 feet in size, connected by sliding doors, the woodwork finished in walnut grain, and well lighted with windows facing to the west and south. These are the reception room and private office of the president of the college. A door to the east side of the private office gives access to the reading room, and from thence to the library.

The original Library and Museum at Michigan Agricultural College, today known as Linton Hall. (CADL/FPLA)

"Opposite these rooms, on the north side of the hall is a room 17 by 31 feet in size, lighted by numerous windows on the north and west, and finished in the same style as those above described. This is the main office of the secretary of the board of agriculture, and it also contains a fire proof vault, 5 by 11 feet in size. Near the northeast angle of this room are double doors opening into a private office of the secretary, a room 17 by 20 feet in size, lighted from the north and east, and finished like those above-mentioned. These are the only rooms that are grained. The finish of the rest of the woodwork of the entire building is in oil, showing the natural grain of the wood. The secretary's office is connected on the south with a wash room, and through this, by narrow halls running south and east, with the main corridor and the library. In the angle caused by the junction of the east wing with the west wing, on the north side, is the private entrance to the building, designed for the use of students. It opens into a small vestibule from which a staircase leads to the second story. On the right is a small 'hoist' for conveying heavy articles to the second story and at the left is a door opening into the library.

A wonderful image of the Michigan Agricultural College Library, at the time of construction it lent a certain degree of permanence to the college, a statement that we are here to stay. (CADL/FPLA)

"Opening from the east end of the main corridor, through large double doors, is the library room, 40 feet in width by 50 feet in length, occupying nearly the entire main floor of the east wing. It is lighted from north and south by five large windows on a side. About 12 feet from the wall, on each side, and running east and west, are two rows of iron columns, eight in all, which support the floor of the second story. From each of these columns book shelves run to the wall, similar to those at the state library, and forming well lighted alcoves between. At the extreme east end is a small room, 11 by 18 feet, connected with the library by an archway, and designed for the assistant librarian. At the southwest corner of the library is a large archway affording access to the reading room.

"This room is in the shape of an L, the main wing running east and west, being 17 by 31 feet, and the short arm 12 feet square. It has two mantels and grates as well as steam radiators, and there are two in the second story. Every room is furnished with steam heating apparatus and perfect ventilation by resistors connecting with the main shaft.

"Ascending the main staircase to the second story the visitor enters from the landing, through large double doors, the museum room, which is located in the east wing, directly over the library, and is the same size—40 by 50 feet. From the floor to the wall plate the height is 14 feet, and from thence the rafters are cased in panel work to a clear story with glass slides, making the greatest height of the room 32 feet. The main roof and clear story are supported by two heavy trusses, running lengthwise, and so constructed that instead of marring the appearance of the room they are really ornamental. The middle sash on each side of the clear story are arranged as ventilators, to be opened and closed by cords. Like the library, it is well lighted by windows on two sides, besides the skylight. All the flooring on the second floor is oiled maple.

"Passing through a short hall, we find at the southeast corner, over the president's room, a model class room finished to the rafters, which are supported by trusses, giving a clear height of 19 feet. The room is 31 by 34 feet in size, rising by low platforms from the center to the walls on three sides, so that every student may have a clear view of the platform on the north side of the room. At the rear of the platform is a set of grooves in which are suspended by pulleys and weights, three blackboards for illustrations, each 11 feet long by four feet in width, and so arranged that one or all may be brought into view at a time. This room is designed for Prof. [Albert John] Cook's classes. Adjoining this room on the north is Prof. Cook's private room, 13 by 17 feet in size and, furnished with radiators, sink, ventilators, etc. It communicates with the main hall by a door on the east, and on the north with the dissecting room, 17 by 32 feet in size, and directly above the secretary's office. To the east of this, and separated by double doors, is the laboratory, 17 by 25 feet in size. All of these rooms are well lighted. Over the private entrance is a small packing room, and from this a staircase that leads to the attic and tower. The entire work on this building challenges comparison with anything of a similar character in the northwest, and established the reputation of Messrs. Fuller & Wheeler as builders, if they could point to nothing else, which is fortunately not the case.

"As sub-contractor, Charles M. Chittenden of this city [Lansing] superintended the entire mason and brick work from cellar to roof, and to say it is a good job does not cover the ground. It is a monument of neatness, strength and skill, and what might be expected from the man who supervised the masons on the state capitol. He is a thorough mechanic and has displayed the same intelligence in his department that Messrs. Fuller & Wheeler have in theirs. The slate roof, which is also a good job, was laid by C.D. Farr, formerly of this city, now in Detroit" (*LR* 2/9/1882).

A postcard view of the library at the Michigan Agricultural College. The tower rose above the campus and was the centerpiece of the college. (CADL/FPLA)

In 2019 the original Library/Museum building is known as Robert S. Linton Hall. The building has been described as designed in the High Victorian Romanesque style or as Daniel Bollman, AIA, stated in the *City Pulse* "expressing the architectural excesses of the Victorian era in embellished Romanesque details" (*CP* 2/24/2016). In a way, I agree with both descriptions, except the "architectural excesses" statement. To me this is a pleasing building that was designed and constructed during a period of growth at the Michigan Agricultural College that lent a sense of permanence to the college. People tend to forget that less than 20 years earlier the University of Michigan fought to have the Michigan Agricultural College eliminated and its curriculum transferred to the University of Michigan. As the University of Michigan President, Henry Philip Tappan stated, "It is better to have one great institution than half a dozen abortions" (*Transactions* 200), but enough about the MSU and UM rivalry and back to the building. There are two elements of the building that are very striking. The first is the massive oriel windows with the large arched pier base located on the north and south side of the T shaped building. The second is the tower. It reminds one of the substantial towers one would have observed as a battlement on a Teutonic Knight's castle in Prussia, oddly the brickwork on the library building is the same color as those used in the Teutonic Knight's castles. Michigan State University has never been strong in regard to historic preservation but Linton Hall is an example of one structure they should be commended for renovating and protecting.

UNIVERSALIST CHURCH

Universalist Church in Lansing prior to the proposed renovation. The church was located on the southeast corner of Grand Avenue and Allegan Street or 203 S. Grand. (CADL/FPLA)

"To Be Modernized. —For some time past the Universalist society has been agitating the subject of remodeling and enlarging the church edifice. Plans have been drafted and presented by William Appleyard, and on Monday the committee having the matter in charge met and decided to recommend the plans submitted by him. The old auditorium will be enlarged by taking out the inside stairway which projects into the room eight feet.

This will give room for six rows of pews. The front will be remodeled by adding a brick projection of eight feet to the west front and at the southwest corner, and the old front above this projection will be remodeled. A tower, eighty feet in height, will be placed at the northwest corner, at the foot of which is the main entrance to the auditorium, by an open porch, reached by a flight of steps and guarded by an ornamental iron gate. From this porch, a flight of stairs leads to the vestibule. The center doors lead directly to the basement, and another door at the southwest corner opens into a small porch, from which a flight of steps leads to the vestibule with a side entrance at the east leading to the basement. On the north side the old pilasters will be turned into a buttress, a pediment will be placed at the center, containing a memorial window, and all the windows will be enlarged, remodeled and filled with stained glass. The entire front will be changed to the Norman style of architecture, and if one may judge from the plans, when completed there will be no prettier church edifice for its size in Michigan. It reflects a great credit on our young townsman, Mr. Appleyard, who has already gained an excellent reputation as an architect. The estimate cost of the improvements is $5,400" (*LRW* 4/26/1882).

"On June 20, the Universalist society awarded the contracts for improvements on their church to White & Castle, at $4,840. Will Appleyard, who made the designs, will superintend the work" (*LRW* 6/28/1882).

"The Universalist church is to have a new roof, and repairs and changes in the front and vestibule. White & Castle commenced the work on Monday morning" (*LR* 5/1/1883).

Regarding the improvements to the Universalist Church, the Society's minutes outlined that there was a disagreement in the church as to whether it was prudent to just repair the church or sell the property and rebuild in another location. The church members decided to repair the church and not to expand the building. The minutes also stated that the church not only employed the services of William Appleyard during the repairs/renovation but also consulted with Israel Gillett, one of the earliest Lansing architects. William was employed to supervise the work to repair the building.[13]

---

[13] Universalist Church Minutes, 3/18/1882 to 10/14/1882. Contact the Universalist Church of Lansing for access.

REFORM SCHOOL DORMITORY

A photograph of the Reform School in Lansing, Michigan, taken from the roof of the Superintendent's residence, the dormitory cottage can be seen in the background

"New Buildings. —William Appleyard is hard at work on the working plans for the new buildings at the reform school. The dormitory cottage is in fact a double cottage, having a brick wall through the center from basement to roof. It will be located at the north end of the main building, will be 72 by 70 feet on the ground and consist of two stories and a mansard roof. The two sides will be duplicates, the ground floor containing an entry, sitting room, and schoolroom, the last 34 by 45 feet in size, and seated for 50 pupils. The second and third floors will be arranged for dormitories on the aggregate of the hospital plan. The superintendent's cottage will be located near the gate west of the new cottage on the north side of the grounds. It will be 56 by 44 feet on the ground, and two stories high. The plan is not fully worked up yet" (*LRW* 5/31/1882).

Enlargement of the Dormitory Cottage at the Reform School.

"Work at the reform school is progressing rapidly. The new cottage for the superintendent has reached the second story, the walls on the double cottage area going up rapidly, and under the careful supervision of Architect Appleyard, they will, when completed, stand as a monument to his skill and taste, and good sense of the board of control" (*LRW* 9/6/1882).

The Dormitory Cottage was designed in the Dutch Colonial Revival style of architecture with a stepped arch gable and a mansard roof. Note how the stepped arched gable with the chimneys, frame the façade and help to define the building's setbacks. There is extensive use of stone in the lintels and the sills of the windows as well as a stone water table near the base of the building. The purpose of a water table was to shed water running down the walls away from the foundation. One important note is the stacking of the windows. Add to this the double entrance and you have a symmetrical building that was appealing to the eye.

Dormitory Cottage at the Reform School known as residences 3-4.

The House of Correction for Juvenile Offenders was established in Lansing in 1855 and at its peak encompassed 300 acres which included dormitories, training workshops, a chapel, hospital, athletic facilities, an administrative building plus a working farm. In 1902, the facility held 700 boys. The organization was based upon the family system with the boys grouped in separate houses, consisting of fifty youths under the supervision of a house steward. There was also a larger group of one hundred and fifty youths accommodated in a bigger dormitory. The boys at the school were between the ages of ten and sixteen and remained at the institution until their release upon reaching the age of seventeen. The youths were taught a trade, i.e. tailoring, carpentry, shoemaking, printing, baking, or farming with the idea that they could easily find employment once they left the institution. The residents could play sports or participate in the choir and it was essential the institution acted as a boarding school with limits (Industrial School 16). Throughout the years, the Michigan House of Correction for Juvenile Offenders went through a variety of name changes, the Michigan Reform School, Boy's Reform School, Boy's Industrial School, Michigan State Industrial School for Boys, Industrial School for Boys, etc. The institution closed on January 31, 1973.

REFORM SCHOOL SUPERINTENDENT'S COTTAGE

Superintendent's Cottage at the Reform School in Lansing, Michigan.

A MODEL COTTAGE

"In August last the Republican mentioned briefly the new cottage then in the process of construction at the reform school for the superintendent and his family. It is a Queen Ann cottage, 46½ by 55½ feet on the ground with two stories and a basement, the first story being 12 feet in the clear, the second 9 feet, and above this is a high and roomy attic. The walls and ceilings are hard finished in the first and second stories, with plaster cornices. The attic is unfinished on the inside. The building stands on the north side of the grounds, near the entrance. The basement walls are of stone, with cut stone water tables. The walls to the height of the second floor are of brick; from this point to the roof the building is frame, covered with red tiles of a beautiful pattern. Two beautifully ornamented gables surmount the south front, with dormer windows. The main entrance is near the center of the south front, and is reached from a veranda, which extends westward about 20 feet. Admission is obtained through a small arched vestibule, with tiled floor, which opens into a hall 11 feet wide by 23 in length, east and west. A stairway, three feet wide rises from the northeast corner of the hall, leaving the hall nine feet in the clear. At the southeast corner of the hall is a grate, surmounted by an ornamental slate mantel, and under the stairway, on the north side are arched recesses containing a lavatory, wardrobe, and chest of drawers.

Superintendent's Cottage at the Reform School. Notice the bargeboards on the gables and the finials at the end of the cresting on the roof ridge.

"The southeast room extending beyond the veranda is the library and study of the superintendent. It is 11 feet 10 inches by 15 feet 8 inches in size. It is lighted by four windows, three on the south and one on the east, each two feet by seven in size. The upper sash in each of these windows is two by two feet in size, and composed of nine small lights of rough cathedral glass in various colors, each window disclosing a different pattern. The lower sashes, which are two feet by five, are composed of a single light of plain plate glass. A similar window lights the main hall, at the west of which, through double sliding doors, the parlor is reached, a room 13 feet 8 inches by 16 feet 8 inches in size, located by the southwest corner. It is lighted by three windows, two of which, opening on the veranda, extend to the floor. Returning to the reception hall, and passing through an arch into a short hall on the north we find, opening from right and left, two rooms, each 13 feet 8 inches by 17 feet 10 inches in size. That upon the right is the sitting room, and the one upon the left is a dining-room, which contains a convenient china closet. Each of the rooms described above has hard-wood floors. The finish is a pure and highly ornamental Eastlake, and the lumber is selected Norway pine. Doors communicate from both sitting and dining-rooms with a short passage in the rear, which leads to the patron, servant's room, rear stairs, and kitchen, which is 13 feet 10 inches by 14 feet 4 inches in size, furnished with a range, a sink with hot and cold water, a flour and meal room furnished with chests, and a dumb waiter running to the basement and second story. From the kitchen, a door opens into the wood-shed, in one corner of which are earth closets. These rooms are all plainly but substantially finished and wainscoted. The four main rooms in the front and the hall are furnished with open grates, and the mantels, with the exception of the hall and sitting-room, are of solid oak, neatly carved. That in the dining-room has two shelves like a sideboard. The entire building is heated by a furnace, and each room has a register. The windows are also furnished with Venetian blinds.

"The second story is a duplicate of the first floor, so far as regards the size, location, and finish of the four front rooms and hall. The ladies' room is in the southeast corner, over the library. The narrow hall extends the entire length of the building north and opens into the principal hall at the head of the main stairway. Large and airy bed-rooms are located over the parlor, dining and sitting rooms, each provided with grates and mantels. The space over the kitchen is divided into a bedroom and an elegant bath-room, and there is a large bedroom for the servant, in the opposite corner, furnished with a grate. Each bed-room and sitting-room in the house is furnished with a closet.

"Descending a short flight of steps from the wood-shed one enters a narrow hall, walled on each side with solid brick, and pierced by arched passages. At the south end of this hall is the furnace. This basement, which is divided into seven rooms, has a concrete floor about six inches in depth. The entire foundation is under-drained and tiled, and the basement is as dry and sweet as the upper floors. Everything, from basement to garret, is constructed in a very neat but most substantial manner, and the attic itself, which is reached by easy flights of stairs, is well finished for a dry-room or play-room for children in inclement weather. The designs and working plans for this beautiful cottage were made by William Appleyard, the contract for its construction was taken by Fuller & Wheeler, the stone and brick work was done by Charles Chittenden, and the finishing of the woodwork and staining of the brick was done by John Voisell. They are all Lansing firms, and each may well congratulate themselves on this beautiful specimen of their combined ingenuity and skill. The cost was about $8,000, and at that price there must have been but slight profit for the contractors" (*LRW* 1/24/1883).

The cottage was described in the *Lansing Republican Weekly* article as being designed in the Queen Anne style, but the building had many Gothic elements in its plan. It is unfortunate that in the above photograph the tree obscures the wonderful front gable dormer and the bargeboards that help to frame the gables. The other interesting aspect of the building is the pattern of the windows. Observe how they are stacked. In one instance three windows on the first floor, two on the second floor and one on the third floor, or one above one or two above two windows, which gives the structure a balanced appearance. The roof cresting ends in a flourish when reaching the gable end. This was a design that any architect would be proud of. The Superintendent's Cottage was torn down in 1973. (*LSJ* 9/6/1973)

EMERY FLATS

200-204 W. Ionia, Lansing, MI.
Observe how the first flat has been converted into a gas station. The service station address was 301 N. Capitol, while the apartment above, usually occupied by the service station's manger, was 202½ Ionia. (CADL/FPLA)

"Wesley Emery has excavated and is laying the foundation for a French flat on his lot at the northwest corner of Capitol avenue and Ionia street. The building will be 73 feet by 35 feet on the ground and consist of two stories and a basement. The two stories will be brick veneered, and when complete it will constitute three distinct houses separated by dead walls, under one roof. The plans, which were made by Architect Appleyard, are exceedingly neat, and when complete the building will be quite ornamental. George Pratt is doing the stone work" (*LRW* 6/25/1882).

"Wesley Emery's new building is rapidly approaching completion. The cornice is on, and the building will soon be ready for occupancy. It will be a decided ornament to that part of the city" (*LRW* 9/13/1882).

Wesley Emery was born in Livingston County, New York on July 18, 1829 and he attended Lima Seminary and Genesee College. In 1851 Wesley married Miss Adelia Gibson in Barry Center, New York and Adelia passed away one year later. Wesley then married Adelia's sister, Miss Laura Gibson, in 1854; the couple had one child, Archibald

M. Emery. Laura died on May 22, 1864. In 1870, Wesley married Miss Sarah Elizabeth Van Der Voort, in Phelps, New York. Early in his career Wesley taught alongside his wife Sarah at the Okemos Union School. They must have made an interesting combination, Wesley with his business sense and Sarah with her political views. Later Sarah became the Superintendent of the Midland school district while Wesley worked as the representative of an east coast publishing firm and traveled the state attending teacher's meetings and visiting schools. For several years, he was the secretary for the Lansing Industrial Aid Society and helped to form the Central Michigan Agricultural Society. In 1873, he established the first bookstore in the city of Lansing, described by many as the finest in the state. Wesley passed away at his son's home on March 19, 1916.[14]

Notice the unassuming nature of the flats and the undersized mansard roof, later a smooth stucco surface was applied over the brickwork of the building. It should be pointed out that it is unclear which Appleyard designed the original three flats on the site, it could have been James or William. It is more likely that William designed the flats, for two reasons. First, William was listed in the 1882-1883 *Lansing City Directory* as an architect and James was listed as a contractor. Secondly, James rarely served as an architect and when that occurred it was noted in the account. The gas station on the east corner was a modification not present in the original design. An additional three flats were added in 1890 and designed by Darius Moon. The flats were torn down between 1940 and 1941.

---

[14] *LSJ* 3/20/1916. Sarah Elizabeth Van Der Voort Emery was the author of the *Seven Financial Conspiracies Which Have Enslaved the American People.*

LANSING IRON & ENGINE WORKS

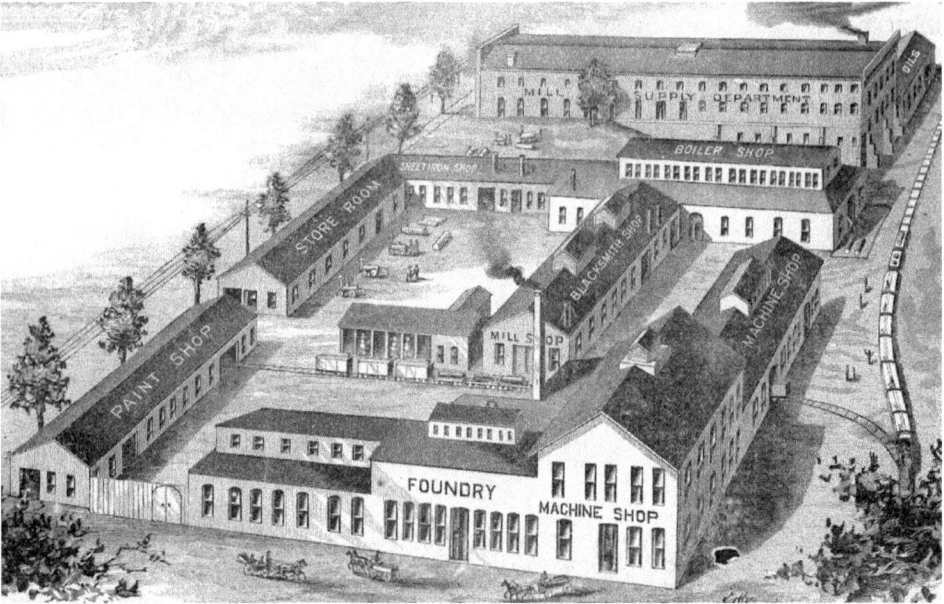

A drawing of the Lansing Iron & Engine Works Plant at 420-422 E. Shiawassee, Lansing, Michigan, circa 1889.

"Wm. Appleyard, architect is preparing plans for the new boiler shop to be erected by the Lansing iron works on the southwest corner of Shiawassee and Cedar streets, and bids are being received for its construction. It will be of brick, and when completed will be the best of its kind in Michigan" (*LRW* 10/1/1882).

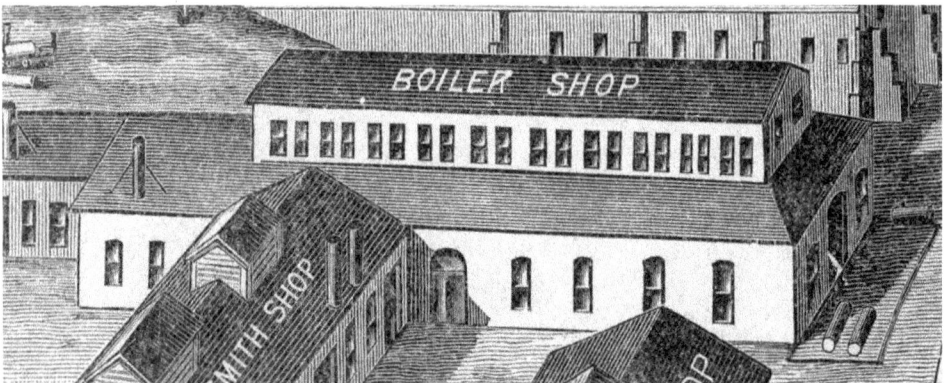

Detail of the boiler shop of the Lansing Iron & Engine Works. Notice the second story windows, an architectural feature, meant to capture the natural light.

The Lansing Iron & Engine Works' boiler shop can be seen at the rear of the first image with the mill supply house beyond it. There is not much that can be said about the design of the shop except like all early industrial buildings there was a heavy dependence on natural light to provide illumination in the workspace. The raised section on the top of the boiler shop is a monitor roof, which maximized the amount of light entering the center of the factory.[15] Artificial arc lighting was first used in factories in 1879, which had an intense light that created shadows which could only be alleviated by increasing the number of lights used, resulting in higher operating cost and increasing the risk of fire. Incandescent lighting was the solution to the problem of interior lighting; it was developed by the Edison Electric Light Company and was first used in 1881. It is doubtful that the Lansing Iron & Engine Works used artificial light at this time, although they did have the capacity to generate the power needed to produce electricity. It is important to remember that although artificial light was available it took many years before it appeared in areas outside the largest cities. Many early factories employed large windows and a center dormer with windows and skylights, as well as artificial light powered by their own steam plant.

The Boiler Shop is the two-story building to the extreme right in the above image. The two-story structure with the cupola was the Machine Shop. Compare this image with the artist's rendering of the plant and you will see it was accurate, except for clutter around the buildings.

The boiler shop was built on an east west axis, which maximized the amount of natural light that could enter the building through the side windows and the dormer, reducing its dependence on artificial light. Unlike many advertising images of a company's plant, the image of the Lansing Iron & Engine Works was an accurate depiction of the plant in the 1880s. This is confirmed when comparing the image to the layout in the 1885 Sanborn maps.

---

[15] I wonder if the term Monitor roof originated from the description of the USS Monitor of Civil War fame that was described as a cheese box on a raft? Only a suggestion.

The 30 HP Portable Engine by Lansing Iron & Engine Works. When you consider the size of this beast it is amazing that this was a portable engine!

"Since our description in the Republican of the Lansing iron works and new boiler shop, a great deal of inquiry has been made as to the architect. It was designed by William Appleyard of this city who furnished the plans for the three new cottages at the reform school, and those designs are attracting much attention for their beauty, solidity, convenience for the purposes designed, and economy in construction" (*LRW* 1/24/1883).

The Lansing Iron & Engine Works was once one of the largest industrial concerns of this type in the country. Besides the production of farm tractors, steam engines and boilers, the firm also had a mill supply house that stocked everything needed to properly equip a mill or a production factory, from leather and rubber belts to brass fittings. The company's management believed that the mill supply department should have any part a mill needed, to eliminate down time due to a broken part. The idea worked; by the end of 1889 the company had reached $150,000 in annual sales or about $4,000,000 in today's money. The firm also produced a compound engine for use in power plants. Lansing Iron & Engine Works engines powered electrical plants in Albion, Jackson and Battle Creek. In 1889, the officers of the company have two names well-known to Lansing residents. The President was Orlando F. Barnes and the Secretary and Treasurer was J. Edward Roe.[16]

---

[16] *SR* 3/19/1889.

A Portable Saw Mill built by the Lansing Iron & Engine Works. Imagine how nerve-racking it was to use this tool. The open blade reminds one of something you would see in a 1930s cartoon.

E.F. Cooley purchased the mill supply department of the Lansing Iron & Engine Works in 1890 and formed the Michigan Supply Company. Orlando F. Barnes was not the same businessman as his father, Orlando M. Barnes. The panic of 1893 placed the Lansing Iron & Engine Works in a dire financial position. It was only due to the intervention of Orlando M. Barnes, who used his personal fortune plus the monies of the bank he controlled, who staved off the bankruptcy of the company. In fact, this was one of the issues that eventually destroyed the Barnes' family fortune. Lansing Iron & Engine Works was reorganized by its creditors as the Lansing Boiler & Engine Works in 1896 and Orlando F. Barnes was not one of the officers of the new company.[17] In 1903, the Lansing Boiler & Engine Works filed for bankruptcy and the Lansing & Suburban Traction Company, the local streetcar company, acquired the property and tore down the factory to construct streetcar barns.[18] In 1936 the site was purchased by the city to be the home of the Lansing Municipal Market, which opened its doors on August 27, 1938 and was later torn down in 2009. Such is the march of progress and the destruction it entails.[19]

---

[17] *Daily Democrat* 4/19/1893, *SR* 4/19/1893, *SR* 8/27/1889, *SR* 8/28/1889 and *DFP* 8/29/1896
[18] Later the Michigan United Traction Company.
[19] *LSJ* 1/1/1936 & *LSJ* 8/26/1938

KALAMAZOO STREET SCHOOL

517 W. Kalamazoo, Lansing, MI.
An early image of the Kalamazoo Street School. Note the placement of the chimneys and the snow sheds over the entrances are evident and interesting. (CADL/FPLA)

"The school board last evening adopted plans and specifications for a new schoolhouse, to take the place of the present union school building and contracted with Wm. Appleyard for details and superintendence, etc." (*LRW* 1/31/1883).

"Architect Appleyard wishes to say to the anonymous 'smart Alec' who wrote him a note in regard to the material and workmanship on the 3rd ward schoolhouse, that the building has not yet been accepted, nor will it be unless the work is satisfactory. He will be pleased to talk with or hear suggestions from any honest 'taxpayer' who is not ashamed of his name, but does not appreciate anonymous letters" *(LR* 11/22/1883).

"The new union school-house was occupied for the first-time Monday. It is plain, but neat and substantial structure, and reflects credit upon the architect. Wm. Appleyard, and the contractors Messrs. White & Castle. The brick and stone work, which was done by Fitzpatrick Brothers will compare favorably with any in the city" (*LR* 1/19/1884).

KALAMAZOO ST. PUBLIC SCHOOL.

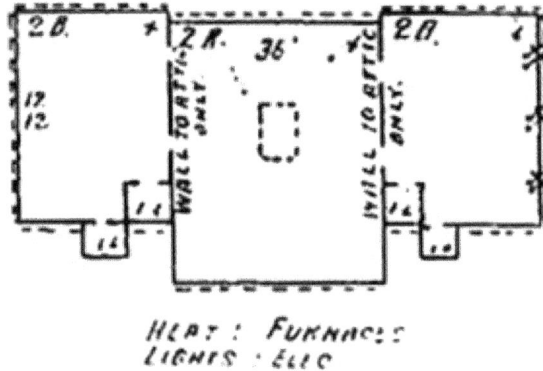

Sanborn image of the Kalamazoo Street School in 1906.

Originally known as the Clark School, the building's name changed in 1888 to the Kalamazoo Street School.[20] William not only designed the building but acted as the Superintendent of Construction for the project. The work on the school was completed in February 1884.[21]

The Kalamazoo Street School was an imposing structure that was the showpiece of the school district. The above photograph of the school shows the building after a later addition in 1909 at a cost of $9,000. The Sanborn image illustration shows the original footprint of the school. Using the first photograph and the Sanborn image the reader can see that the original building consisted of the front part of the building in the photograph facing Kalamazoo Street.

---

[20] The best I can determine is the school was originally named after Oscar W. Clark. Although this may be the result of some confusion of the property sites. In the *Record of Deeds: Land Transactions of the Lansing School District from 1843 to 1980* it is noted that the property on Block 161 Lots 1-4 were the Clark Lands, site of the 3rd Ward school located on South Walnut Street between Hillsdale and St. Joseph streets.

[21] *LR* 8/28/1883 and *LR* 2/5/1884

517 W. Kalamazoo, Lansing, MI.
The Kalamazoo School after the addition in 1909. (CADL/FPLA)

The school was torn down in 1923 and replaced with West Junior High School, which later served as the Administrative Offices of the Lansing School District. It is interesting to compare the image of the Kalamazoo Street School to Appleyard's later school building designs, created for the state of Michigan and in those he submitted to the state of New York school design competition. The imposing central structure and the two wings presented a balanced façade. Observe how the two entrances to the building are almost hidden when viewed from the street, the focus of the passerby is drawn toward the central part of the school. Notice the stacking of the facade windows in the center structure, three over three over two over two. While on the east and west wings, the facade windows are arranged one over three over two over two. Oddly the patterns seem to work. Observe the placement of the bell tower. It is interesting to note that Appleyard placed the bell tower back away from the front of the building, a departure from previous school designs.

CHARLES DAVIS RESIDENCE

1326 E. Michigan, Lansing, MI.
Strangely there are few photographs of the Davis home.

"Chas. J. Davis will erect a beautiful brick cottage, Queen Anne style, on his property on Michigan avenue east, the coming season. It will contain 14 rooms, finished in the latest style, and when complete will be one of the neatest residences in the city. Appleyard is the architect" (*LR* 3/3/1883).

"A few rods east of this is Mr. Davis' building, a large house, with two stories a roomy attic and a massive basement. It is about 44 by 63 feet in size on the ground, and is in a style that is called the Queen Anne cottage, being brick up to the second story, and from thence shingled to the cornice in imitation of tiles. The interior is arranged for all modern conveniences each sitting room containing a grate, and hot air ventilation flues extending from the furnace in the basement through each room, including the attic. ... The architect is William P. Appleyard. Martin & Hilliard are the contractors" (*LR* 8/28/1883).

"Charles J. Davis is moving into his elegant new residence on Michigan avenue east a description of which was given in the Republican last summer. It is one of the neatest and most convenient of the many fine homes in this city, and a credit to its genial and happy owner, as well as to the architect and superintendent, William Appleyard of this city. It is in every respect a cozy home, furnished with every practical modern convenience. Open grates are found in all the rooms, and the interior wood-work is of choice ash and pine, all-natural color and neatly carved" (*LR* 1/19/1884).

The above image is a slightly different view of the Davis home. Note how the entry porch is hidden away and not the main focus of the home.

The Davis home was an intriguing mixture of the Queen Anne and Gothic style architecture; it reflects a hybrid style of design that is often overlooked from this time period. The striking aspect of the residence is the center hip roof with a flat center section enclosed by ironwork cresting that is surrounded by three chimneys in a triangle pattern. The small porch at the front is almost hidden and blends with the structure of the home. On the gable end the windows have a traditional stacking pattern. The ornate bargeboards at the gable ends offer a pleasing design element which are difficult to see in the photographs. The small shed dormer over the entrance porch is also intriguing; did it provide light to the stairwell? When you consider the importance of the Davis home, it is remarkable that the site is now a parking lot. Frankly it is tiring to note that an architecturally significant building or home was torn down to create a parking lot or a sterile office building. One wonders what Lansing could have been like if the historic homes and buildings in the city were not demolished. We may have rivaled other state capitals like Nashville, Madison, or Austin. Instead Lansing offers few significant historical architectural wonders aside from the Capitol. People visit historic sites, not parking lots.

Charles J Davis 1845-1924

Charles J. Davis, former Lansing Mayor, railroad pioneer, businessman and renowned naturalist, passed away at Sparrow Hospital at the age of 79 on March 25, 1924. Davis was born in Paris, Ontario, Canada on March 22, 1845 and came to the United States at the close of the Civil War. Davis settled in Saginaw, Michigan where he worked as a surveyor selecting and plotting lands for lumber companies and it was at this time Davis became a United States citizen. In 1874 the Jackson, Lansing and Saginaw Railroad, later the Michigan Central Railroad, received a grant of land from Congress to become one of the first 'land grant' railroads in Michigan. Davis who was an assistant to Orlando M. Barnes, was responsible for much of the work related to the land grant. As a direct result of his work, Davis moved to Lansing where he employed in the land grant office. In 1897, Davis was elected mayor of Lansing. His first term was under an old Lansing ordinance, which limited the mayor's term to one year but in 1898 that law was changed expanding the mayor's term to two years. In 1898, Davis was reelected again by a large margin. Davis was also a distinguished naturalist and his home at 1326 E. Michigan had a zoological garden on the rear portion of the property. The garden was populated with many specimens of animals both living and stuffed. In fact, when Theodore Roosevelt visited the M.A.C. he was amazed to see a giant stuffed black bear on Davis' front lawn. Davis also owned over three thousand books, many of which were priceless including a Double Elephant Folio of Audubon's *Birds of America*.[22] Given what we know about Charles he seemed like a delightful character who must have been a joy to talk to. In 1874 Charles married Miss Amelia Hurd in Saginaw, Michigan; the couple had two children, Anna Morelle and Charles Hurd Davis.[23] After the death of her father, his daughter Morelle

[22] It is unknown what happened to Davis' copy of the Double Elephant Folio of the *Birds of America*.
[23] *LCN* 3/26/1924 and *LSJ* 6/25/1924.

Davis Brayton occupied the home. Morelle was a gifted woman who studied art in Dresden, Germany, but had one odd habit of never throwing anything away. In today's terms she was a hoarder. After Morelle's death in 1948 the contents of the home were put up for auction on July 24, 1948. The auctioneer was amazed at the assortment of items present in the home; there was Charles J. Davis' prized collection of stuffed animals, Hepplewhite furniture, Windsor Arrowback chairs and many other antiques.[24] The home was torn down in March 1949, a great loss for the citizens of Lansing.

M.A.C. FACULTY HOMES

On the campus of Michigan Agricultural College, Faculty Row No. 9 house, built 1884. Notice the small triangle dormer, used to bring light in to the upstairs rooms or illuminate a stairwell.

"Prof. Satterlee was authorized to secure from Mr. Appleyard plans & specifications for a Prof's house to be veneered with brick total cost inclusive of heating and Architects fees not to exceed $3000. Plan to be submitted to building Com June 26th."[25]

"New Dwelling— It was resolved that Secretary Baird Superintend & take charge of the erection of the New House [designed by Appleyard] now under Contract."[26]

---

[24] *LSJ* 7/8/1948.
[25] Offices of Board of Trustees and President MAC, Meeting Minutes, June 11, 1883.
[26] Offices of Board of Trustees and President MAC, Meeting Minutes March 18, 1884.

217 Beech Street, East Lansing, MI.
Faculty Row No. 9 house after it had been moved to its new location. Observe how the central chimney has been shortened and lacks the ornamentation of the original chimney. Note the overhang of the eaves, which seems quite deep.

Robert Gardner Baird was appointed Secretary to the State Board of Agriculture in August of 1875 and served in that position until his death 10 years later on August 5, 1885. It was odd that Baird supervised the construction of the home and not Appleyard. This may have been a result of Appleyard either overseeing the construction of the Baraga County Courthouse or the Congregational Church in Perry, Michigan.

The structure seems to be an extended Ell home in the Gothic style. There is little to be said about the home except for wonderful triangular dormer which resembles an eyebrow dormer. The Gothic bargeboards on the facing pediment of the gable and the side gable ends are an attractive element of the home's design. The residence was moved to 217 Beech Street in 1924.[27] The structure was originally constructed with a brick veneer, but after the move the house was sided in clapboard. The hipped dormer seems to have been added after the move or it may have been obscured in the first image by the tree, but it works and only adds to the elegance of the residence. The home is still standing in 2019.

---

[27] The is based upon an article in the *LSJ* 7/11/1924 that stated all the Faculty Row buildings would be removed. In fact, they were not. The date of the move of Faculty Row No. 9 house to 217 Beech Street is still unknown.

LIEDERKRANZ HALL

526 N. Grand, Lansing, MI.
Notice the simplicity of the building. Constructed in a north south axis the large windows take advantage of the early morning and late evening sunshine. (CADL/FPLA)

"A New Hall—Among the many building operations now in progress and in contemplation, showing the substantial growth and prosperity of our beautiful city, we noticed the plan and drawings by Architect Appleyard, for a new hall for the "Lansing Liederkranz" society, on its grounds on Grand street at the foot of Lapeer, which is 75 feet long and 36 feet wide, in the gothic style, and surmounted by two towers, and will be provided with a stage 17x36 feet, with all the equipment necessary for holding of amateur concerts, musical and dramatic entertainments, also apartments for a resident janitor" (*LR* 7/7/1883).

"The contract for the new Lieder Kranz (sic) hall was let on Saturday, to William Martin, at $3,548. The society has purchased a lot adjoining its present property, which will be enclosed and improved when the new building is completed" (*LR* 10/2/1883).

The first Liederkranz Hall was an unassuming Gothic style building. Because of the limitations of the photographic evidence all that can be said is that the bargeboards on the gable ends were plain without ornamentation with a simple entrance on the south side of the building. What is not shown in the photograph is that the building extended eastward toward the river with a structure that was equal in size to what is shown in the above image. The Liederkranz Club was formed in 1868 by a group of German immigrants to promote German culture and more importantly to sing. The club first met at the home of Christian Ziegler, and the first clubhouse was built on North Grand Avenue in 1872. After a fire in 1883 it was rebuilt based upon the design by architect William Appleyard and the new hall was dedicated January 15, 1884. (*LR* 1/15/1884). In 1903, another fire occurred at the clubhouse and Darius Moon was hired to redesign the building. Moon added a second story, which contained a ballroom and stage on the second floor and clubrooms on the first floor. The building was sold in 1919 to John Morrissey who planned to establish a theater on the premises. The structure's conversion to a theater never occurred, and the building served as the home of the Cadillac Athletic Club and for a brief time as service station (*LSJ* 9/25/1919). The Liederkranz Hall was torn down in 1939 and the site is now Adado Riverfront Park. (LSJ 8/3/1939) Many people in Lansing do not realize that the Liederkranz Club still endures in Lansing and the club is now located at 5828 S. Pennsylvania Avenue.

MICHIGAN SCHOOL FOR THE BLIND

The above image is of the main entrance of the Michigan Female College in Lansing, Michigan, after it was acquired by the Odd Fellows. The photograph shows the building being updated for the Odd Fellows into a Second Empire structure. Observe the scaffolding at the center. The design for the modifications to the building were by Saginaw architect John B. Dibble. (CADL/FPLA)

"THE SCHOOL FOR THE BLIND—On Tuesday last Architect Appleyard presented his plans for the extension of the main building of the Michigan school for the blind to the state board of health, for examination as to heating, ventilation, and drainage. They were examined by the full board and approved in nearly every particular. The proposed extension consists of two wings, running north and south from the building constructed by the Odd Fellows, each 40 feet 6 inches by 44 feet 6 inches. Across the ends of each of these wings extend other wings or pavilions, each 40 feet by 6 inches by 96 feet 8 inches. The entire structure will consist of three stories and a basement. From the grade line to the first course of the water table the wall will be faced with rock-faced ashlar; above this, with fine white brick, relieved with red brick arches and belt courses. The whole will be made to harmonize with the old building as nearly as possible. The north and south pavilions will have verandas, eight feet wide, running the entire length, and also the rear of the north and south wings. All the main walls of the building are solid brick, resting on concrete footing. Through the wings and pavilions run corridors, 7 feet 6 inches wide, from which, on each side, open rooms. The south wing, on the first floor will be occupied exclusively by girls, and the north corridor by boys.

The north and south additions and the two-story veranda can be seen at the left and right in the image. Notice how the central core of the building and the wings have been updated by Lansing architect William Appleyard. (CADL/FPLA)

'The first floor of the south wing will be used for school, work, apparatus, music, and bedrooms, and also for the library. On the second floor, will be located the hospital, sitting rooms, music rooms and bedrooms. The hospital will be isolated by double doors and a passage between. The entire third floor will be fitted for sleeping-rooms. Each floor will be furnished with a complete suite of water-closets and bathrooms. Iron fire-escapes will be placed at the rear of each pavilion, running from the ground to roof. The north wing will be a duplicate of the south, with the exception that the business office will be located on the first floor of that wing. The building, which is entirely heated by steam, by which fresh air is heated and supplied to every room, independent of the others, and the whole will be thoroughly ventilated. If the plans as adopted are fully carried out the result will be gratifying to the state and a monument of which the architect may be proud" (*LRW* 7/12/1883).

The rear view of the School for the Blind, notice the tiered walkways and how plain the rear of the structure was.

It is time to explore what is known regarding the School for the Blind structure that was updated by Appleyard. The building originally functioned as the Michigan Female College and was designed by Detroit architects, Albert Jordan and James Anderson. The Michigan Female College was the first institution in state to provide women with a college level education and was founded by Abigail and Delia Rogers in 1858. The college building consisted of a central core and a wing to the north which served as a dormitory for the students. In 1869, after the death of Abigail Rogers the building was acquired by the Independent Order of the Odd Fellows to serve as a home for its indigent members.[28] With the Odd Fellows' acquisition of the property, the main building was expanded with a wing to the south, designed by Saginaw architect John B. Dibble and updated to the Second Empire style that was popular at that time. In 1881, the state of Michigan purchased the property from the Odd Fellows and engaged William Appleyard to modernize the building. The old wing on the north side of the structure was torn down and replaced with a new wing while on the south side a new wing was constructed. The improvements also included the addition of fire escapes and the extensive fresh air porches. The large, barrack like dormitories were eliminated.

---

[28] Delia Rogers died in Chicago on December 18, 1887. Delia was one of the founding members of the Ladies Library and Literary Society so in a way she helped to establish the Lansing Public Library. *Michigan Historical Collections*, 13 197.

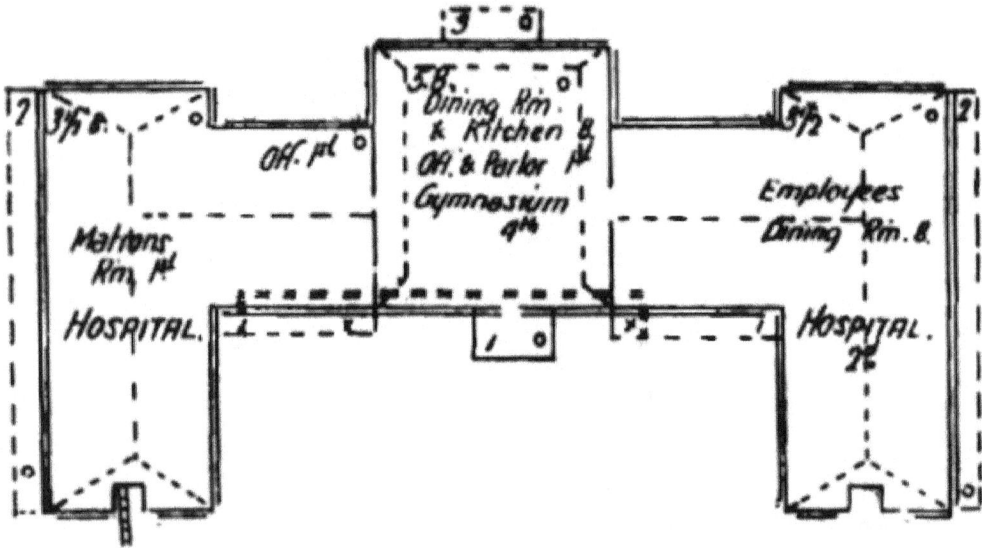

School for the Blind 1898, the two-story verandas on the North and South sides are represented with the dotted line as well as the single-story veranda at the rear of the building. The two new wings are both labeled 'hospital', one for females and the other for males.

The south wing was constructed in 1883 and contained two schoolrooms for women, a teacher's library, museum, two work rooms, nine piano rooms, four teacher's rooms, a women's hospital, bakery, twenty-three dormitory rooms and bathrooms on each floor. The large dormitories were eliminated. The new wing was occupied on September 18, 1884 (*Biennial Report* 42). The old north wing, part of the Michigan Female College, was torn down after the construction of the south wing and rebuilt in the same style. The firm of Farr & Vincent of Grand Rapids were the contractors (*Biennial Report* 7).

Appleyard's main building for the School for the Blind was torn down in 1916 and replaced with the Bowd designed structure that stands on the site today. It seems Bowd designed several other buildings that resemble the School for the Blind building including the Ionia Poor House, the Jackson Odd Fellows Home and the Michigan School for the Deaf in Flint. These structures all had the massive classical portico that was a signature of Bowd's work.[29] The Michigan School for the Blind closed its doors in Lansing in1995. The School for the Blind structure still stands in 2019 but is slated for conversion into apartments.

---

[29] There is quite a bit of misinformation concerning Bowd's life. For example, it has been stated that he attended Orset College in Dover, England but there was no Orset College in Dover. His full name was Edwyn Alfred Spencer Bowd, and he spent his childhood in Cheltenham, England. (MacLean E-mail)

One of the writer's favorite images of any building in Lansing. It demonstrates how imposing and yet graceful the enterance for the School for the Blind was, and the child sitting on the porch creates a piognancy appealing to this writer. (CADL/FPLA)

You can observe how the additions of both wings by Appleyard matched seamlessly with the French Second Empire architectural style of the original building. Accomplishing the merger of the old and new structure was one of William Appleyard's notable achievements. Notice the flow of the windows and how they are balanced in the two, three, four patterns across the facade. Frankly it is disappointing that the current Bowd designed building replaced the Appleyard building. The writer relishes the style of the Appleyard building versus the sterile almost clinical Germanic design of the Bowd structure. The Second Empire towers with the Mansard roof create an imposing facade that in some ways reminds one of a gothic horror movie.

FRANK WELLS HOME

306 W. Ottawa, Lansing, MI.
The image is from 1944 after the home was moved to 209 Seymour. Observe the architectural details on the front porch. (CADL/FPLA)

"Architect Appleyard is sketching plans for a $3,000 dwelling house to be erected on the corner of Seymour and Ottawa streets for Frank Wells, the druggist" (*LR* 8/25/1883).

"Ground was broken on Wednesday morning for Frank Well's new residence on Ottawa street north of the capitol building" (*LR* 11/27/1883).

The Well's house was originally located at 306 W. Ottawa and was moved to 209 Seymour in 1920-1921. The home was originally situated on the east half of Lots 5 and 6, Block 94 on the Original Plat of Lansing and faced Ottawa Street. In 1920-1921 the structure was moved to the back of the lots, reoriented, and became 209 Seymour. There is no listing for 209 Seymour before 1921.

Notice the Queen Anne style windows on the second-floor facade. The smaller panes on the upper sash of the window contained colored glass. (CADL/FPLA)

In that year it is listed as a home with two apartments. No city record of the home being moved has been discovered indicating a permit may not have been required because the structure was being moved on the property. The Sanborn maps confirm that the home at 306 Ottawa in 1898, 1906 and 1913 had the same footprint as the home at 209 Seymour on the later Sanborn maps. In 1919-1920 Drs. McNamara & Carr built the Medical Office building on the southeast potion of the lot, while Dr. E.I. Carr owned the home on the northeast section of the property. It is highly unlikely that the doctors would have built a home in such a dated style to serve as a set of apartments. It is far more likely that they moved the existing home to the back of the lot. The Medical Office building still stands today and serves as the offices for the Diocese of Lansing. The structure at 209 Seymour became the Diocese of Lansing Tribunal building. Take a closer look at the current building and you can observe some of the basic features of the home.[30] The Wells house was a perfect example of an architect combining architectural elements from a variety of

[30] The Stebbins' card listed the home at 209 Seymour as being built in 1895, but the 1888 *Lansing City Directory* placed the Frank Wells' residence at the northwest corner of Ottawa and Seymour Streets.

styles to design an organic structure. The house contains elements of the Gothic and Queen Anne styles. Notice the flaring over the porch in the first two images, an attempt to blend the awkward small bump out over the porch with the rest of the facade. It is surprising that the flaring was not continued around the home as a design element. The Gothic bargeboards were original to the home, but at a later date the one on the small front gable changed to a collar beam style ornamentation.

The final image of the home at 209 Seymour displays the home in all its barren beauty. Thankfully the home was not torn down, and it is understandable why the Diocese of Lansing chose to simplify the structure. Maybe one day it can be returned to its original state.

Francis Bradstreet Wells, one of Lansing's early businessmen and former chairman of the State Board of Health, died of typhoid fever at 5:30 am on January 20, 1905. Frank Wells as he liked to be known was born in New York in 1832, the son of Leonard and Susannah A. (née Frost) Wells. His parents moved to Ohio, where Frank attended the Huron Institute in Milan, Ohio. After graduation, Frank moved to Howell, Michigan and opened a drug store. Ten years later he relocated to Lansing where he established a drug store at 122 S. Washington. Frank subsequently acquired an interest in a jewelry business, which he combined with the drug store, under the name of Wells & Morgan. He also established the Wells & Clear Ice and Coal business. Like many men of this time, Frank was attracted to the study of science. He wrote *History of Investigations Concerning Micro-organisms, and the Germ Theory of Disease*, an early examination of the subject. In 1891, Governor Winans appointed Frank to the State Board of Health and two years later he was elected chairman of the State Board of Health, a position he held until his death. Frank married Miss Lydia Jones in 1867, the couple had three children who survived to adulthood, Bertha, Helen and Frank G. Wells. Frank's wife, Lydia passed away on July 17, 1879. Lydia was the daughter of Zephaniah Jones, a contractor who helped to build the old 'Ram's Horn' Railroad. Lydia attended the Michigan Female College and studied under Abigail and Delia Rogers. Frank never remarried.[31]

---

[31] There is some question about the location of Frank B. Wells death. The *State Republican* indicated that he died at the home of Henry S. Bartholomew, 103 W. Main Street, while the *Lansing Journal* had Frank Wells passing away at the home of Judge Edward Cahill, 101 W. Main Street. The death certificate lists 103 W. Main as the place of death. See *LJ* 1/20/1905 and *SR* 1/20/1905. For Lydia's death see *LRW* 7/23/1879.

LENAWEE COUNTY COURTHOUSE

309 N. Main, Adrian, MI.

"Architect Appleyard visited Adrian on Friday with plans for a new county house" (*LR* 11/2/1883). Unfortunately for William Appleyard his plans for the courthouse were not accepted. The contract for the design of the courthouse was awarded to Edward Oscar Fallis, an architect from Toledo, Ohio. Fallis also designed the Noble County Courthouse in Albion, Indiana, the Paulding County Courthouse in Ohio and the Monroe County Courthouse in Michigan.

MICHIGAN SCHOOLHOUSE DESIGNS

Country Schoolhouse (1882) Notice how the bell tower and the rear chimney are connected by the cresting on the crown of the roofs ridge. There is even cresting on the side clipped gable which ends in a finial. Beautiful, but impractical.

In 1882 William Appleyard presented a paper to the State Teachers' Association on Country Schoolhouses. What follows are some excerpts from the paper, which outline Appleyard's views on how a county schoolhouse should be designed.

"In view of the necessity of better school-house construction, what changes to be made? How are we to construct buildings, which shall combine economy with good hygienic qualities? The form of the building will be to a great extent, depend upon the amount to be expended and the number of scholars to be accommodated. It is unnecessary that a school-house be highly ornate or stately. I consider that tasteful simplicity should enter into all its parts. It should be interesting to the children who come to occupy it each day, and it should be made to reflect the nature of its surroundings. Nowhere then in the country are the surroundings better fitted to bring out the elements of art, which make a simple building attractive. There are woods, the fields, and a pure atmosphere, made blue by distance, while the building is childhood. Therefore, I say that of all school buildings, those in the county districts, should be artistic."

A rear view of Appleyard's design for a County Schoolhouse (1882)

"So, I say, if a school building must have plain outlines, give it color. If brick is to be used in the walls, then I would choose red brick, and in default of these stain the brick red and pencil the joints with dark brown. If the roof must be of shingles, then paint them in imitation of tiles or red slate; it not only has a good effect but it is economy. If the building is to be frame, then paint the sides sap-green and relieve it by painting the corner-boards, window-casings, and cornice a dark green, and in this case an excellent effect may be produced by striping the window-sash with Venetian red. Above all, I consider white paint on a country school-house an abomination; it soon blackens with age and is cold and uninteresting while it lasts."

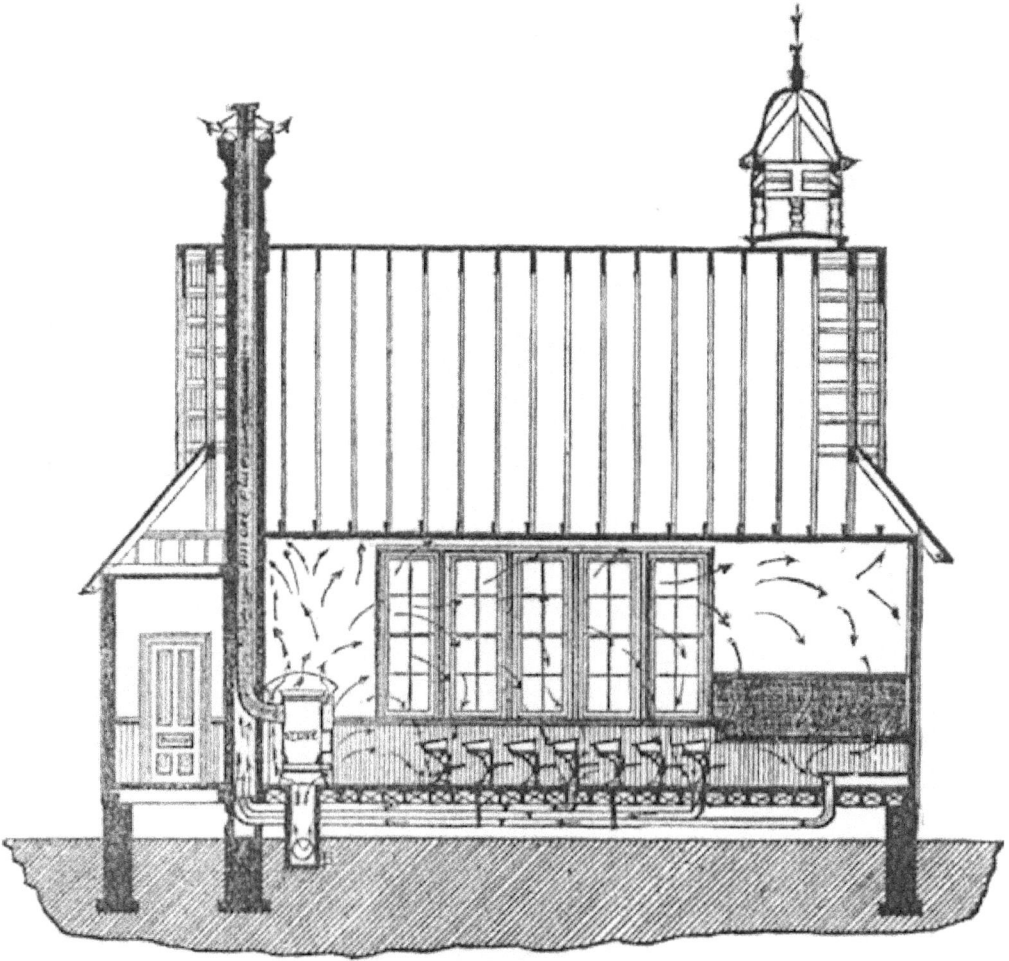

A view of how the heat from the stove circulated in an Appleyard designed Country Schoolhouse, circa 1882.

"Lighting is a part of school hygiene much neglected. For our guidance in the proper lighting of school-rooms, let us take into consideration some natural and scientific facts. It is a fact that the world and the objects in it are lighted from above, and that the light by which we see objects is reflected from them to the eye. Again, our eyes are protected from the intensity of the original light above them by lids, so that it may not interfere with and overcome the less powerful reflected light, and if this wise provision in the human economy was no proof we would need but the sense of an overstrained optic nerve to tell us that direct light in your eyes is injurious. Light should not come directly from the rear, for you would not turn your back to a window to read, because your head and shoulders would cast a disturbing shadow upon the page. You would involuntary stand so that the window would be at side and slightly to the rear. But in the act of writing you would sit so that the light would fall directly upon the moving pencil and the matter being written, thus causing the light to come from the left side."

"In view of these facts, I would say that the working-light of a school-room should come from the left side and above the height of the eyes. We know that the best light from a window comes through the upper panes, because if we darken the lower half of a high window, while reading, the light is almost insensibly diminished while it is more pleasant to the eye; therefore, the window heads should be as high as possible and their sills should be four feet from the floor."

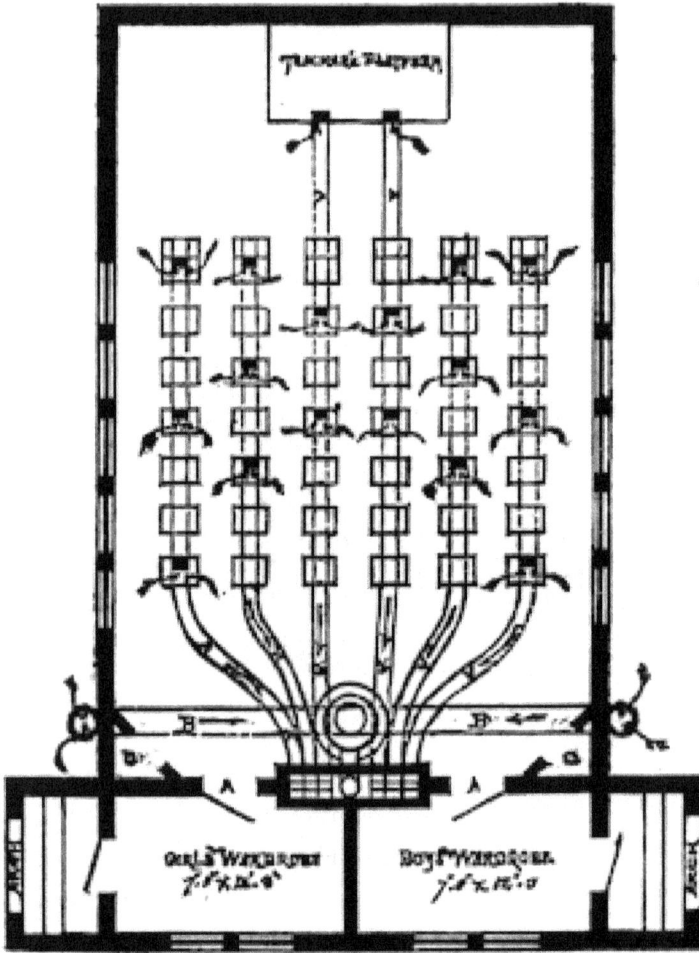

PLAN OF SCHOOL ROOM

Appleyard's Country Schoolhouse design from 1882, showing how the flow of heat circulated in the building.

"For convenience sake, suppose we are required to heat and ventilate a single school-room containing 50 scholars. If we supply to each scholar 300 cubic feet of air-space—and I consider this none too much—we would have a room containing 15,000 cubic feet. Now a stove, to heat this amount of air, should be large enough to do so without becoming red hot; therefore; it should have a large fire-pot, —I mean so large that there would be no temptation to heat it red hot, and the radiating surface should be proportion to the fire-pot. I cannot insist too strongly upon having a large stove, for upon its size depends altogether its success as a heater, and it is obvious that a large radiating surface, moderately heated is far more effective and healthy than a small surface heated red hot. The stove should be completely encased by a sheet iron jacket, leaving a sufficient space between it and the stove to admit the necessary amount of fresh air, which should be brought from outside the building at a point three feet above the ground. It should be conducted through a glazed clay pipe, and introduced to the room beneath the stove, passing it between the stove and the sheet iron casing, thus warming it before it reaches the pupils. The air in the school-room should be kept moist, and for this purpose a pan of water should be placed on top of the stove, so that the fresh air in leaving it may take with it the proper amount of moisture. The casing around the stove should have a moveable dome-shaped top, made of wire cloth, with meshes about one-quarter of an inch square. This will serve to check the upward current of fresh air, allowing it to become warm and gather moisture. Now that we have a supply of fresh warm air, to make it useful, we must ventilate the room, and to do so properly, we must supply to each pupil at least 2,000 feet of fresh air each hour, and as we have 50 pupils, we must supply each hour 100,000 cubic feet of air for the entire room. The contents of our school-room is 15,000 cubic feet, therefore; we must change the entire air of the room about seven times each hour."[32]

The reader may wonder why this long description of rural school house is important to this work. First, it is a view into Appleyard's theory on what impact the physical interior environment of a school-room has on education, and by simply improving the surroundings in the school-room helps to boost the learning potential of the students. Secondly, we hear for the first and only time Appleyard's own voice on the importance of the design of a structure to its placement in the landscape. In the preceding drawings, it is interesting to note the ornamentation that Appleyard envisioned for the exterior of the structures. In the first image the ornate entrance, the clipped gable on the side and the cresting on the roof are wonderful elements. While in the second image the fish scale siding on the gable end, the inlayed stick work and eyebrow dormer make this an attractive building. But these were all expensive extras that many rural school districts simply could not afford, or they chose not to include. The members of many rural school district boards were practical men, with an eye for the cost of a project, especially when they were paying for it. The embellishment of their local school house was not usually their top priority. No school houses based on Appleyard's designs outlined in the paper were ever used by any school district in the state of Michigan, but the writer is still looking.

---

[32] *Forty-Sixth* 295.

METEOROLOGICAL STATION

Meteorological Station on the west lawn of the Michigan's Capitol in Lansing, Michigan. The round instrument is a Draper self-recording thermometer, and two barometers running vertically located at the right in the image. (CADL/FPLA)

"A building for the meteorological instruments of the state board of health is about to be erected on the lawn west of the capitol, after the plans drawn by Wm. Appleyard. It will be about four feet square, and a little more than 10 feet high, and very neatly ornamented. Excavations for the concrete are now being made" (*LR* 3/29/1884).

"In order that more accurate results might be obtained, a new shelter for instruments was made in accordance with improved plans and placed in the southwest corner of the Capitol yard, where it is comparatively free from the influence of the building; and from July 1, 1884, separate observations were taken in the old and in the new shelter till the close of the year. The instruments in this new shelter are 4 feet from the ground" (Baker 21).

For many years the prior image has been incorrectly labeled as being on the campus of the MAC; all the Meteorological stations on the MAC campus were located on the building's rooftops. The image matches those elements outlined in the above article. The State Board of Health began taking readings in 1879, but the results were suspect since the station was located right next to the Capitol to allow for reading to be taken by just opening a window. The new station was located at the southwest corner of the Capitol and readings were taken at 7:00 a.m., 2:00 p.m. and 9:00 p.m. In 1904, the State Board of Health ceased recording the weather because of the expanded role of the U.S. Weather Service. This is a structure with a great deal of consideration behind the design; the ventilator on the roof with its center location and louvers allowed for the structure to cool especially when coupled with the louver walls that kept out rain, direct sunlight and allowed air to pass through. It is unclear when the meteorological station was torn down. It may have been in 1905 after the State Board of Health stopped recording weather related data.

The old Lansing, Michigan, Post Office/Federal Building, the meteorological station can be seen in the upper left, atop the tower. (CADL/FPLA)

The Signal Service opened an office in Lansing in January 1887 to record the weather at the Old State Office Building at 200-204 S. Washington Avenue. The office remained in place until July 1891. The Weather Bureau, the successor to the Signal Service, did not take over until February 1895 and placed a meteorological station at the old Post Office/Federal Building located on the northeast corner of Michigan and Capitol Avenues. In 1903, the Weather Bureau closed its site in Lansing, transferring the weather observations to Grand Rapids. In 1910 the Weather Bureau established a building at the Michigan Agricultural College, located on the northern part of the campus. A new office was established at Capitol City Airport. It has been said that the base of the Meteorological Station was still present at the southwest corner of the Capitol, but given the current construction at the Capitol, in 2018, it is doubtful that the base survived.

PERRY CONGREGATIONAL CHURCH

128 E. Second, Perry, MI.
Notice the fieldstone foundation and detailed stonework on the base of the chimney. The upper portion of the chimney has been rebuilt. Image from 2014.

"Architect Appleyard is drawing plans for a $3,500 church to be built by the Congregationalists at Perry, Shiawassee county. He is also drawing plans for a circular roof to be placed over the Lansing gas works. This roof will be 60 feet in diameter and requires a high order of architectural skill for that reason that it must be self-supporting" (*LR* 4/15/1884).

An early image of the Perry Congregational Church; the paintwork on the steeple is remarkable. Compare the chimney in this image with the previous image and observe the change in the chimney cap. Image circa 1909.

The Perry Congregational Church was dedicated in late 1884. The Reverend M. Foster directed the construction of the church and the total cost of the building was $4,000. Today the structure is the home of the Perry Congregational Christian Church (Lowery 1836 16).

The stout tower and overall style of the structure harkens back to the style of earlier Congregational churches built in the United States. What is odd is the placement of the chimney at the front of the building. Notice how the structure of the chimney has changed from the early image to the photograph taken in 2014. The original fish scale siding is still visible on the front pediment while the fish scale roofing on the steeple has been removed. The fieldstone foundation of the church gives the structure a sense of strength and stability, all traits desired by the church members. The bell tower roofing pattern almost resembles the time of day, dark in the morning, progressing toward full sunlight and the sunset in the evening.

The level of detail on the spire of the church is remarkable. Observe the triangle pattern on the ornamentation on the spire, mimicked on the gable end. You can also see that the louvres, capped with a sunrise motif, are in a waved pattern and not straight like a traditional louvre.

LANSING GAS WORKS

215-225 N. Grand, Lansing, MI.
The Gasometer to the right was built of brick, while one to the left was constructed out of iron.
Appleyard designed the circular roof for the brick gasometer.

"Architect Appleyard … is also drawing plans for a circular roof to be placed over the Lansing gas works. This roof will be 60 feet in diameter and requires a high order of architectural skill for that reason that it must be self-supporting" (*LR* 4/15/1884).

Lansing Fuel & Gas moved from 215 N. Grand to its new site at North Chestnut Sreeet and the Grand River in 1910. In 1926 Consumers Power Company acquired Lansing Fuel & Gas and currently owns the site on the Grand River. The gas storage tank was known as a gasometer and functions by employing water as a seal for the tank and to provide pressure to help distribute the gas.

Appleyard's design for a cover is unique because it was fixed and self-supporting. It is curious that gasometers were usually constructed away from the center of the city, which may explain why Lansing Fuel & Gas chose to relocate the gasometers to Willow Street.

BARAGA COUNTY COURTHOUSE

29 N. 3rd Street, L'Anse, MI.
Observe on the front dormer the two small windows on the front closed gable end and above the windows the trefoil motif.

"Wm. Appleyard, the capable architect of this city, has prepared plans for the new Baraga county court house at L'Anse, and they have been adopted by the board of supervisors. The building will be about 50 feet square and will present a very fine appearance" (*LRW* 1/24/1884).

"An act of the Michigan Legislature established Baraga County on February 19, 1875. L'Anse was named the county seat. County officials rented commercial space in the village until 1883 when a county jail, constructed at the cost of $8,000 was completed. The following year Baraga County commissioners accepted a bid for $11,945 to build a new brick courthouse. William Appleyard, a Lansing architect drew the plans. John B. Sweatt of Marquette served as the building contractor. The Baraga County Courthouse remains the seat of county government."[33]

---

[33] The above information was captured from the State Historic Preservation website in 2012,

Baraga County Courthouse rear view. Notice how the style employed on the front of the structure is carried through on the rear of the building.

Located upon a hill overlooking the town of L'Anse, the Baraga County Courthouse is an example of a late Victorian structure with Gothic elements. The building is of red brick; notice the arched first floor windows and the brick coursing that surrounds the building at the base of the first and second floor windows while also being employed over the first-floor windows. The third-floor dormer with the chimney has a Gothic style element on two of the gables, which one might see in the vaulting of a church. While not as large or ornate as many of the county courthouses built in Michigan during this time period the Baraga County Courthouse is a graceful structure with fine strong lines. The building is still in use today.

---

http://www.mcgi.state.mi.us/hso/sites/2742.htm. Unfortunately, when the SHPO was moved under MSHDA the information was removed from the website. The Internet is an incredible tool, but it is not an archive. You can see the information at the WayBackMachine, https://web.archive.org/web/20120612201620/http://www.mcgi.state.mi.us/hso/sites/2742.htm Other sites reverse the order with John B. Sweatt as architect and William Appleyard as the contractor.

SCHOOL FOR THE BLIND SUPERINTENDENT'S COTTAGE

Superintendent's Cottage, Lansing, MI.
Oddly the state of Michigan seems to have no photographs of this structure.

"The cottage built for Supt. [James F.] McElroy of the School for the Blind is one of the handsomest, most conveniently arranged, and most elaborately finished private residences in the city. Wm. Appleyard is the architect, and the completed building will sustain his growing reputation as a model draughtsman. The house is heated by steam and will be lighted by the Edison incandescent electric system. One of the features of several of the rooms is the elegant wrought wood mantel pieces for the fireplaces, which were made at the shop of D.W. & M.J. Buck. They are fine pieces of workmanship. Fuller & Wheeler are the builders of the house, and of course there is not a defect in the construction" (*LRW* 5/15/1884).

The superintendent's cottage at the Michigan School for the Blind was a massive structure, unlike the later superintendent's residence, designed by Edwyn A. Bowd. The Appleyard designed building was meant to impress. The white brick coursing at four levels around the building first attract the passerby eye. The triple chimneys and the extensive roof tell onlookers that this is a building of importance. The appropriation for the building was $4,500 but the bids came in much higher.

The Superintendent's Cottage at the School for the Blind was of considerable size but plain structure devoid of almost all ornamentation. The stacking of the windows was conservative and symmetrical. Unfortunately, the motif of the gable ends cannot be established.

The Lansing firm of Fuller & Wheeler was engaged and the cost of the building was increased to $7,500 (*Biennial Report* 7). The superintendent's cottage designed by Appleyard was just to the north and west of the current superintendent's cottage. Michigan Public Act 332, 1913 appropriated $8,500 for the construction of a new superintendent's cottage plus $6,022 to convert the current superintendent's cottage into a dormitory. The old building was expanded to the north and the dormitory accommodated 32 boys, with new bathrooms and living area. (*LSJ* 8/24/1914) The building functioned as a dormitory for many years and was torn down, best estimate between 1950-1951. In 1953 the site was occupied by the new Lion's Hall.

Electric lights, or as the article described them Edison Lights, were a huge advancement in 1884. In 1879, Thomas Edison created the first incandescent light bulb that could be mass produced. This may have been the first use of electric light in a Lansing residence. It was not until 1889 that a system was set up in Lansing to provide incandescent lights in residences and businesses (*LJ* 4/26/1889). The powerhouse at the School for the Blind provided a consistent source of power for the lighting at the Superintendent's cottage.

LANSING CITY HOSPITAL

827 N. Washington, Lansing, MI.
This was a wonderful Italianate home, the cupola couple with the gently pitched roof coupled with the ironwork balconies made this one of the most attractive homes in the city. (CADL/FPLA)

"The idea of erecting a hospital at Lansing, as advocated by Dr. J.A. Post and others during the recent sanitary convention, is meeting with universal favor among our public-spirited citizens. Father Van Driss has expressed a desire to substantially aid in its construction, as have many others, and Wm. Appleyard, the architect, has generously offered to take charge of any building which the recently organized association may desire to erect for the hospital purposes, and will render his services free of charge. There is no doubt that if the committees take hold of the matter energetically they can secure the means for the institution of the kind named that our city will be proud of" (*LRW* 3/25/1885).

It was four years before the dream of a hospital was realized in Lansing. In September of 1889 Orlando M. Barnes and Father Louis Van Driss purchased from the heirs of

Schuyler F. Seager Lots 1, 2 and 3 of Block 51, or 827 N. Washington for $6,000.[34] It is unknown if William Appleyard's plans were used in the renovation of the property, but it is worthwhile to include a description of the hospital building.

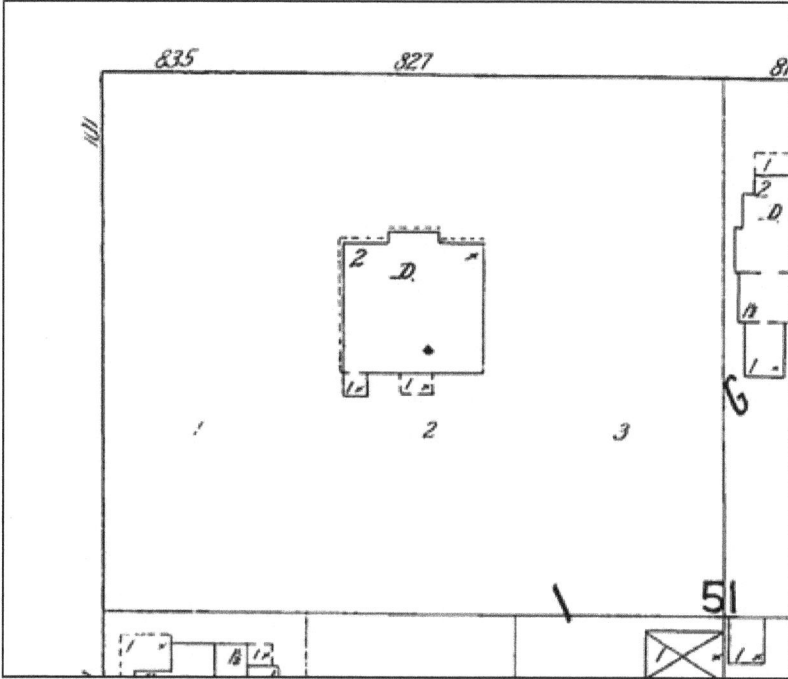

Lots 1, 2 and 3 Block 51, later Lots 1 and 3 was sold and separate residences built.

LANSING CITY HOSPITAL IS NOW DOING BUSINESS
A Brief Description of its Interior-Neatness, Convenience and Coziness it's Striking Features-The Hospital Staff

"Lansing's city hospital opened this morning, and a crowd of visitors have been viewing the many admirable arrangements all day, under the guide of the sisters in charge. There are four of the sisters, with Sister Gabriella, the superior. They all come from the Mother's house in Cincinnati, except Sister Magdalena, the chief nurse who is directly from the Good Samaritan hospital of Cincinnati. Sister Gabriella, superior, Sister Magdalena, principal nurse, and Sister Mary Frances and Sister Rancratia complete the force. They all wear regulation black habits. Sister Gabriella kindly conducted the STATE REPUBLICAN representative around. The entrance of the hospital leads into a great hall, running back the full length of the building. To the right, as you enter, is a double reception room, prettily carpeted and furnished; everything spotlessly neat without being

---

[34] *ICN* 9/26/1889

glaringly so. A very pleasant place to sit for a few moments is the visitor's natural comment. Across the hall is the general ward, containing five beds of snowy whiteness, with the prettiest little medicine stand close by the head of each. On each stand is a tray covered with snowy linen and containing a pitcher, glasses, etc. Each bed has an accompanying chair. The bed-posts are eight feet high, made so in order that the patient might be enclosed with a canopy, if he so desires. At the west end of the ward is a mantel and fireplace, and above a magnificent stained-glass window that throws color into the room, making the general effect extremely pretty. Upstairs, at the front of the house on each side of the long hall are two private corner rooms as pretty and cozy as any to be found in a private home. Splashers, vases, and the little odds and ends that go so far towards making a house pleasant are not wanting. The front window of each opens upon a cute little balcony, and the view is a most pleasant one. Back on the south side of the hall is another ward for two patients, and opposite are the sister's rooms and adjoining a bathroom.

"The third floor is not in use yet. In the basement is a model little dining room and kitchen. The whole hospital is well lighted and ventilated, and admirably heated by the hot water system. The rooms are all freshly frescoed, painted, and delightful cornices ornate the entire interior. The bare floors of the ordinary hospital are not here. Even in the general ward, the bare floor is relieved with carpet running the length of the ward at the floor of the beds. The exterior of the hospital is about the same as has always greeted Lansing's citizens when the property was owned by the late Schuyler Seager, except at the front a large portico has been added, and it is the intention to run a crescent shaped driveway from the north end of the front up to the portico and out at the south-east corner. The refurnishing and finishing cost $3,000, making the total cost to the donors, $9,000 or $3,000 each. Hon. O.M. Barnes is president; Father Van Driss, visitant; E.W. Sparrow, treasurer. Dr. Geo. E. Ranney has charge of the medical department, and Messrs. A.O. Bement, O.F. Barnes, S.L. Smith and Dr. W.H. Haze are the board of visitors. The hospital was given to the sisters furnished and ready for occupancy, and if, at the end of three years, the hospital appears to meet a demand in the community the three-year lease will be made into a perpetual grant. The advantages of such an institution to the physicians of the city are invaluable, and there is no doubt but what the hospital will be readily patronized" (SR 3/8/1890).

The hospital closed on September 1, 1893 when the Sisters of Charity withdrew their staff. Why did the sisters leave? There were several reasons, the indifference of the majority of the citizens of Lansing to the hospital, a reluctance of some physicians to send patients to the facility and finally, the property owners' (Barnes, Sparrow and Van Driss) unwillingness to deed the property directly to the Sisters of Charity.

827 N. Washington, Lansing, MI. Note the brackets under the roof line and the arch windows. All that is missing is an extensive wrap-around veranda. (CADL/FPLA)

The sisters were willing to improve the property if they owned it; they planned to add an elevator and surgical ward. The property owners were willing to commit to these terms if the property was used in perpetuity as a hospital, a condition the sisters could not guarantee. So, the hospital closed.[35]

A style of home not seen often in Lansing, the structure was a mixture of Renaissance Revival and the Italianate Styles. Appleyard did not design the home and the name of the original architect is still undiscovered. The home was at one time one of the most striking residences in Lansing. The quoins strangely only extend from the water table to the beginning of the second floor; usually the quoins would extend to the roofline. [36] The same pattern is repeated at the front entrance where the quoins only extend to the beginning of the second floor. To the passersby on the street these elements reinforce the

---

[35] See *SR* 8/23/1893, *SR* 8/31/1893, *SR* 9/2/1893, *SR* 8/5/1893 and *SR* 9/23/1893.
[36] Masonry blocks at the corner of walls used to strengthen the structure and as an added feature provide detail to the structure.

notion that this was a home of someone important in the community. Above the main entrance is a small ironwork porch that is framed by pilaster columns. At the corners of the second floor, the pilaster columns wrap around the building and the architectural term for this type of pilaster column is canton.[37] These components are an interesting mix of architectural elements; the original architect deserves great credit for his seamless use of both quoins and pilasters on the facade of the building. The styles of windows used in the structure are an interesting mixture of circle top windows on the first floor and the graceful arch windows on the second floor except over the entrance where two narrow circle top windows are employed with a center column. The residence was torn down in September 1960.

The home at 827 N. Washington was originally built for Daniel L. Case in 1857. Case came to Lansing as the Deputy Auditor General and in 1858 was elected Auditor General. The property was later sold to Schuyler F. Seager where he lived until his death in 1883. It has often been stated that the property was sold to Seager after Case's death, in fact Daniel Case passed away at his home on High Street on November 24, 1898.[38] The misunderstanding may have arisen as a result of confusing Daniel L. Case Jr. with Daniel L. Case Sr. Daniel L. Case Jr., who served with the 78th New York Volunteer Infantry, was captured and served 10 months in Confederate Prison camps, passed away on December 10, 1870 due to wounds received during his war service.[39]

---

[37] See Ching 266.
[38] *SR* 11/25/1898 and *ICD* 12/8/1898.
[39] For a full biographical account of Case's life see *Portrait* 640.

WILLIAM ENNIS HOME

616 W. Genesee, Lansing, MI.
The home was originally located at 311 W. Allegan and was moved in 1932 to 616 W. Genesee with the construction of the new Post Office/Federal Building. The above image is of the home after it was moved. (CADL/FPLA)

"Wm. Ennis will shortly commence the erection of a fine residence on Allegan street opposite the capitol building. The architect is Wm. P. Appleyard. Which is as good as a guarantee of first-class work in every respect, and the building when completed will cost $3,500. The house will be finished in Queen Anne style. The contract for the woodwork has been given to Fuller & Wheeler, and the mason work to James Hilliard" (*LRW* 4/15/1885).

"The house of Wm. Ennis on the opposite side of the capitol grounds is on Allegan street, between Townsend and Walnut, and although still in course of erection has so nearly reached completion, that the visitor has no difficulty in assuring himself that it will be one of the finest residences in the capitol city. The building is of the Queen Anne style of architecture and was designed by the popular young architect, Wm. P. Appleyard. The builders were Fuller & Wheeler and the masons, Hilliard & Barrett. The structure is three stories in height, and is surmounted on the front side by a tower rising from the first floor. It is painted dark brown to the second story, at which point two narrow belts of light drab run entirely around the building. Above this to the shingles the color is a darker drab, and the roof as well as the shingles on the side are stained with creosote. The trimmings are of light drab and the panels over each window and the porch are green. The front porch, at the northeast corner of the building, opens into the main hall. On the left-hand side of the hall a winding stairway leads to the floor above, while sliding doors at the right denote the position of the parlor. This well-arranged room has double windows fronting on the street and a handsome fire-place with a square brick arch, which will be finished in black ash. The parlor opens to a bedroom in the rear. The entrance to the living room is at the south end of the hall, and this is also provided with double windows. The kitchen back of this room will contain a force pump and boiler by means of which every floor can be supplied hot or cold water. This floor, like the one above, is bountifully supplied with large closets and also contains bath and toilet rooms, woodshed, etc. About midway up the front stairway is a window of a decidedly unique pattern. The center is of cathedral glass surrounded by small panes of stained glass in a "crazy" pattern, all set in heavily-carved frame. The second floor contains four commodious bedrooms. Two of them being provided with double windows, affording magnificent views of the city, and a store room, but the third floor will not be divided into rooms at present. The cellar extends the entire length of the house, and will contain the Richardson & Boynton furnace, which will be used for heating purposes. The building has unusually complete ventilating and sewerage arrangements, and will be supplied with gas, speaking tubes and many conveniences of a similar nature. The structure, taken as a whole, is not only one of the most attractive dwelling houses in Lansing, but also one of the best made. In the near future, the Republican will have something to say of the other residences that have been constructed this season" (*LRW* 7/15/1885).

William Ennis was born on November 20, 1842 in Centerville, St. Joseph County, Michigan, the son of David and Elizabeth Caroline (née Magee) Ennis. On April 21, 1869 William married Miss Rebecca M. Hasbrouck in Centerville, Michigan, the couple had one child Harry H. Ennis. In 1872, the family moved to Lansing when William received an appointment to work in a state office. William held the position of bookkeeper with a variety of state offices, served as Justice of the Peace and at one time administered the safety deposit vaults at the City National Bank. First and foremost, in William's life was his affiliation with several Masonic organizations. On March 31, 1901, William's wife Rebecca passed away at their home. William lived another 16 years occupying his time by staying active in the Masonic orders. William Ennis passed away on March 15, 1917.[40]

---

[40] *LSJ* 3/15/1917

A later view of the house at 616 W. Genesee after its move. Originally the home was constructed with a spire on the tower, that may have been removed to help ease its relocation. (CADL/FPLA)

With the construction of Lansing's new Post Office/Federal Building the Ennis home was moved from Allegan Street in February 1932 to 616 W. Genesee. In many ways, this is a remarkable house. First, it is the only home that survived from the 300 block of West Allegan Street, once one of the premier sites in Lansing given its location just south of the Capitol. Secondly, the home still has many of the exterior architectural features that allow the researcher clues as to its original appearance. The tower was originally capped with a more pronounced peak than what currently exists on the home. Next, the front porch extended across the entire front of the building. The entrance has also been changed, the original entrance was set back a little further, and there is also a small addition on the north east side on the rear of the home that was not originally present when the house was located on Allegan Street. The current owners should be commended for their attempts to renovate the house.[41] The home is still standing in 2019.

---

[41] See the LSJ 10/16/1949 for an image of the home before the renovation.

M.A.C. VETERINARY BUILDING

Veterinary Building at the Michigan Agricultural College; East Lansing, Michigan. Note what seems to be a weather station on the roof.

"Architect Wm. P. Appleyard of this city in 22 days prepared the full plans and specifications for the new assembly hall, Veterinary and mechanical laboratories, and residence to be erected at the state Agricultural college, and did it well. This is a remarkably short time when the amount of labor which was of necessity crowded into it is considered and shows Mr. Appleyard to be possessed of an unusual faculty for hard, earnest work" (*LRW* 6/17/1885).

What an interesting building. In many ways the Veterinary Building resembled the Mechanical Laboratory that was built at the same time. The color scheme in the above postcard image is noteworthy, especially when compared to the next image. You can discern that the brickwork, on the gables and tower shingles, have been painted. The painting did not subtract from the structure but only added to the architectural appeal. The circle top windows on the first floor were mimicked on the second floor with segmental windows with an arched brick lintel and made the facade of the building striking. Notice the small decorative towers on the building's corners and the gables and how the towers flow into the pilasters. The brick coursing that surrounds the building at the bottoms and tops of the windows coupled with the location of the pilasters frame the building. If you look closely you can see the weather station located on the roof of the building, in the first image, but in the photograph below only the base is visible.

Veterinary Building at the Michigan Agricultural College, the structure to the left of the entrance was used to house animals that were being treated by the students.

Prior to 1910 the Michigan Agricultural College, oddly enough, did not offer a degree in veterinary medicine. That changed on October 21, 1909 when the State Board passed a resolution that authorized the college to establish a division of Veterinary Science. Prior to this the college taught classes in zoology and veterinary science but did not offer a full course of study in the subject. Why did it take so long for the Michigan Agricultural College to establish a Department of Veterinary Medicine? Well it had not been mandated by the Michigan Legislators. On May 22, 1907, the state legislators passed Public Act 97 that allowed the establishment of a "Department of Veterinary Science at the M.A.C."[42] The Veterinary Laboratory building was replaced in 1915 with a new structure which was built just east of Farm Lane. The old Veterinary Laboratory was demolished in August 1930, for no other reason than it was in the way of a new road that was to be run near the Agricultural Laboratory, a big loss for the college and the public. (*LSJ* 8/20/1930)

---

[42] *Offices of Board of Trustees and President Meeting*, Minutes, October 21, 1909 *MAC Record* 11/2/1909.

M.A.C. MECHANICAL LABORATORY

Mechanical Laboratory, Michigan Agricultural College

REPORT OF THE DEPARTMENT OF MATHEMATICS AND ENGINEERING
By R.C. Carpenter, Superintendent.
THE BUILDING

"The building was designed by myself [Rolla C. Carpenter]. I also prepared with aid of student's specifications and drawings. Mr. William P. Appleyard, the architect of the other buildings erected in 1885, acted as superintendent of construction. The building was erected by Fuller & Wheeler, contractors for $7,800."[43]

"It was moved and carried that the following offer of Mr. Wm. P. Appleyard be accepted. To prepare plans and specifications for the Armory and Assembly Hall, the Veterinary Laboratory, the Professor's Residence and to examine the plans and specifications of the Mechanical Dept. prepared by Prof. Carpenter making such suggestions as he thinks best. Also, to superintend the construction of all of the above-mentioned buildings for the sum of five hundred dollars ($500)."[44]

---

[43] *Twenty-Fifth* xlviii.
[44] Offices of Board of Trustees and President, *Meeting Minutes* April 20, 1885.

Mechanical Laboratory and Shop, note how the brickwork detail on the chimney is extended downward, terminating between the first and second floors.

"In 1885, the first machine shop and foundry was erected, having been designed by Professor R.C. Carpenter. Portions of the buildings were used for class rooms. The veterinary laboratory was erected in 1885; the upper portion after a while was used by Dr. Marshall for bacteriology. On March 5, 1916, the Engineering Building at the MAC was destroyed by fire; the machine shop and foundry, which was located just east of the Engineering Building, was also destroyed" (*LSJ* 3/6/1916).

Mechanical Laboratory and Shop. Observe the number of windows, this view is from the east, which allowed for a tremendous amount of natural light to enter the building.

It is clear based upon the previous texts, that Professor Carpenter designed the Mechanical Laboratory and Shop, with William Appleyard acting as a consultant, and superintendent of construction of the building. The rear of the structure has the appearance of the typical factory that was constructed at this time period. The classroom building was situated on a north south axis, while the foundry wing had an east west alignment. The structure was laid out in this manner to maximize the amount of natural light that would enter the building through the rows of windows and the center skylight. The tower at the front of the structure had elegant triangle dormers that seemed to fade into the structure of the tower. The layout of the laboratory and shops was an efficient design. The view of the structure to the passerby was pleasing and fit well with the other buildings on campus. The Mechanical Laboratory was 30x60 feet across the front, with a mechanical lecture room and laboratory on the first floor and on the second an open drafting room. The rear wing was 50x60 feet and contained a machine shop on the first floor and a wood shop on the second floor. The tower was 16x16 feet with offices on the first and second floor. The third floor of the tower served as a student study room.

The Mechanical Laboratory and Shops during the fire which also destroyed the Engineering Building and damaged Wells Hall on March 4-5, 1916

Rolla Clinton Carpenter was born in Orion, Michigan on June 26, 1852 the son of Charles K. and Jennette (née Coryell) Carpenter. Rolla graduated from the MAC in 1873 and obtained a Master's Degree from the University of Michigan in 1875. He was a professor of Civil Engineering and Mathematics at the MAC from 1875-1890. Carpenter accepted a position at Cornell University in 1890 where he was an associate professor of Engineering until 1905. Considered one of the foremost engineering experts in the United States, Carpenter served as a judge at several World Fairs and as an expert witness in several important cases. He published several works and was best known for his books on *Heating and Ventilating Buildings: A Manual for Heating Engineers and Architects* (1895) and the *Internal Combustion Engines: Their Theory, Construction and* Operation (1908) with Herman Diederichs. In 1915, Carpenter was part of the commission to inspect the Culebra Cut landslide at the Panama Canal. On May 25, 1876 Rolla married Miss Marian Dewey in Greenville, Michigan, the couple had three children; George D., Charles K., and Naomi J. Carpenter. On January 19, 1919 Rolla Clinton Carpenter, a principal figure in MAC history, passed away at his home in Ithaca, New York.[45]

A view of the front of the Mechanical Laboratory after the fire, the ruins of the tower are quite visible. The fire began in the cement laboratory in the Main Engineering Building.

After the destruction of the Engineering Building and Mechanical Laboratory, both structures were quickly rebuilt, helped in part by a $100,000 donation by Ransom E. Olds. The new Engineering Building, named R.E. Olds Hall in 1917, and the Mechanical Laboratory were designed by Lansing architect Edwyn A. Bowd to be fireproof buildings.[46]

---

[45] *Post Standard* 1/20/1919, *Beal* 417 and *Iron Age* 1/23/1919 p. 280.
[46] Offices of Board of Trustees and President, *Meeting Minutes* April 19, 1916.

M.A.C. ARMORY BUILDING

A view of the Armory Building that shows the smaller arched windows on the southside of the structure. Note the position and height of the chimneys on the facade and how this pattern is repeated on the rear of the structure.

"It was moved and carried that the following offer of Mr. Wm. P. Appleyard be accepted. To prepare plans and specifications for the Armory and Assembly Hall, the Veterinary Laboratory, the Professor's Residence and to examine the plans and specifications of the Mechanical Dept."[47]

In 1885 Fuller & Wheeler, of Lansing, built a low, broad building for military drills and other college functions. The Armory was also used as an auditorium, gymnasium, chapel, and lecture hall, for campus dances and countless other events. The Armory was connected to the bathhouse by an enclosed addition, which made sense given the nature of the users of the building. In many ways, the Armory was a nondescript building with an interesting two-tone brick color scheme which in some ways mimicked that of the Veterinary Building. The circle top windows and entrance framed by the brickwork creates an attractive contrast with the lighter brickwork.

---

[47] Offices of Board of Trustees and President, *Meeting Minutes* April 20, 1885.

Armory Building at the Michigan Agricultural College. Observe how the height of the chimney on the left closest entrance has increased, just why the chimney was added to is unknown.

The interior had an extensive wood floor and tie rods spanning the interior above to strengthen the structure. The location and function of the chimneys are interesting with the chimneys sloping in height from left to right with the angle of the roof. In 1928, a new Armory was built on campus, known today as Demonstration Hall. In 1939, the old Armory building was torn down to make way for the new $200,000 Music Building built with a Public Works Administration grant (*LSJ* 12/19/1938).

M.A.C. FACULTY HOMES

Michigan Agricultural College, Faculty Row, Dwelling No. 10 built in 1885.

"Architect Wm. P Appleyard of this city in 22 days prepared the full plans and specifications for the new…residence to be erected at the state Agricultural college and did it well" (*LRW* 6/17/1885).

"It was moved and carried that the following offer of Mr. Wm P. Appleyard be accepted. To prepare plans and specifications for the …the Professors Residence … Also, to superintend the construction of all of the above-mentioned buildings for the sum of five hundred dollars ($500)."[48]

"Resolved that the Board do hereby approve of the plans and specifications for the Veterinary Laboratory as submitted by Messrs. Fuller & Wheeler and do also approve of the plan and specifications for the new dwelling to be erected for the Professor of Mechanic Arts being substantially the plan used for the house of now occupied by Prof. Johnson." [49]

---

[48] Offices of Board of Trustees and President, *Meeting Minutes* April 20, 1885.
[49] Offices of Board of Trustees and President, *Meeting Minutes* April 20, 1885.

"Moved and carried that Mr. Appleyard be authorized to have the specifications of the new buildings printed. Moved & carried that the time of completion of the new buildings at the suggestion of Messrs. Fuller and Wheeler be as follows. [Time Limit to Contracts] Residence Sept 15th Armory and Assembly Hall Nov. 15th Mechanical Building Dec 15th, and Veterinary Laboratory Jan 15th".[50]

"For Professor Lewis McLouth, a large dwelling, No. 10, in Faculty Row, was erected in 1885". (Beal 271)

This all seems pretty straight forward except for the statement in regard to the plans submitted by Messrs. Fuller & Wheeler. It is unclear what this statement means: "substantially the plan used for the house now occupied by Prof. Johnson". The exterior of the Faculty Row home at No. 8 does not resemble the final appearance of the Faculty Row home at No. 10. The home at No. 10 seems to be a completely new design. The stumbling block is that Fuller & Wheeler, besides being contractors, also designed houses. Consider the fact that No. 10 also resembles the work Appleyard did for the state of Michigan at the School for the Blind and the Boy's Industrial School and you see the conundrum. Was Appleyard so overworked that he subcontracted the design of these two structures? Or is it the case that Fuller & Wheeler receiving board approval for Appleyard's plans? Faculty Row, Dwelling No. 10 was torn down in 1922.

The first resident of Faculty Row, Dwelling No. 10 was Professor McLouth. Lewis McLouth, the son of Farley and Mary (née Doty) McLouth, was born in Rochester, New York on September 21, 1835. Lewis attended Oberlin College and later graduated from the University of Michigan in 1858 with a Master of Arts. In 1860, he received a Master of Penology from the State Normal School [Eastern Michigan University]. After graduation, he taught at an assortment of educational institutions in Michigan, from being principal at an academy in Lapeer, Michigan to an instructor at the State Normal School. Lewis accepted a position at the MAC in 1885 as president of the Mechanical Arts Department. However, in 1896, Lewis resigned his position at MAC to become president of the South Dakota Agricultural College [now South Dakota State University]. During Lewis' tenure he oversaw the growth of the campus at South Dakota Agricultural College, expanded curriculum and establishment of many new departments including the founding of the School of Pharmacy. In July of 1894 student unrest and politics resulted in the regents of the college requesting Lewis' resignation, but he did not leave until 1896. In regard to his personal life, Lewis married Miss Sarah A. Doty in Ann Arbor, Michigan on December 30, 1860, the couple had nine children; Lawrence A., Bessie C., Lewis C., Marnie C., Sadie, Farley, Ida, Burnie and Fanny C. McLouth. After leaving South Dakota Agricultural College, Lewis served as Dean of Faculty of the Home Correspondence School of

---

[50] Offices of Board of Trustees and President, *Meeting Minutes* June 8, 1885.

Springfield, Massachusetts. While visiting his daughter Sarah, in New Britain, Connecticut Lewis passed away suddenly on March 16, 1909. Long forgotten, Lewis McLouth should be remembered as one of the founders of the Engineering School at the Michigan State University.[51]

TERRACE HOUSE

An example of a Terrace House in Lansing, Michigan, that was located at 515 E. Shiawassee; there is no indication that Appleyard designed this structure. The date of construction of these flats was between 1885-1887. Note the superb pattern on the pediment of the two front gables.
(CADL/FPLA)

"Wm. P. Appleyard, the architect has completed the designs for an original terrace house, which will probably be erected in this city during the coming fall. The architect's plan is one which seems destined to become popular with those who have an idea of building a row of dwelling houses, the structure being designed as a double building, each half perfect in itself, and while roomy and attractive both inside and out, can be erected at a very moderate cost" (*LRW* 8/19/1885).

Appleyard's plan for a terrace house may or may not have been built in Lansing. There are two options for the terrace home, the only ones built in Lansing during this period are

---

[51] Beal 425 and the *MAC Record* 3/23/1909.

515 E. Shiawassee and 409-411 W. Ottawa. The building at 515 E. Shiawassee was an odd structure. Although architecturally the building is pleasing to the eye, the lack of windows on the facade and the sides of the structure would have made these residences stuffy and very dark with little light penetrating into the interior of the building. The location is now the site of a parking lot.

409-411 W. Ottawa, Lansing MI.
A striking double home. The structure was symmetrical, with two story canted bay windows on the facade. Notice the eye for detail the architect had, the elegant narrow columns on the porch, which do not overwhelm the entrance. (CADL/FPLA)

Another option for Appleyard's design of a terrace house in Lansing is 409-411 W. Ottawa. The structure was built for George M. Dayton, an early Lansing developer, to serve as his principle residence.[52] The Dayton residence with its traditional design may be a better candidate for the terrace residence designed by Appleyard. The date of construction for both structures was circa 1885-1887, but the lack of any collaborating evidence makes either of these structures as the terrace house that Appleyard designed in 1885 purely speculative. A *Lansing State Journal* article in 1958 stated that James Appleyard designed and built the terrace house at 409-411 W. Ottawa in 1890. The date for construction was based upon Lansing City Assessor records from that period, a source

---

[52] For a short biography of Dayton see MacLean 64.

that is known to be imprecise. It is possible that William Appleyard drew up the plans for the terrace house on West Ottawa and it took several years for his father to build the structure. The article also mentions the site where the sandstone used in the construction of the home may have been quarried, one location was across from Moores River Park below the dam, just south of Glenn Island, the other quarry was west of the MLK (Logan) Street Bridge. The residence was torn down in 1958. (*LSJ* 1/12/1958)

TURNER BLOCK

408-410 E. Michigan, Lansing MI.
One of the finest examples of a symmetrical set of business blocks still standing in the city of Lansing. Observe the rusticated, surround lintels over three of the single windows on the second floor complimented by the two arched lintels over the double windows.

"Jas. M. Turner has broken ground for the erection of his two new stores on Michigan avenue opposite Lapham & Longstreet's mill. The building will be 75 by 43½ feet in size and two stories high with a 15-foot basement. The west store will be occupied by Myron Cline, the well-known marble dealer of Mason, who will transfer his entire business to Lansing. The front designed by W. P. Appleyard, will be exceedingly tasty" (*SR* 6/12/1886).

Note the brick pilasters on the side of the building, and how they frame the first and second floor windows. A striking and inexpensive design feature by Appleyard, which was important given that this side of the building was viewed by the public.

James M. Turner was one of Lansing's most distinguished and respected residents. He was elected to the Michigan Legislature in 1879 and served two terms as Lansing's Mayor, 1889 and 1895. James was also one of Lansing's leading businessmen. James worked to establish the Jackson, Lansing & Saginaw Railroad, later was President and General Manager of the Chicago & Northwestern Railroad and was involved in the Iron Range & Huron Bay Railroad. James was born in Lansing on April 23, 1850 the son of James M. and Marion (née Munroe) Turner. After attending Lansing schools, James was sent to study at the Cazenovia Seminary [Cazenovia College] in New York where he stayed for one year. When he returned to Lansing James worked as a clerk at Daniel L. Case's general store. After two years of business experience James went to work in the land office of the Jackson, Lansing & Saginaw Railroad where his father was the Land Commissioner. James was hired to supervise the construction of the Ionia & Lansing Railroad. Shortly afterward James' father died and James, age of 19, served as paymaster and cashier of the Ionia & Lansing Railroad.

James M. Turner 1850-1896

James established a general land business with Dwight S. Smith in the early 1870s, where he worked as the surveyor while Smith ran the office; it was at this time that James became familiar with northern Michigan.[53] In 1889 James was elected mayor of Lansing and one year later nominated as the Republican candidate for Governor, James lost the election to Edwin B. Winans by 11,000 votes. After the election, James started Springdale Farm on 2,000 acres south east of the city. Portions of the farm later became Fenner Nature Center, and Crego Park. In 1895 James was again elected Mayor of Lansing by a large majority. On September 20, 1876, James married Miss Sophia Porter Scott in Chicago, Illinois, the couple had two sons; James and Scott.[54] On July 7, 1896 James M. Turner passed away at the Alma Sanitarium at 4 am. His body arrived in Lansing the same day and Governor John T. Rich and Mayor Russell C. Ostrander met the train out of respect for one of Lansing's famous citizens.[55]

---

[53] Dwight S. Smith died in Jackson, Michigan on November 24, 1897.
[54] Scott Turner had a remarkable life. He was aboard the RMS Lusitania and survived the sinking of the ship in World War One. Scott spent his life traveling the world, but he never forgot Lansing. Because of his efforts, Lansing has Fenner Arboretum and Scott Woods. Remember that when you walk the River Trail.
[55] *SR* 7/7/1896 and *LRW* 7/10/1896

GRAND RIVER BOAT CLUB

Grand River Boat Club located at the foot of Ottawa Street and the Grand River in Lansing, Michigan. As someone who once was a member of a crew team, launching off this dock may have been a challenge. (CADL/FPLA)

"Architect Wm. P. Appleyard is preparing plans for a new club house for the Grand River Boat club" (*SR* 7/31/1886).

"Plans for the new boat house, to be built by the Grand River Boat Club, have already been completed by Architect, William Appleyard and several bids for its construction have been presented under seal. The new boat house, which will be located at the end of Ottawa street, will be a one-story building 78x22 feet in size. The main room will, of course, be the boat room. This will take up 21x50 feet of the space and will be supplied with a barge, two gigs and two shells. Besides the boat room there will be a pleasant club room, 11.9x21 feet in size, and the remainder of the space will be filled by a conveniently situated dressing room, 6x8 feet and a bath room of the same dimensions. Facing the river an eight-foot veranda and balcony will be built, adding greatly to the comfort and pleasantness of the house. The building will cost about $1,000. Work will be commenced after the election excitement is over and the structure will be ready for occupancy by the middle of May. The 40 enthusiastic members of the boat club are looking forward anxiously for the time when they can enjoy the healthful exercise of their shells, and they expect as a result, without doubt, to capture some of the prizes in the famous regatta of the N.W.A.R.A. [Northwestern Amateur Rowing Association]" (*SR* 4/1/1887).

"The Grand River Boat Club are somewhat excited over the fact that the firm of Bement & Son's contemplate suing out an injunction prohibiting them from erecting their new club house. Mr. Bement in an interview this afternoon said: 'The injunction is liable not to be issued, and there are no facts about it that I wish to have made public'" (*SR* 4/18/1887).

"The new boat house of the Grand River Boat Club will be completed by next Thursday" (*SR* 5/9/1887).

Just what was built for the Grand River Boat Club and when it was built is one of the greatest mysteries in Lansing history. Many times, throughout its past the Grand River Boat Club commissioned several architects to design a clubhouse/boathouse to be completed for the organization. However, the great majority of these commissions were never built. The Grand River Boat Club filed its articles of association on July 19, 1872. The club purchased its first boats, an eight-oared barge and a four-oared shell from the Neptune Club of East Saginaw.[56] The barge was christened the William A. Barnard after the Vice President of the organization and rowed with great success by the club. The first race that the club participated in was in Grand Haven, Michigan on August 12-13, 1874, when the organization won the race but lost due to the judge's decision. On July 4, 1875, the club won its first race when it defeated the Goguancs Club of Battle Creek on a race held in Lansing by 1 minute and 8 seconds with a 20 second handicap. Two days later the organization joined the Northwestern Amateur Rowing Association. Rowing in the decade of the 1870s was as popular as the NFL is today. Large amounts of money were wagered on the events and cities sought to have the best rowing club in the nation. In the 1880s although popular interest in the sport of rowing waned, the Grand River Boat Club continued as a rowing club and as an important social organization in Lansing. The Grand River Boat Club's annual banquet was considered one of the highlights of the social season. But as sporting tastes changed and as the old guard of the club passed away the organization fell from prominence and disbanded in 1907.[57]

---

[56] The barge was a much heavier boat than the eight-oared sweep, which is in use today in competitive rowing.

[57] *LJ* 7/7/1876, *SR* 12/30/1898, *SR* 4/22/1907 and *LSJ* 12/16/1920.

JACOB STAHL BLOCK

213-215 N. Washington, Lansing, MI.
Note the advertisements of the side of the building. (CADL/FPLA)

"Plans have been completed for the construction of a new three-story block to be built by Stall [Stahl] & Forrester on Washington avenue this summer. The building is to be 66 x 100 feet and will be made of pressed brick with cut stone trimmings. The first floor will be occupied by Messrs. Stall & Forrester for hardware and fancy goods stores; the second floor will contain offices, and the third will be used as lodge rooms, the Odd Fellows have already secured part of it. It is expected that the building will be completed by November, and work will be commenced on it in a few weeks" (*SR* 4/1/1887).

"The trouble between Messrs. Stahl and Forrester yesterday was occasioned by Mr. Merrifield's refusal to lend Mr. Forrester certain sums of money as previously agreed upon. The refusal came at the last moment after Mr. Appleyard had the plans drawn and after arrangements for the building block were about completed. The question to be settled is: Who shall pay Mr. Appleyard, the architect? Mr. Forrester says that Mr. Appleyard's plans are for a building of twice the value he and Mr. Stahl said they wanted, and since he [Mr. Forrester] withdraws on that account, Mr. Stahl wants him to pay all of the architect's bill. The case will probably get into the courts, as each side is determined" (*SR* 5/20/1887).

"Mr. Stahl gave his side of the Stahl-Forrester block embroglio [complicated situation] this morning to a reporter of the *STATE REPUBLICAN*. "He has, so affirms no specific agreement as to the amount of money they should pay for the block before the plans were drawn but gave Mr. Appleyard instructions to draw up plans for a good block and 'if it was too rich for his blood,' he could cut down before building. The parties were to build as partners each on his 33-foot lot, with a common stairway between the two buildings. Mr. Forrester failed to secure the funds he expected Mr. Merrifield to procure for him from the Connecticut Mutual Life Insurance Company, and then backed out of the partnership, after contracts for brick, joist, and other materials had been signed. Mr. Stahl proposes to go on and build alone, but must necessarily have new plans, for different arrangements for a stairway must be made and other changes as well. He claims that Mr. Forrester's withdrawal makes the original plans of no avail to him, and that therefore he should pay for them, and also for half the wall next to his land. The matter will likely get into the courts" (*SR* 5/21/1887).

"Messrs. Stahl and Forrester will build separately. Mr. Appleyard still whistles for his pay" (*SR* 5/24/1887).

Notice the architectural carved flourishes over the third-floor windows and the 13 small corbeled arches along the pediment, an odd number to have since the number was considered unlucky in a building, but not in the Masonic world. (CADL/FPLA)

ELEGANCE AND BEAUTY
MARK THE NEW APARTMENTS OF CAPITAL LODGE I.O.O.F.

In Jacob Stahl's New Block on Washington avenue—The will be no Finer Rooms in the State—A Well Furnished Building from Top to Bottom, a Credit to Mr. Stahl and to Lansing.

"Jacob Stahl believes what is worth doing is worth doing well and has carried this idea out thoroughly in the construction of his new building on Washington avenue. From basement to garret the building is the most complete in its appointments, and in detail of finish and convenience of arrangement, will compare favorably with any similar building in the State. Mr. Stahl expects to occupy the elegant new store himself about the first of April, and he will have a place that is a credit both to him and to Lansing. The second floor has been rented by George B. Richmond, the dentist, and he will undoubtedly have the very finest offices in the city. On this floor are two sets of offices, in the front and rear of the building, which are exact duplicates of each other, except in the view afforded. The offices are provided with all the modern conveniences, and although Mr. Richmond has taken the entire floor, it is probable he will sublet the back suite. The new lodge room of Capital Lodge, I.O.O.F. will be on the third floor, and their apartments will undoubtedly be the most elegant in the state. It is entered by a broad and splendidly lighted stairway of easy assent. The door opens into a hall, which leads from one end of the ante-room and from the other into a kitchen. Between the kitchen and dining-room is another ante-room. This is connected with the dining room by large folding doors, and folding doors open from the dining-room to the first ante-room. The main hall is a spacious room 36½x60 feet, fronting on Washington avenue, off which are the coat room, closets, small office and a room for the very private of the order and the concealment of the inevitable goat. Then the closets, wash-room, and in short, all modern conveniences. It is the intention of the Capital Lodge to commence preparing their rooms for occupancy in a short time, and in doing this something over $1,000 will be expended. The members of the Lodge are certainly to be congratulated on having secured these elegant apartments, than which there are no finer in Michigan" (*SR* 3/3/1888)

"Undoubtedly the finest hardware store in central Michigan is that recently erected by Jacob Stahl at 211 Washington avenue. The work on the construction of the building was begun a year ago. The plans were prepared by Wm. P. Appleyard, and the contract was let to Fitzpatrick Bros. and Jackson & Huff. The building is 33x100 feet, outside dimensions, and 27x97 inside and is 68 feet high. The front of the building is pressed brick with Lake Superior red stone and terra cotta trimmings. Of the three floors the first will be occupied by J. Stahl as a hardware store; the second by Dr. G. B. Richmond for dental parlors and the third will be a hall of the Odd Fellows.

An interior photograph of Jacob Stahl's Hardware store from 1890. Notice how the business carried almost everything a person could need. (CADL/FPLA)

"The first floor is trimmed in red oak and black ash, and the other two in pine. The ceiling of the first floor is fifteen feet high. On the north side of the room are drawers, shelves and boxes for holding the hardware stock, and on the south side are glass cupboards and paint and oil tanks. At the west end are the boxes for bolts. Perhaps the most attractive feature of the building is the show window. It extends into the street five feet from the store line and is of the finest plate glass. The doors two in number, one on each side of the window, are models of beauty, the transoms being of pebble plate, perhaps the most costly of plate glass. Aside from the apartments already mentioned there are the basement and tin shop. The former is eight feet deep and runs the entire length of the building and will be used for a storeroom. The tin shop is but a few feet in the rear of the building and is two stories high. The first floor will be used as a storeroom and the second for a tin shop" (*LR* 4/11/1888). The building was torn down in 1968.

Well over time one finds one's mistakes when one writes a book. In *Darius B. Moon: The History of a Michigan Architect 1880-1910*, I thought that Moon handled the remodeling of the third-floor when the G.A.R. moved to the building in 1895, but I also implied that Moon may have designed the structure because the building had many architectural elements that Moon used in other structures. (MacLean 151) Now you understand the difficulty in attributing the design of a building to a specific architect based upon the fact that a building exhibited architectural components used by an architect in another building.

Note the date of construction of the Stahl Building, it was 1887.

So, it seems Moon was responsible for the remodeling of G.A.R. rooms and not the design of the structure. It begs the question, did William Appleyard's architectural designs influence the work of Darius B. Moon? The building was definitely designed by William Appleyard, and what a building it was. The Stahl building was asymmetrical; the tower entrance which serviced the upper floors was an exceptional architectural element that is complemented in the narrow-recessed arch that continued upward until it reached the parapet to match the thirteen smaller arches. Notice how the lintels of rusticated stone extend across the facade and are balanced by the thinner rusticated stone sills. The second-floor widows over the store are oriel windows and are a later addition, maybe the result of the Moon remodel? Over the second-floor windows was a motif, not as elaborate as the one over the third-floor windows, but a pattern of three small boxes over three of each individual window. One facet that was overlooked in the Moon book was the date of construction over the transom to the door leading to the upper floors, it reads 1887.

Note the pattern of motifs under the third-floor windows, twenty-four to be exact. Was it Masonic? Stahl was active in many Masonic organizations in Lansing.

Born in Germany on August 23, 1845, Jacob Stahl immigrated to Cleveland, Ohio in 1867. In Cleveland he served as an apprentice in metalworking profession at the C.C. Ironworks; he advanced in the shop rising from machinist to the position of foreman. On January 21, 1868, Jacob married Miss Kate Hessert in Cuyahoga County, Ohio, the couple had two sons; Frank and Louis. In 1871 Jacob started a hardware store in Amherst, Ohio; after ten years, he relocated his business to Lansing where the hardware firm of Stahl & Son was established. Jacob served on the boards of the Boys Industrial School, the Lansing Electric, Light and Water, was the treasurer of the Lansing, St. Johns and St. Louis Railroad Company, and a director of City National Bank. Jacob personally selected the stock for his hardware store, much of which was purchased on his trips to back to Germany. His hardware business had one of the finest selections of toys in Michigan, which must have made his store the centerpiece for the dreams of all the children in Lansing. Jacob Stahl had an interest in music and the arts, he was one of the principal financial organizers for the Lansing Conservatory of Music. Jacob Stahl died on October 13, 1922 in Battle Creek, Michigan surrounded by his family. The pallbearers at his funeral included B.F. Davis and Frank L. Dodge; both respected Lansing citizens who along with Stahl placed civic duties in the forefront of their lives.[58] The Stahl Hardware store was eventually sold to the VanDervoort Hardware Company, in 1939, by Merritt J. Stahl the son of Frank J. Stahl.[59]

---

[58] *LSJ* 10/13/1922, *Lansing Capital News* 10/13/1922 and 10/14/1922.
[59] *LSJ* 8/28/1939.

USA FORRESTER BLOCK

219-221 N Washington, Lansing, MI.
What is interesting is the motifs on the facade between the second and third floor coupled with those above the third-floor windows. They were an inexpensive detail to enhance the front of the building. (CADL/FPLA)

"Messrs. Stahl and Forrester have as good as concluded to pay half and half on the plans for their joint block, and then build separately with a joint wall between their buildings. Mr. Stahl will build of pressed brick with cut stone trimmings at an expense of about $10,000; Mr. Forrester, of ordinary red brick, at the cost of some $7,000; and Dr. Hull, who owns the balance of the land in that location, will put up such a structure as Mr. Forrester's. They will all build at once" (*SR* 5/27/1887).

Stahl and Forrester Stores, 213-219 N. Washington, in the late 1950s. Observe how the decorative parapet on the Forester building has been removed. (CADL/FPLA)

"The contract for the mason work on the Forrester and Hull buildings has been let to the Fitzpatrick Brothers. It is estimated the buildings will cost about $15,000. The Stahl contract is not yet let" (*SR* 6/9/1887).

Usa H. Forrester was one of Lansing early businessmen whose life is more akin to that of a character in an adventure novel than that of a Lansing merchant. Born in either Japan or China, Usa was brought to the United States by General Edward Forester, who rescued him from execution during the Taiping Rebellion 1850-1864. The General employed the young man as an aid to his steward and named him USA after the United States of America. When General Forester returned to the United States, he enrolled Usa in school in Clayton, New York. Many years later Usa was interviewed about his early life and gave this account:

> "'My parents lived in a place called Zing, in the interior of China,' said Mr. Forrester, a day or two ago, during an interesting chat upon his rather eventful history. 'We seemed to be in danger and had determined to leave the city. We traveled all night, going in the direction of the mountains, where we thought we would be safe, when we fell into the hands of the rebels. I remember that I ran back to town, but they followed me, and took me prisoner. When I tried to get away again a soldier stabbed me in the leg. After that I went with the rebels peacefully. They kept me prisoner, as near as I can fix the time, about eight months, when the city where we were stationed was captured by General Forester.'"[60]

In *An Account of Ingham County*, Frank Turner relates in Usa's short biographical sketch that as a young man Usa was educated in New York Schools and worked for the Forester Retail and Wholesale Dry-goods store. In 1869 Usa moved to Lansing where he found employment at Fred M. Cowles dry goods store but soon left to work for Herbert A. Lee's dry goods business. Next Usa partnered with H.P. Hitchcock in a book, stationary and wallpaper business at 130 S. Washington, the partnership lasted for five years, then Usa formed a new book and stationary business with Wesley Emery. By 1882 Usa had opened his own stationary store at 235 N. Washington, in one of the business blocks that was part of the Opera House building. On February 3, 1880, Usa married Miss Sallie Amos of Philadelphia; they had one child, a daughter, Margaret. Sallie Forrester died at her home September 11, 1911, as a result of appendicitis and heart failure.[61] Usa's daughter Margaret married William E. Wood on December 24, 1912 in Lansing; the couple had two children, Monte and Robert. Tragically, in 1918 Margaret contracted Spanish influenza. It was speculated that in a distraught state, she feared exposing her family to the sickness, Margaret jumped off the Shiawassee Street Bridge and drown in the Grand River.[62] While visiting his winter home in Miami, Florida, Usa H. Forrester passed away

---

[60] *Interesting Record of a Young Chinamen's Life in America.* Hawke's Bay Herald, Volume XXXII, Issue 10616, 22 May 1897, Page 2.
[61] *LSJ* 9/11/1911
[62] *LSJ* 10/23/1918

from heart disease on May 12, 1931. Much of Usa's early life is unknown, the census lists his date of birth in 1849 and that he was of Japanese ancestry. His obituary related that he was taken from his native land by a sea captain. Other versions recount that he was brought to the United States as a boy in the capacity of body servant (valet) to a William K. Rogers or that he was saved by William R. Kissane who made him his body servant.[63] It is well known that General Edward Forester visited Usa in Lansing. Just who Usa H. Forrester was may never be known. Recorded in Usa and Sallie's marriage record is the notation that Usa was colored and Sallie was white. It seems that the racist environment that existed in the United States at that time seemed to have no effect on Usa, Sallie or their child, either socially or in his business.[64] The subject of racism in Lansing throughout the later 19th and early 20th century is a topic that needs to be studied further, especially when compared with the prevailing atmosphere in the United States in 2019.

[63] William K. Rogers or William Rogers Kissane were in fact the same person. William Rogers Kissane's life is the stuff of legend. But it is unlikely that Usa had any dealings with Kissane although Usa claimed to know him (*Times-Picayune* 4/13/1887). General Forester, who resembled Kissane claimed to know him, which confuses the matter. Before I get too far off on a tangent, if you are interested in Kissane's life see (Kissane William Kissane Rogers)

[64] For Usa death see *LSJ* 5/13/1931. Usa's second wife Anna passed away in Miami, Florida on December 31, 1932. (*LSJ* 6/7/1933)

FIRST PRESBYTERIAN CHURCH

203 W. Allegan Street, Lansing, MI.
Observe the street light with the globe bulb design. A subtle elegance that is missing in city planning today. (CADL/FPLA)

"…To this end the building committee has presented its ideas to numbers of architects who have returned plans for inspection. Among the competing architects was Mr. L.B. Valk of New York City, who is one of the most noted artists in his line in America.[65] It was he who originated the semi-circular seating plan for churches, which he put into use in the great Tabernacle of Talmage in New York, one of the largest churches in that city.[66] His plans were accepted by the church here. The new church will far surpass any of the local houses of worships, and will indeed be a marvel of architectural beauty, comparing favorably with any similar structure in the State. The lot selected for its erection is the south-west corner made by the intersection of Capitol avenue and Allegan street, just a block from the handsome Congregational building. It will be 125x60 feet in size. The style of architecture will be the beautiful Norman. The material to be employed is Amherst stone, whose superior properties for church building purposes are well-known. The skillful architect has made the most of his opportunities and every point appears to advantage. The structure is no barn like building with four blank walls, but the parts rise gradually, higher and higher, to the great central tower, with its four-dial clock. On the north, south and east are the three great windows. The main entrance is to be on Allegan street, and about [surround the doorways will be marble pillars. Perhaps the interior is the most wonderful part of the building. The main part of it will be occupied by an auditorium, 57x50 feet, seating over 500 people. The floor is boled [straight] and the seating semicircular. A suitable pulpit platform and a choir and organ loft will be arranged, and on either side of them will be fireplaces. Back of the organ loft on either side will be the choir room and pastor's study. Sliding doors separate the auditorium from the Sunday school room, which will seat about 300 people, and around the room there will be smaller class rooms and parlors separated from it by glass doors that rise and fall; so, that by opening the auditorium sliding doors and raising the glass doors of the smaller rooms, one vast room may be made of the whole, with a total seating capacity of 1,000. The cost of the building will be from $30,000 to $50,000 and necessary funds will be secured…" (*SR* 4/8/1887).

"The contract for building the new Presbyterian church has been awarded to Claire Allen, of Ionia, for $28,000. Architect Appleyard, of this city, will oversee the work. The church will be built of Ionia stone with Lake Superior sand stone trimmings. Granite pillars will be furnished by Hon. O.M. Barnes, a member of the church" (*SR* 6/3/1887).

---

[65] Lawrence B. Valk designed several churches in the United States. The Church of the Disciples in New York, St. Paul's (Zion's) Evangelical Lutheran Church, Red Hook, New York, Christ Church Cathedral, New Orleans and many others.
[66] Also, known as Talmage's Tabernacle, the building burned down in 1889. Thomas De Witt Talmage was one of the prominent forces in American religion during the last half of the 19th Century.

This was a fantastic church, one of the most striking that ever stood in Lansing. Note the empty space for the clock on the tower. (CADL/FPLA)

IN THEIR NEW CHURCH
The First Presbyterian Church Dedicated with Imposing Ceremonies.
WORK OF THE BUILDING COMMITTEE
A Liberal Contribution Almost Frees the Society from Debt—Evening Services
"Sunday was a red-letter day in the history of the Presbyterian church in Lansing.… At the commencement of the work Wm. Appleyard was chosen superintendent of construction and upon his removal from the city, A.G. Dorrance took charge of the work. The plans for the church were drafted by a celebrated New York architect, and approved by the church March 17, 1887. The contract for the building was let to Claire Allen, the price being $27,000, and the ground was broken May 31, 1887. The corner stone was laid in due form Oct. 31, 1887 and the work proceeded without interruption to its completion. The stone used in the edifice is known as Ionia sandstone, with Lake Superior stone in the arches of the windows and doors. The red granite columns at the front entrance are from the granite quarries of Nova Scotia" (*LJ* 6/10/1889).

ELEGANT TEMPLE
The New First Presbyterian Church Dedicated Sunday

"…The building which is of the modern Gothic style has a ground area of 125x66 feet, the main front facing Allegan. The walls of the main or central structure, which is nearly square, rise 22 feet above the basement. Height of clock tower from basement line to center of clock face, 83 feet; from the basement to the top of the spire 130 feet. The tower is 17 feet square, and is not in any sense a spire, having been designed with reference to placing a clock there at some future time. There is a large circular arched window of stained glass on each of three sides and several smaller ones. The foundation of the building is of field stone reaching to the water table, three feet above grade. The superstructure of Ionia sandstone trimmed with Lake Superior red stone. East and west of the central structure are wings in the same general style, the walls of the east wing being ten feet high and those of the west wing eight feet. The main roof is of slate, and those of the wings of tin, with galvanized iron cornices at the roof angles. The main entrance on Allegan street is by double doors, opening on universal hinges, in an arch, through the base of the tower. They are surmounted by a stained-glass transom bearing the name 'First Presbyterian Church'. There are also smaller doors at either end on Allegan street, opening into the ladies' parlor and the choir room, one on [toward] Townsend street, to the pastor's study, and a hooded Moorish door on the south side, leading to the auditorium from Capital avenue.

"The Interior. At the main entrance beneath the tower is a vestibule, 12 feet square, with doors on three sides and winding stairs running from the basement to the top of the tower. At the right hand is the auditorium, at the south the vestry or Sunday school room, and on the east a small parlor, all reached by double doors. The auditorium which is the central or main room, is square, 54 feet on a side, and resembles in general appearance the parquetted [seating on the main floor] of a modern opera house, the floor descending towards the platform with a pitch of one foot in ten, and the seats being arranged in a semi-circular form, so that the platform, which also has a semicircular front, and elevation of two and a half ft., a radius of nine feet, and it entirely open with the exception of a small reading desk, is visible from all sides of the house. Two main aisles approach it from the north and south doors, and a center aisle runs from the rear to the center of the auditorium. The choir and organ loft in the rear of the reading platform are about 14 inches higher and are separated from the platform by a richly carved rail. The organ stands in an arched alcove, 10 feet deep from the wall line. The roof is supported by groined arches resting on four pillars and is beautifully frescoed. The work was done by the well-known Walthew Bros., of Detroit —a guarantee for its taste and beauty. The interior finish is of pine, natural color, with wainscoting of the same. The pews are of red oak cushioned with figured red, and the platform seating, consisting of two decorated chairs and a divan, are of red oak upholstered to correspond with the pews. On either side of the platform is an open grate, surmounted by ornamental mantels in oak. In the rear of the auditorium on either side of the organ loft are the choir room and the pastor's study, appropriately furnished and having grates and mantels in each.

"The auditorium is separated from the Sunday school room and ladies' parlor by sliding doors and sashes which can be opened, thus converting three-fourths of the entire building into one room and more than doubling the capacity of the auditorium proper, which will seat 425 people. The acoustics of the building are believed to be perfect, as well as the ventilation and heating, the first of which is entirely controlled by the janitor. From his position near the main entrance he can open or close all or any of the ventilators or windows by means of a system or wires and levers, which are invisible. The heating is performed by three Walker furnaces, and the grates, heretofore mentioned, which are designed for temporary use. The auditorium will be lighted when necessary by two elegant brass chandeliers of 48 and 12 lights respectively. The Sunday school room which is connected with the auditorium by sliding doors as previously mentioned, is flanked on two sides by small rooms, connected with it by sliding sashes of ground glass, which will be used as class rooms. The whole is well lighted and ventilated. To the east of it and separated by wide ground glass sliding sash is a ladies' parlor—an elegant little room, connected with the street by a vestibule and door. It is carpeted and fitted with a grate surmounted by a mantel in which is inserted an elegant beveled glass mirror. The entire ground floor is carpeted with a body Brussels [a style of carpet] of one pattern selected expressly for the purpose. The basement is as well finished as an ordinary dwelling. The furnaces and coal bunkers occupy a circular space in the center, and surrounding them are closets, a large dining room, a kitchen and a pantry. The kitchen is furnished with a gas range, sink, and water from the city works. It has been fully furnished by the ladies, with cooking utensils and tableware, including silverware, and it can be lighted by gas. Taken as a whole, it is probable that Lansing has the model church building of the State, at least for its size, and it is hoped the readers of THE REPUBLICAN will derive much pleasure from viewing its interior tomorrow and will show a substantial appreciation of the enterprise of the congregation that erected it" (SR 8/10/1889).

Of interest are the small circular coves on the gables at the peak of the tower. Were they decorative or did the function as bird coves as they in Medieval church architecture? (CADL/FPLA)

The church was sold in 1945 to Ransom E. Olds who intended to build a 14-story office building. After four years of delays in trying to obtain approval from the city for the office building the church was torn down in late 1949 and replaced with a parking lot. (*LSJ* 12/14/1949) So much for city planning, the site is one of the most desirable locations in the city and on it, sits a parking structure. Architecturally this was one of my favorite churches in Lansing and its description in the previous articles accurately portrays the church. No further comments need to be added except that its demolition was a loss for the city. But it is doubtful however, that the Presbyterian Church would have survived the intense fire which stuck down its neighbor, the Plymouth Congregational Church on February 25, 1971.

M.A.C. HOWARD TERRACE

Howard Terrace at the Michigan Agricultural College. Above the entrance are four narrow arched windows which provided natural light to the staircase and second floor landing.

"The plans for the professors' cottages or flats to be built at the Agricultural College are about completed by Mr. Wm. Appleyard. The building is two stories high, about 100 by 50 feet in size and is to be built in an artistic Queen Ann style, with an ornamental front. Large open porches and other embellishments are to be arranged on the outside, while the inside will be supplied with grates and all modern improvements and appurtenances. The flats will be veneered with brick, probably red. The number of sections is eight, each being supplied with a parlor, living room, bed chamber and kitchen, a good vestibule, and front and back stairs. The plans for the other buildings provided for in the recent appropriation are not yet drawn" (*SR* 6/24/1887).

Howard Terrace for many years was the residence of unmarried college instructors. With the growth of the attendance of women at the MAC, the building was converted to be a residence hall for females. Howard Terrace was known as the 'incubator' to distinguish it from the main women's building which was referred to as the 'coop'. It was one of most beautiful dormitory buildings that existed on the campus of the Michigan Agricultural College.

Howard Terrace at the MAC had recessed balconies under the front and rear gables. Note the wonderful arched entrance and the sixteen chimneys. (LOC)

Imagine seeing the structure in person, the subtle arched entrances with the detailed brickwork that formed the arch. The rusticated stone foundations and the use of stone sills, note how the sills seem to form a banding around the building, these are all architectural elements that were inexpensive to incorporate into a structure. Appleyard's design of the Howard Terraces was a successful compromise between style and controlling the construction budget of building, the modern acceptance of the idea of Cost Overruns did not exist at this time. The building was torn down in July of 1922 to make way for the new Home Economics Building that was designed by Lansing architect Edwyn A. Bowd at a cost of $450,000.[67]

The Howard Terrace could almost be described as resembling an army barracks. This is not a criticism of the design, because it was an elegant building. Notice the stacking of the windows and the symmetrical appearance of the structure.

Sanford Howard was born in Easton, Bristol County, Massachusetts on August 7, 1805. He worked on his father's farm until 1829 when he moved to Hallowell, Maine. In that same year, he married Miss Matilda Williams on August 22, 1829, the couple had six

---

[67] See *LSJ* 5/2/1922 and *LSJ* 7/12/1922.

children. Howard became a frequent contributor to the agricultural magazine, the *Maine Farmer*. In 1837 Howard relocated to Zanesville, Ohio where he remained until 1843 when he moved to Albany, New York to work for Luther Tucker, where he wrote for the publication, the *Cultivator*. In 1852 Howard was recruited by Otis Brewer to become the agricultural editor of the *Boston Cultivator*. It seems during this era in United States history, experts on agricultural matters were the sports stars of their time, sought after and lured from position to position.

Sanford Howard 1805-1871

Howard was renowned for his ability to select the best quality stock for farms, whether cattle or horses, and was employed between 1857 and 1864 selecting livestock for a variety of large landholders in the United States. During that period Howard visited Ireland, England and France, purchasing stock for his employers. In 1864 Howard accepted a position with the State Board of Agriculture of Michigan, for whom he prepared the State Agricultural Reports. On March 1, 1871 Howard suffered a stroke which disabled his right side, and rendering him unable to speak, Howard lingered for eight days and passed away on Thursday March 9, 1871 (*LRW* 3/16/1871).

M.A.C. HORTICULTURAL BUILDING

Horticultural Laboratory at the M.A.C. soon after its completion. This is one of my favorite buildings at Michigan State University. Note the arched window on the side with the recessed brickwork mimicking the shape of the window and ending with decorative stone blocks.

Builder's Proposals Wanted

"An Apartment House building [Howard Terrace], a Dormitory building [Abbot Hall] and a Laboratory building [Horticultural Laboratory], ...Plans and specifications can be seen at the office of Wm. P. Appleyard, Architect, Lansing, Mich." (*SR* 9/1/1887).

"The contract for the three new buildings at the Agricultural College—the dormitory, horticultural laboratory and department [apartment] building—was let at an aggregate estimate of $30,500" (*SR* 12/1/1887).

"The time for the construction of the apartment and horticultural buildings at the State Agricultural College has been extended to October 1. The dormitory will be ready for occupancy August 1. The contractor was unable to secure sufficient material to complete all three buildings at the same time" (*SR* 12/22/1887).

In this image of the Horticultural Laboratory you can see the greenhouse attached to the building, which was not present in the first image. The small silo gives the building an almost storybook flair. Notice the low arch over the entrance and how it is almost hidden from view.

This building was the first purpose-built Horticultural Laboratory in the United States and today is the second oldest academic building on the Michigan State University campus.[68] What can be said about this building? First, this is my favorite building on the campus of Michigan State University. Second, the peasants should storm the Hannah Administration Building, carrying pitchforks if the university ever attempts to tear down this structure. Third, I am surprised in a way that Appleyard's design for this building was accepted. The building has been described as a mixture of Queen Anne, Richardsonian Romanesque, and Shingle Style, but there also is an element of idealized British farmhouse architecture, picture Tolkien's vision of Hobbiton. Today the building is known as the Eustace–Cole Hall, home of the Honors College and is on the National Register of Historic Places.

---

[68] Linton Hall is the oldest academic building on the campus of Michigan State University (MSU), some believe the Cowles house is the oldest building at MSU because two interior walls and the foundation were used in the construction of the new President's residence. The writer finds that argument rather weak.

M.A.C. ABBOT HALL

Abbot Hall at the Michigan Agricultural College has been described as a Colonial Revival building and in many ways, it was. Note the pilaster columns, which may actually have been structural rather than decorative. The effect you can see on the facade columns is a result of the placement of the downspouts.

Builder's Proposals Wanted

"An Apartment House building [Howard Terrace], a Dormitory building [Abbot Hall] and a Laboratory building [Horticultural Laboratory], ...Plans and specifications can be seen at the office of Wm. P. Appleyard, Architect, Lansing, Mich." (*SR* 9/1/1887).

"The Hall, named for President Abbot, was designed by the late William Appleyard of Lansing. It was built in 1888 by Cleveland & Ward, of Flint" ..."The building is two stories high, of a modified colonial style, the walls made of red brick" (*Beal* 271-272).

Theophilus C. Abbot was born in Vassalboro, Maine on April 29, 1826 to Joseph R. and Rachael (née Capra) Abbot. Theophilus attended Waterville College, known today as Colby College, Maine, where he became an instructor in Chemistry and Greek. In 1858 Theophilus was appointed professor of English Literature at the Michigan Agricultural College and less than five years later, Theophilus became president of the Michigan Agricultural College. In 1860 Theophilus married Miss Sarah H. Merrylees; the couple had two children Mary M. and Joseph Rodney Abbot. Theophilus served as president for 22 years, resigned the presidency in 1885, and continued to teach at the college until his retirement in 1889. Sarah's sister Mary was married to Oscar Clute, who later served as President of the Michigan Agricultural College 1889-1893. On Monday, November 7, 1892, Theophilus C. Abbot passed away at his home, 327 (317) Seymour Street at the age of sixty-six. After Theophilus' death, Sarah moved to San Gabriel, California, where she resided with her son, Joseph until her passing on June 22, 1911. Her sister Mary and her husband Oscar lived with the family in California.[69]

The four narrow arched windows on the second floor over the entrance, a pattern Appleyard employed in the design of Howard Terrace and how he used the recessed brick banding around the entire building above the second-floor windows, an inexpensive but agreeable embellishment.

Abbot Hall served as a men's dormitory until 1896, when it was converted to a women's dormitory. In 1928, the building was turned over to the Music Department to be used as a practice hall. In October 1938, Abbot Hall was slated for demolition, to be replaced by a new auditorium funded by a Public Works Administration grant. With the announcement of the news, the college received such a storm of criticism from students and alumni that the college was abandoning its past. Plus, it dawned on the college administration that if they placed the new auditorium on the site of Abbot Hall, there would be no parking for the auditorium. So, the new auditorium was built on Farm Lane and Auditorium Road. Abbot Hall became the Music Practice Hall and operated in that role until 1967 when the university decided to tear down the old Abbot Hall and construct a five-story music rehearsal building, with ninety practice rooms, forty office studios, three classrooms, one lecture hall seating for two hundred people and two music laboratories to study the effects of music on people. The destruction of old Abbot Hall began on June 26, 1967 oddly enough there were no protests by students or alumni.[70]

---

[69] *SR* 11/7/1892
[70] See *LSJ* 10/9/1938, *LSJ* 10/14/1938, *LSJ* 6/15/1967 and *LSJ* 6/26.1967.

CHAPIN COTTAGE

The Chapin Cottage in 1897, designed by Appleyard, before it was replaced by a Mead designed cottage. This is the only image that has been discovered of the cottage.

"Architect Wm. P. Appleyard is preparing plans for the largest cottage at Harbor Point, to be built next spring for Chas. A. Chapin, of Niles" (*SR* 9/8/1887).

"Architects Mead & White of this city prepared plans... The same architects are preparing plans for a summer residence for C.A. Chapin of Niles to be built at Harbor Point" (*SR* 5/30/1899).

In 1886 Charles A. Chapin purchased Lot 15 at Harbor Point. Throughout the history of Harbor Point it was not unusual for a cottage to be built, then within a short period of time, torn down and replaced with a much grander structure. A "large" cottage in 1887 would be small when compared to the cottages built just ten years later. A person's position and ego had a lot to do with this decision to tear down and rebuild, it seems human nature does not change. So, it was quite natural that Chapin would engage Appleyard's services, then within twelve years commission Earl Mead to design an even larger cottage. In 1929 the Chapin family sold the cottage to J.R. Frances. Inez T. Chapin, the wife of Roy D. Chapin of Hudson Motor Car fame, purchased the property in 1936. The two Chapin families were not related (Creecy. 99).

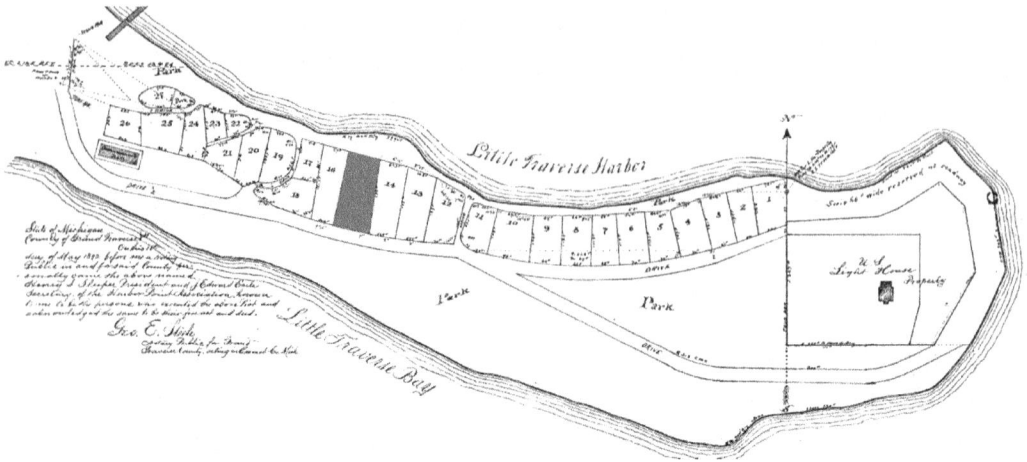

Charles H. Chapin Cottage at Harbor Point, near Harbor Springs, MI., Lot 15 is shaded in grey

Charles Augustus Chapin was born in Edwardsburg, Michigan on February 2, 1845 to Henry A. and Ruby N. (née Nooney) Chapin. The following year Henry moved his family to Niles, Michigan where he opened a general store. Charles attended Niles High School and with his father Henry, opened the H.A. Chapin & Son Insurance and Real Estate Business. The company owned the Ohio Paper Company Mill in Niles, an electric company in South Bend, Indiana, the I&M [Indiana & Michigan] Electric Company and real estate in Alabama, Illinois and Michigan. In 1879 iron ore was discovered on property Chapin owned in Michigan's Upper Peninsula, where the Chapin Mine at Iron Mountain, Michigan was established and operated until 1934. It is believed that the royalty paid by the Menominee Mining Company to the Chapin family was between $100,000 and $300,000 a year. The family accumulated a tremendous amount of wealth, which was overseen by Charles after Henry's death on December 16, 1898. Charles was President of the Indiana & Michigan Power Company and acquired extensive property holdings in Chicago that included the Unity Building. Charles married Miss Emily M. Coolidge on June 4, 1874 in Niles, Michigan; the couple had eight children. Charles' health began to fail in 1912 and he made two trips to Europe seeking a cure. While visiting his cottage at Harbor Point, he was stricken with organic heart disease and retuned to Chicago by special train. Charles Augustus Chapin died at his home at 616 E. Goethe Street in Chicago on October 22, 1913. It was believed that at the time of his death Charles was worth $15,000,000.[71]

---

[71] *Niles Daily Star* 10/23/1913, 10/25/1913 and *Michigan Historical* 24.

HOYT LIBRARY

Hoyt Library, Saginaw, Mich.

501 Janes Street, Saginaw, MI.
A wonderful structure that is still standing today. The above image does not do this beautiful building justice.

It is always best to have a bit of uncertainty in a book. There is conflicting evidence as to which Appleyard, James or William, served as the Superintendent of Construction for the Hoyt Library in Saginaw, Michigan.

"W.P. Appleyard, who is superintending the construction of the Hoyt library building, fell in a hole up to his neck yesterday and was dragged out by some masons working near by" (*SN* 12/7/1887).

"E.S. Crawford will go to church at Lansing tomorrow in company with James Appleyard, of that city, who is superintending the construction of the new Hoyt library on Jefferson street" (*SN* 12/24/1887).

"William P. Appleyard, superintendent of construction of the Hoyt Library building in this city, one of the state's most successful architects and builders, together with his assistant, E.A. Bowd, recently of this city, now of Lansing..." (*SN* 1/10/1888).

Today if you visit this building the entrance has been relocated to the side where the main structure connects to the wing. Van Brunt & Howe design of the building is timeless and functional, the structure is still used as a library today. (LOC)

"James Appleyard, who has been superintendent of the Hoyt library building, having completed his work returned to his home in Lansing Saturday. He has left a pleasing monument of his ability behind him" (*SN* 10/1/1888).

The Hoyt Library in Saginaw is one of the state's most stunning examples of Richardson Romanesque architecture. The library was a gift to the city of East Saginaw, now part of Saginaw, by Jesse Hoyt, the son of James M. Hoyt. James and his brothers were some of the early developers of the area of East Saginaw. Jesse left a bequest of $100,000 to build the library in 1882. The architects, Van Brunt & Howe of Boston designed the structure which was opened to the public in 1890. Henry Van Brunt and Frank M. Howe were known for their design of the Union Station in Portland, Oregon and the Cambridge Massachusetts Public Library, which bears a remarkable resemblance to the Hoyt Library. One interesting aspect of the Appleyards' work is that this was one of three large library buildings that they would act as the Superintendent of Construction and in one instance serve as the architect. As a result of William's injury during the early stages of building the library, James replaced his son, so it seems both James and William operated as a team while they supervised the construction of the Hoyt Library.

NEW YORK SCHOOLHOUSE DESIGNS

PERSPECTIVE VIEW OF STUDY SUBMITTED BY WM. P. APPLEYARD, AND E. A. BOWD, LANSING, MICH.

"FIRST PRIZE," ESTIMATED COST, $2500.

New York School Building design competition. Class IV $2500 Building. First Prize. Observe the flaring of the bell tower and how the triple openings on the tower flow towards the ground. Much like the Horticultural Laboratory at the MAC, the entrance to the building blends into the structure.

In 1887, the New York State Superintendent of Public Instruction held a design competition between architects and solicited plans and specifications for a series of school buildings ranging in cost from $600 to $10,000. William Appleyard along with his partner Edwyn A. Bowd submitted plans for three classes of school buildings, for which they captured first place with all their entries.[72]

"The New York State Board of Education invited architects to make competitive designs for school buildings costing from $600 to $10,000. There were six classes of buildings to be designed, each plan to embody the best arrangements, sanitary condition and highest beauty. Architects could compete in one or more of the classes. Wm. P. Appleyard, of Minneapolis, formerly of Lansing, sent designs for three classes of buildings, all of which received first prize. The Michigan State Board of Health is endeavoring to secure plans for model school houses for country districts in Michigan, and plans presented by Mr. Appleyard received less criticism than those of any other architect" (*SR* 7/25/1888).

---

[72] See *Documents of the Assembly of the State of New York* 921ff.

PLAN Nº13

PLATE 2

CLASS IV

$2500

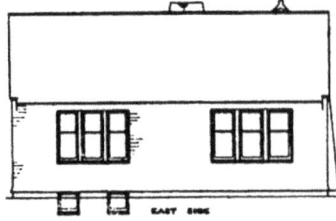
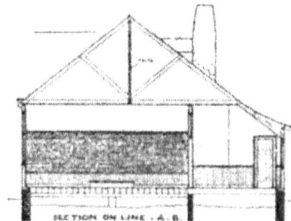

1ST PRIZE:

Wm. P. Appleyard & E.A. Bowd. Lansing. Mich.
[DOTHEBOYS']

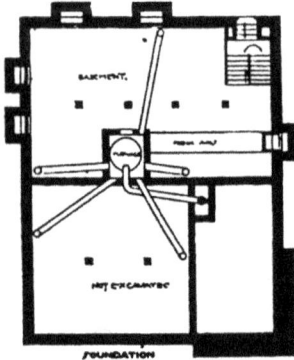
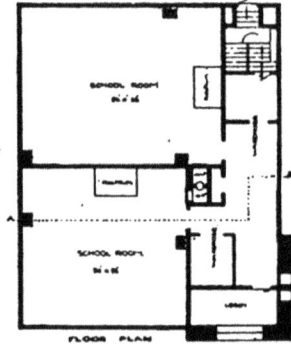

PLANS ELEVATIONS & SECTIONS

New York School Building design competition. Class IV $2500 Building. First Prize.

"In noticing the architectural work of W.P. Appleyard in Wednesday's *STATE REPUBLICAN* the name of E.A. Bowd was unintentionally omitted. He helped prepare the designs and is also deserving of the credit equally with Mr. Appleyard" (*SR* 7/26/1888).

The structure for a Class IV school house designed by Appleyard and Bowd was an ornate structure with a building cost of $2,500, quite a sum in a rural community. The plan, while pleasing to the eye, raised a serious design issue. The flaring along the main structure and the bell tower would have resulted in a large amount of water around the building. Unless the school was built on an elevated site there was the potential for quite a bit of water around the structure and in the basement. The design of the school building harkens back to Appleyard's plan for the Horticultural Laboratory, with the squat silo shaped tower. Underneath the architect's names in the drawing is this the notation "DOTHEBOYS" a reference to Dotheboys Hall in Nicholas Nickleby, a novel by Charles Dickens. It is odd that this notation was added, Dotheboys Hall in Dickens was not a nice place, overseen by the malicious Wackford Squeers.

State of New York School Building design competition. Class I, $600 Building. First Prize.

The simple design of the $600 school house structure should have resulted in quite a bit of demand for this style building. The large windows on both sides of the structure would have flooded the classroom with natural light. If you look carefully at the image and the plans for the Class I school you can observe that the architects included a chimney brace to secure the chimney to the roof bracing, something Appleyard had not employed before. Appleyard & Bowd designed a building in a reversed Saltbox style, with a long-pitched roof that faced the front, with the shorter steeped roof facing the rear.

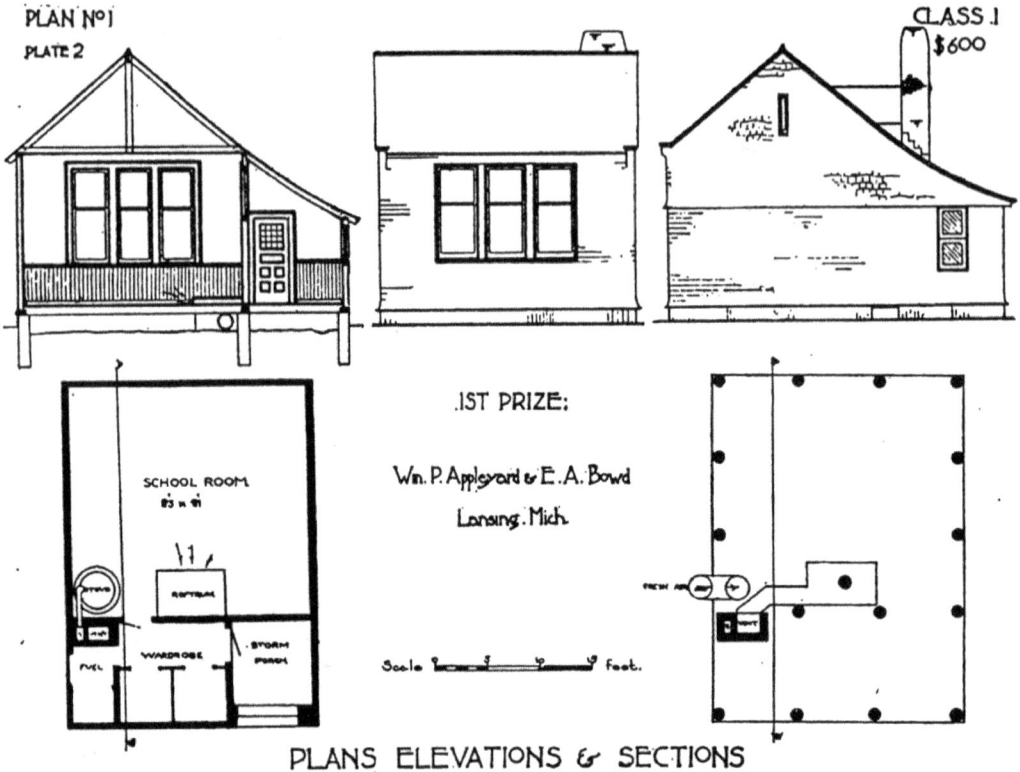

PLAN N°I
PLATE 2

CLASS I
$600

SCHOOL ROOM

.IST PRIZE:

Wm. P. Appleyard & E.A. Bowd
Lansing. Mich.

Scale _____ Feet.

PLANS ELEVATIONS & SECTIONS

State of New York School Building design competition. Class I, $600 Building. First Prize.

In the architectural plans for the Class I school the Saltbox shape of the structure is clear. It is curious that that the triple banks of windows are not present on three sides of the building, only two. The location of the furnace is interesting. The furnace room has a footprint of at least 20% of the floor space of the school. What was the function of the space at the rear of the furnace? The ductwork below the floor resulting in the warmest section of the school was at the front of the classroom. Was this an incentive for students not to sit in the back row? One other observation, the reversal of the footprint of the saltbox structure would have resulted in water pooling at the front of the structure, given that fact that the larger roof footprint on the front of the building shed water forward not to the rear, the traditional advantage of the saltbox building.

New York School Building design competition. Class II $1000 Building. First Prize.

With all the Appleyard & Bowd designs for the New York State design competition, there is a recessed entry, probably in respect for the New York winters. The entire second floor structure is curious. What role did it serve except for making the building aesthetically pleasing? Did the upper windows allow more natural light to enter the classroom? One other observation: an experienced carpenter was needed to construct this building. The peaks and valleys of the roof line, coupled with the position of the chimney and the flaring rooflines and gable end required a carpenter of exceptional skill. In many ways, the structure resembles a home, not a school house.

New York School Building design competition. Class II, $1000 Building. First Prize.

Mirroring the Class I design, the Class II plans place only the triple banks of large windows on two sides. It can be observed on the architectural renderings that there is a bank of four windows on the false second level on the side without a triple bank of windows on the first floor. Did they provide light to the interior? The Appleyard & Bowd designs for school houses were exceptionally beautiful, but were they practical? I can find no evidence that any of the Appleyard & Bowd designs for school houses were ever built in New York.

NEW CAREER

William P. Appleyard left Lansing in April of 1888 to accept a position with Adam L. Dorr, a Minneapolis architect. (*LJ* 4/3/1888) William had sold his architectural business in Lansing to Edwyn A. Bowd. (*SR* 4/10/1888) The 1888 *Minneapolis City Directory* listed William as a partner in the firm of Appleyard & Dorr architectural business located at 608 Boston Block Building, William purchased a home at 3032 Pleasant Avenue. William's partnership with Adam L. Dorr offered William a chance to become his own man out from under his father. Think about it; William wanted to find his own way as an architect. The question is what triggered this desire of William's to leave Lansing and eventually leave the architectural profession? Was he tired of the whims of his clients? Did he view the railroad industry as the future? Or maybe he just wanted a regular paycheck and not one based upon commissions? None of these questions can be answered, William's personal papers do not survive.

William P. Appleyard was a talented architect. The architectural history of Michigan State University and the city of Lansing may have been quite different if William had stayed in Lansing and was given the commissions that later went to other local architects, specifically Edwyn Bowd. The Horticultural Laboratory and Howard Terrace at the Michigan Agricultural College were beautiful structures. The Frank Wells and William Ennis residences demonstrated William's ability to design attractive residential homes. With his work at the Michigan Agricultural College, his schoolhouse designs coupled with William's work in renovating and expanding the Michigan School for the Blind building established his vision as an architect and created his legacy. In many ways William may not have been a happy man, which may have played a role in his leaving Lansing. He would have always been in the shadow of his father or he may have lacked the passion to be an architect. William's death was unusual when you consider that he had worked in the railroad industry for more than 16 years, he knew the risks regarding walking on a rail line. Given all of these factors, the fact that William left the architectural profession was a loss for Mid-Michigan.

❧CHAPTER THREE❧

RUFUS ARTHUR BAILEY

Rufus Arthur Bailey, better known as R. Arthur Bailey was a respected architect and entrepreneur. He was born in Lansing, the son of Rufus Alonzo and Sarah Jane (née Richardson) Bailey, on May 6, 1867. His father was a distinguished Lansing businessman who came to the city in 1857 and established a shoemaking business which grew in to a large retail shoe company. Rufus Alonzo Bailey was born in Orleans County, New York on September 13, 1830. As a young man he moved west where he married Miss Sarah Jane Richardson in Twinsburg, Ohio on March 9, 1853; there were nine children born to the couple. Their son, Rufus Arthur Bailey, attended Lansing Public schools and after graduation he studied architecture under William Appleyard, his brother-in-law. Bailey's architectural style undoubtedly was influenced by William, as well as James Appleyard, William's father.

Rufus Arthur Bailey left Lansing for Detroit in late 1887 to study architecture and work at some of Detroit's leading architectural firms. The 1888 *Detroit City Directory* listed Bailey as a draftsman working for G.W. Lloyd architectural firm. Bailey undoubtedly found employment with architect Gordon William Lloyd through an introduction by James Appleyard. In 1889, the *Detroit City Directory* recorded Bailey as working for the Mason & Rice architectural firm as a draughtsman and a year later Bailey is listed in the 1890 *Detroit City Directory* as a practicing architect in his own right.[73] By 1891 Bailey was again working as a draughtsman, this time for J.E. Bolles & Company, a manufacturer of interior/exterior iron elements for architectural firms. The 1892 *Detroit City Directory* recorded that Bailey had returned to Lansing, where he opened an architect office. The *State Republican* in 1893 noted "Arthur Bailey, superintendent of the new post office is today moving his office from the Jerome block on Michigan avenue to the sixth floor of the Hollister block" (*SR* 8/23/1893). The 1894 *Lansing City Directory* listed Bailey as an architect residing at 211 S. Capitol Avenue, the home of his brother Walter S. Bailey.

---

[73] The Detroit Public Library has a photograph of the Draughting Room of the architectural firm of Mason & Rice from July 30, 1888. Present in the image are: R. Arthur Bailey, Charles Kotting, George W. Nettleton, Mary Chase Perry (later Mary Chase Perry Stanton) and Albert Kahn. All later became well known architects in their own right or in Mary Perry Chase's case founded Pewabic Pottery. It is unknown if Bailey maintained a relationship with any of his former co-workers.

It is unclear why R. Arthur Bailey left Lansing again for Detroit. The *State Republican* in 1895 noted, "R. Arthur Bailey has closed his office in the Hollister block, and as soon as he can finish the work he has on hand he expects to leave for New York and Boston to continue the study of architecture" (*SR* 8/16/1895). But Bailey continued to work in Lansing for a year afterwards and there are no indications that he ever studied architecture in New York or Boston. Bailey had a successful architectural firm in Lansing; however, the return of architect Darius Moon to Lansing from Chicago may have played a role in his decision to leave. Simply there may have been too many architects in Lansing, or the business prospects were far better in Detroit.

Detroit Package Wagon, produced by the Detroit Commercial Car Company, formed in 1915 by John H. Mead, Walter S. Bailey and John S. Gafill.

Bailey moved to Detroit in 1896 with his brother Walter and together they formed the Bailey Company, which sold art stationery, statuary and home furnishings. The Bailey Company was incorporated in 1899 with $7,000 in capital and the principle shareholders were R. Arthur Bailey, Florence Huson and Samuel J. Weil.[74] The firm was located at 34

---

[74] See *DFP* 8/12/1899. Dr. Florence Huson was a force in women's medicine in Detroit. Dr. Huson graduated from the University of Michigan in 1885 and opened a practice in Detroit with an office in her home at 506 Cass Avenue. Although she had a private practice as an obstetrician, Dr. Huson was involved in treating the city's poor. She was Vice President of the Women's Free Hospital and President of the Free Dispensary, which she organized in 1893. Dr. Huson served as President of the Y.W.C.A., Priscilla Inn, St. Agnes Home and was one of the founders of the Detroit Association of the University of Michigan. Dr. Huson founded the Blackwell Society, an association of women physicians in Detroit and was Vice President of the Michigan Medical Society. Florence Huson was born in Ann Arbor on June 17, 1860 to Frederick and Mary (née Bradiss) Huson. Florence committed her life to service, in fact in many ways that was the cause of her death. Against the advice of her friend, Dr. Huson kept up her frantic work pace and suffered a stroke on August 12, 1915 which resulted in her death. (*DFP* 8/13/1915) Samuel J. Weil was a bit of a mystery. The text in the newspaper article is unclear, it is either Samuel J. Weil or Samuel J.

W. Fort Street in 1898, moved to 224 First Street in 1903 and later relocated to 220 Twenty First Street in 1906. Walter later established W.S. Bailey & Company, which produced automotive accessories and afterward formed the Detroit Commercial Car Company, which designed the Detroit Package Wagon, a delivery vehicle.[75] One interesting facet of R. Arthur's life was his involvement in the burgeoning automotive industry. In 1910, along with O.R. Cumback, Bailey formed the Cumback Motor Company to build delivery trucks; Bailey served as President and Treasurer, along with his brother Walter. The principal advantages of the Cumback delivery vehicle, were that it weighed only 1000 pounds, cost $1000 and the interchangeable body could be removed from the chassis in five minutes.[76] Only one vehicle was produced by the company and the Cumback Motor Company disappeared sometime in 1911. In the 1910 *Detroit City Directory* Bailey is listed as President of the Bailey Company as well as President of the Bailey Auto Livery (Taxis, Touring Cars, etc.) located at 647 Cass Avenue. The Bailey Auto Livery was sold by Bailey the following year.[77] So ended R. Arthur Bailey's brief venture into the booming automotive world.

Ravine Hotel after the addition to the rear of the structure, Oxley, Ontario, Canada

The Bailey Company closed its doors in 1911, after which Bailey disappeared from the Detroit City Directories. It seems Bailey left Detroit to develop his new commercial enterprise, a resort hotel. In 1902, he purchased the Stephen Julien home in Oxley, Ontario and converted the residence into the Ravine Hotel.

Well. In the 1899 Detroit City Directory Samuel J. Weil operated a bazaar at 231 Woodward Avenue and lived at 429 (2700) Third Avenue. By 1900 there is no listing for a Samuel J. Weil at the address for his place of business or his home. I have found no listing for a Samuel J. Well, but most search tools read Weil as Well.

[75] Walter Bailey died in Detroit on September 19, 1949, *LJ* 9/20/1949.

[76] See *DFP* 10/23/1910.

[77] For the Cumback Motor Company and Bailey's role see Carter 4.

The Ravine House in 1907.
Oxley, Ontario, Canada.

The Ravine Hotel was situated on 20 acres of land which Bailey bought, combining the Julien and Harris properties into the resort. The hotel was situated on a bluff, 65 feet above Lake Erie, with views of Pelee and Put-In-Bay islands.[78] In 1911 Bailey moved into the hotel to supervise its expansion, which included a three-story addition to the hotel and a dining room expansion. The hotel was a success and operated until 1970, under the management of Mrs. Priscilla Rawson Blair, Bailey's daughter, who ran the resort after her father's death.[79]

By 1914, Bailey returned to Detroit and resumed working as an architect. In his later career in Detroit, Bailey had many important architectural commissions. For example he designed a residence for John Henry Smith owner of Peter Smith & Sons, and a home for A.G. Holland, owner of White & Holland Wallpaper & Paint Company. The structures Bailey designed after 1914 are beyond the scope of this work. There is a wealth of information regarding his later designs that should be explored.

[78] *DFP* 3/16/1902
[79] See *DFP* 8/24/1996.

A cottage that Bailey designed in 1923 for Albert W. Kludt located on Franklin Road in Birmingham, Michigan across from the Birmingham Golf Course.

One example is the Kludt Cottage, designed in 1923. Bailey received a commission from Albert W. Kludt, to design a summer cottage in Birmingham, Michigan. Kludt was a well-known Detroit optometrist, with an office in the Metropolitan Building and a home in Highland Park.[80] It is amazing to consider that Detroiter's once considered Birmingham cottage country.

The Kludt cottage still stands at 1752 Northlawn Boulevard, Birmingham, MI. The street name must have changed from Franklin to Northlawn at a later date.

The Kludt cottage is a fantastic residence. The chimney is reminiscent of the type you would have seen as part of an English cottage or at a small ironworks. The chimney cap is the reverse of a standard chimney bonnet, in this case moving from narrow at the base to

---

[80] Drawing from the *DFP* 5/6/1923. Kludt passed away April 30, 1951, see *DFP* 5/2/1951.

wider at the top. The gentle rise to the gable end roof lends an almost whimsical appearance to the home. The fieldstone and beams help to form the four-window bank on the first floor. Overall this is an idyllic cottage that demonstrated Bailey's work at its best. The home is still standing in 2019.

COTTAGES **BAILEY'S BEACH** RAVINE HOTEL

There is also a beach where the Ravine House wass located that is named after Bailey.

On March 2, 1897, Rufus Arthur Bailey married Miss Grace Carey McGrath in Detroit, Michigan; the couple had two children; Rufus and Priscilla Bailey.[81] Rufus A. Bailey, one of Lansing's early architects, died at his home in Grosse Pointe Park, Michigan on October 21, 1948. Like many parts of Bailey's life there are inconsistencies concerning his death; the *Detroit News* listed his date of death as October 21, 1948, while the *Free Press* recorded October 22, 1948 as Bailey's date of death.[82]

---

[81] On May 29, 1898 Rufus and Grace lost an infant son who was unnamed. (*DFP* 5/31/1899)
[82] *Detroit News* 10/23/1948, *DFP* 10/23/1948 and Burton 5: 940. Bailey's Death Certificate listed October 21, 1948 as his date of death.

POST OFFICE AND FEDERAL BUILDING

124 W. Michigan, Lansing, MI.
The Post Office and Federal building were placed upon the empty lot that was located across from the Capitol, suggested as the most valuable piece of real estate in the city. Note the weather station on the roof of the tower. (CADL/FPLA)

The first design of the new Lansing Post Office/Federal Building envisioned a one-story structure with an attic. Those plans changed in 1892 when funding for a second story was allocated by congress.[83]

"Arthur Bailey, formerly of Lansing is in the city figuring out the iron work for the new post office building for J.E. Bolles & Co. of Detroit" (*SR* 11/25/1891). J.E. Bolles Iron & Wire Works specialized in the manufacture of ornamental iron work.

On August 5, 1892, the United States Congress passed a sundry civil bill to appropriate an additional $25,000 to add a second story to the new Lansing Post Office. All construction ceased while the design was modified (*SR* 8/6/1892). The new plans for the post office arrived in October of 1892 and construction resumed in the spring of 1893 (*SR* 10/24/1892).[84]

---

[83] For a full description of the original plan for the building see, *SR* 11/13/1891.
[84] With most Federal projects, there was some controversy over the awarding of contracts and the materials used in the construction of the building; see *LJ* 12/26/1891 and *SR* 8/7/1892.

In this image, you can see the United States shield at the peak of the gable. (CADL/FPLA)

In the following article from the 1894 *State Republican*, there is a full description of Lansing's new Post Office and Federal Building.

TIS DONE
The Federal Building Completed Today
ONE OF THE MOST SUBSTANTIAL STRUCTURES IN THE STATE
Erected at a Cost of $125,000 and Every Dollar of the Money Well Spent
SEVERAL LANSING FIRMS WERE INTERESTED IN THE CONSTRUCTION OF THE
BUILDING WHICH IS A MODEL OF CONVENIENCE

The Lansing Lumber Company had put up an Exceptionally Fine Piece of Work—Brief Write-up of the Building and those Interested in the Construction—Postmaster Rowley will be Handing out Mail in the New Building One Week from Tomorrow.

"Within the next few days another handsome monument to the growth and advancement of the capital city will be dedicated to the public in the shape of the new government building, which is now practically finished and which Contractor Bassett will deliver to Col. Ed. Roberts of Washington, Uncle Sam's representative, Monday.

In the motif at the peak of the gable of the post office you can see the United States shield.

"The building, an excellent cut of which appears with this article, is situated on the northeast corner of Michigan and Capitol avenues, directly under the shadow of the state capitol, and occupies one of the handsomest sites in the city. It faces both avenues, with a double door entrance on each, the main entrance being on Michigan avenue. The building is surrounded by a broad stone walk, is a model of convenience and fully up to the requirements of a progressive and growing city like Lansing. The original appropriation for the building of $100,000 was made by the 51st congress, the bill being introduced by Senator F.B. Stockbridge, who was largely instrumental in securing its passage, at a time when many other like bills were being shoved under the table. The first work was the selecting of the site for the structure and after looking the situation over thoroughly and securing an expression from the leading business men and property owners, the choice fell on the site now occupied, and nearly everyone concedes now that the selection was a wise one. Bids were advertised for and on the 11th of December 1891, the contract was awarded to N.M. Bassett of Austin Ill., at $68,356. The original plans called for a one-story building, but after the building was started, it was deemed too small and "squatty," and after much persistent effort, Senator Stockbridge secured a second appropriation of $25,000 for an additional story, and the wisdom of such a move is now fully appreciated. Contractor Bassett arrived on the ground February 14, 1892, and a very pleasing valentine has he proved himself to Lansing. The building, as it is turned over to the public, is a monument that will stand for many years to the skill of the builder.

"Of the $125,000 appropriation, not a dollar will remain when the work is completed. The building and furnishings have cost $94,000, the site $17,500, and the balance has been paid to the superintendents of construction and the inspectors, but it is worth every dollar it has cost. When postmaster Rowley and his assistants take possession next week they will step into one of the neatest and best appointed public buildings in the country. The building was built entirely of Ohio blue stone, with carved and ornamental trimmings of the same material. No particular style of architecture was followed in the plans; the building being put up with reference more particularly to solidity and convenience. It occupies a ground space of 54x88 feet, and a tower on the northwest corner rises to a height of 70 feet. Entering from the Michigan avenue side through the immense arch, one is at once impressed with the beauty of design and elegant finish of the whole structure and a trip through the building but confirms this impression.

"The first floor contains the lobby and office proper. Both are spacious and the appointments are excellent. The boxes, stamp windows and deposit boxes are directly in front while the money order department is to the left and facing Capitol avenue. On the right is the postmaster's private office, which is connected with the work room by call bells and a large door. The screen that separates the lobby from the workroom is as handsome a piece of work of its kind as was ever put up in the state. It is of solid, quarter-sawed white oak, beautifully carved and ornamented. It extends nearly the entire length of the building and to the ceiling, the top six feet being plate glass. [85] The woodwork of the entire building is in contrast to this screen, this part of the work being built by the Lansing lumber company, who have made the entire contract a sample job. The solid oak staircase leading up from the first floor in the tower was also built by this firm and is a dream. The work room of the office is spacious and well lighted and will contain every modern convenience for handling the big business of the office. New furniture and appliances, including revolving cases, distributing boxes and table, pouch-holders, and everything that will tend to better service has been placed in the building. There are two large vaults on the first floor, with burglar-proof locks, for storing of books and valuable packages.

The Second Floor

"The entrance to the second floor is via a handsome winding staircase in the tower. To the left of the landing is the lavatory, which is wainscoted five feet high with pink Tennessee marble. There are five elegant office rooms on the second floor with vaults,

---

[85] William Martin Aiken, a Supervising Architect of the United States Treasury, designed the screen for the post office.

one on the north side having been designed for sessions of United States court business. On this floor, the same elegance is manifest that characterizes the entire building. From this floor a winding stair leads to the top of the tower. The basement contains another lavatory and heating apparatus. Steam is used for heating, both the direct and indirect system. The apparatus was furnished by the Herendeen manufacturing company of Geneva, N.Y.

"N.M. Bassett [Nelson M. Bassett], the contractor, who will finish his work today, and an excellent likeness of whom appears in this issue, has certainly left nothing undone to give Lansing an excellent job. The inspectors who have visited the building from time to time during its construction speak but words of the highest praise for Mr. Bassett and the manner in which he has done his work, and their reports to the department at Washington have been full of the same praise. There has been no attempt to shirk or scale the plans. Where they have called for a bevel-edge, gilt-cornered, hammered brass, gold-mounted trimmings, they have been put in, and every sub-contractor was given to understand all material and work must be of the very best quality.

"Mr. Bassett came to Lansing a stranger, but there are few good people here now that he doesn't know. He is of genial disposition, a good judge of human nature and pure spring water, and appreciates good company and plenty of it. He is about as young a man for his years as ever sat for a photograph, and the friends he has made here will deeply regret that he is soon to take his departure. During the [Chicago] world's fair, he chaperoned a party of young Lansingites while in Chicago, and while there was dubbed "papa" by the gang. The name has clung to him, and at a recent gathering of friends Roy G. Jones recited a poem he had dedicated to Mr. Bassett. The following is the last verse and very partly expresses the good feelings Lansing friends have for Mr. Bassett.[86]

> *Soon Papa Bassett's work will be done,*
> *And his face will be turned to the setting sun:*
> *Soon he will leave us, and when we part*
> *We'll keep for papa a place in our heart.*
> *And papa, when you're discouraged and blue,*
> *Think of us, papa, and we'll think of you.*
> *And in each of our mem'ries the tenderest spot*
> *Will be for Pa Bassett, the best friend we've got.*
> Work of Lansing Firms

"Two Lansing firms, besides the Lansing Lumber company, have had much to do with the

---

[86] Nelson M. Bassett acted as contractor for the Post Offices in Des Moines, Iowa, Leavenworth, Kansas, St. Joseph, Missouri and Fort Scott, Kansas. He was born in Dutchess County, New York on June 4, 1838 and passed away on January 15, 1917.

construction and beautifying of this building, Gordon & Black, plumbers, and Joseph R. Larose, painter. Their work speaks for itself. Suffice to say it is of the very best and must be seen to be appreciated. Another sub-contractor whose work shows to advantage and greatly to his credit is John McGoff of Kalamazoo, who did the plastering. His work has been described in these columns before. The tiling and marble work was done by Sherman & Flavin of Chicago; the glass was furnished by H.M. Hooker & Co. of Chicago; ironwork by the Dearborn Foundry Company, Chicago; stone, E.R. Brainard, Chicago; and the slate by Albright & Co. of Saginaw.

"The excellent work of James M. Skinner, the superintendent of construction of the building, with the exception of a few months last winter, must not be overlooked. Mr. Skinner was appointed because of his qualifications for the place, and his work was highly satisfactory and commendable.[87] His successor, R Arthur Bailey, also gave excellent satisfaction. The carrier system has greatly simplified the work of the metropolitan post offices, and the general public knows but little of the inside work of the department such as Lansing has. This system does away with the thousands of calls for mail each day, and the number of private boxes is therefore reduced to a minimum, and it is believed ample provision has been made in this regard for years to come. Four hundred and sixty-eight handsome Yale boxes and a number of extra-large-size drawers for the capitol departments and the newspapers have been supplied. Postmaster Rowley says he will be doing business at the new building Sunday April 1" (*SR* 3/24/1894).

[87] James Madison Skinner died at his home at 426 W. Ottawa in Lansing on Thursday, March 19, 1936. James was born on September 19, 1863 in Windsor Township, Eaton County, Michigan to Ormal D. and Lydia M. (née Reeves) Skinner. James' grandparents and parents were early settlers of Eaton County and had extensive property holdings just southeast of Dimondale, Michigan. James attended local county schools and later Lansing High School. After graduation, he worked as a carpenter and joiner learning the building trade from the ground up. On April 18, 1888 James married Miss Myrtie E. Baker in Lansing, Michigan; the couple had one child, Clarence M. Skinner. In 1894 James was appointed United States Superintendent of Construction for the new post office. He also was the building superintendent of the Lansing City Hall. James also oversaw the construction of the Olivet College Library, Wells Hall at MAC, the McKinley House at the Boy's Industrial School, the Oakland Building, Pilgrim Congregational Church, Lansing Cold Storage and the home of Horatio H. Larned. In 1920 James was designated superintendent of construction of the Cass building. Later he was appointed to the State of Michigan Building Department by Governor Alex J. Groesbeck and served for eight years in that capacity. James also served two terms as a Lansing city alderman. *LSJ* 3/19/1936.

An image of the old Post Office being torn down circa 1957, the current City Hall and Police Headquarters in the background. (CADL/FPLA)

The residents of Lansing viewed the new Post Office/Federal Building with immense pride. Prior to the building of the Federal Building and Post Office, the citizens of Lansing were served by several smaller post offices accommodated in a variety of buildings. The construction of a Federal Building in the city confirmed the position of Lansing as a progressive and upcoming city. James H. Windrim, who acted as the Supervisory Architect, designed the Lansing Post Office; Windrim was a well-known Philadelphia architect who designed the Philadelphia Masonic Temple, National Saving and Trust Company Building in New York and numerous other public buildings throughout the United States. Modifications to the plans were carried out by the architect Willoughby James Edbrooke of Chicago, who with his partner Franklin Pierce Burnham designed the Georgia State Capitol Building in 1884. The Federal Building/Post Office building was one of the finest examples of Richardsonian Romanesque style of architecture that occurred in the city. R. Arthur Bailey assumed the position of Superintendent of Construction of the building in August 1893 and was paid $6 per day for his work.[88] The Lansing Federal Building/Post Office was an architectural treasure of the city, which was tragically torn down to build the glass and steel modern style city hall and police headquarters building between 1956 -1959.[89]

---

[88] *DFP* 8/5/1893.

[89] Information on the on the design of the Lansing Post Office provided by the National Archives

MICHIGAN AGRICULTURAL COLLEGE LIBRARY

The old library building on the campus of Michigan State University, East Lansing, Michigan, now known as Linton Hall.

"Arthur Bailey of Detroit has secured the contract for the alterations in the agricultural college library for his Detroit firm" (*SR* 2/10/1891). The Detroit firm must have been J.E. Bolles Iron & Wire Works; Bailey had left the firm of Mason & Rice in 1890.

In 1891 parts of the library building caught fire due to poor wiring and Bailey handled the restoration work on the building (Beal, 95). The library was originally designed in 1881 by Charles H. Marsh. James and William Appleyard completed the design of the edifice after Marsh's death. The building housed the Library, Museum and the Office of the College President (Beal, 270). Known today as Linton Hall, the building currently hosts the College of Arts and Letters at Michigan State University. The structure has been described as being in the Victorian Romanesque style, an interpretation that is correct. The central tower is the greatest feature of the building. In many ways, it reminds me of the fortresses built by the Teutonic Knights of Prussia, the tower replicated a watchtower with medieval hoardings to ward off attackers.

---

and Records Administration from the Records of Public Building Service, Record Group 121.

CANNELL & EDMONDS STORES

107-111 E. Allegan, Lansing, MI. (CADL/FPLA)

"Cannell & Edmonds will erect two fine brick stores in the spring, on Allegan street east, just across from engine house No.1" (*SR* 2/23/1891). Engine House Number 1 was located at 108-111 E Allegan and was Lansing's original fire station.

"Arthur Bailey of Detroit has prepared plans for Cannell & Edmond's proposed block of stores on Allegan street east" (*SR* 3/7/1892).

The property records for this period are unclear as to what the property Cannell & Edmonds owned jointly in 1892. What is known is that James Edmonds, John's son, inherited from his father the South ½ of Lot 7 Block 111, or 107-111 E. Allegan Street in 1894-1895. The Lansing City Assessor lists the date of construction of 107-111 E. Allegan Street as being 1928. However, a review of the Sanborn maps from 1892 and 1898, shows that 107-111 E. Allegan Street was built after 1891, which places the construction in line with Bailey designing the building. The survey for the 1892 Sanborn map was completed in late 1891 to allow the publication to get to press in time. Put simply, the building is far older then the Lansing City Assessor records. Notice how the windows facing Allegan are not symmetrical, the usual stacking of the widows by the architect is ignored and the odd second floor arrangement of the windows is not repeated on the third floor. The recessed panel on the second floor, between the single window and the triple window is something never seen before which created an unbalanced facade. The stone banding over the corbelling helps to soften the large area over the third-floor window. It is interesting that there are seven bands over each block and the seven windows in each block when counting the second and third floor. Was this just an odd coincidence? The building is still standing in 2019.

Charles Cannell, an early Lansing businessman, died at 11:25 pm on Wednesday December 27, 1905 of chronic gastritis. Charles was born in Liverpool, England in 1829 and immigrated to United States in 1849 where he first settled in Rochester, New York. In 1856 Charles came to Lansing, Michigan and established the Cannell & Edmonds harness and trunk business with John Edmonds. In 1861 Charles married Miss Frances W. Hickox; the couple had five children, Arthur W., Winifred, Mary J., Charles William and Maud. Charles was a commissioner on the city Water Board and was an active member of the choir at St. Paul's Church.[90]

---

[90] *SR* 12/28/1905.

107-111 E. Allegan, Lansing, MI. Image from 2017.

John W. Edmonds was born in New York City on December 28, 1833 to John W. and Marilla J. (née Pelton) Edmonds. In 1854 John moved to Lansing, Michigan and with Elisha Coolidge established a harness business. Two years later Elisha decided to devote more time to his farm and John acquired a new partner in Charles Cannell, a relationship which lasted until John's death. John was an alderman for the Second Ward in 1861 and 1862 and a member of the school board. George K. Grove along with John were instrumental in creating Lansing's first volunteer fire department and John served as the foreman of the organization for twenty years and later as Fire Chief for nine years. In February 1865 John married Miss Marilla J. Pelton, the couple had four children; James P., Robert G., and Perry H., another son John W. died at the age of one in 1880.[91] The name James P. Edmonds may be familiar to those with an interest in Lansing history. James was an avid collector of historic photographs and he authored the work, *Early Lansing History*. John W. Edmonds died at his home on August 15, 1894.

---

[91] *SR* 8/15/1894.

DR. JOHN S. MOFFETT STORE

228-232 S. Washington, Lansing, MI.
You can observe how the business blocks were separated by a double wall. Notice the reflection in the building windows of the structures on the east side of Washington Avenue.

"Arthur Bailey of Detroit is drawing plans and specifications for a $6,000 store to be built by Dr. Moffatt [Moffett] on the second lot north of Washtenaw street on Washington avenue" (*SR* 5/11/1892). The Moffett's purchased Lot 27 Block 115, 228-230 S. Washington in the Board of State Auditors Subdivision for $4200. In 1924-1925 the structure that Bailey designed was torn down and replaced with the two-story building which currently occupies the site. The above image is the only known surviving photograph of the building. In 1908, 228 S. Washington was occupied by the Cadillac Cigar Store; 230 S. Washington housed the Arthur Hurd, Men's Furnishing Store, finally 232 S. Washington accommodated the Little Downey Restaurant. The structure Bailey designed for Moffett has a simple exterior appearance, except for the corbelling along the parapet and the recessed panel along the facade, and there is little to set this building apart from any other structure on Washington Avenue. No interior images of the building have been discovered.

John S. Moffett was born in Ohio in 1848.[92] During the Civil War, Moffett served with the 10th Ohio Cavalry; he enlisted on October 13, 1862 and mustered out on July 23, 1863 at Louisville, Kentucky. The 10th Ohio Cavalry was organized by Colonel Charles C. Smith and served with the Army of the Cumberland in Tennessee, under the command of General Ulysses S. Grant. Moffett left the 10th Ohio Cavalry before the Battle of Chickamauga. John later attended the Pennsylvania College of Dental Surgery and graduated with the class of 1871-1872 where he studied under Dr. C.P. Coffee and specialized in the treatment of tartar. In 1874, John arrived in Lansing and began his dental practice that was located on the southeast corner of Michigan and Washington Avenues. With a thriving practice John became a director of the Ingham County Savings Bank. Unfortunately, John failed in his role as a board member for the Ingham County Savings Bank. The bank closed its doors in August of 1896 and John, a director and shareholder of the financial institution, withdrew his assets in the months before the collapse. He also used his bank stock that he knew to be worthless to purchase property in Detroit where he moved in 1896.[93] John continued to work as a dentist in Detroit until his retirement. On December 23, 1873 John married Miss Viola G. Brown in Leslie, Michigan and the couple had one child: William N. Moffett. John met Viola when he was a boarder at U.L. Brown's hotel in Fayette, Ohio; Brown was Viola's father. John S. Moffett passed away on February 25, 1926 at his home in Detroit. A month later Viola passed away in West Palm Beach, Florida on March 22, 1926, while visiting her granddaughter, Harriet Wood Moffett.[94]

---

[92] John S. Moffett's last name appeared in records with several variant spellings, Moffett, Moffitt, Moffit and Moffatt.
[93] Brooks 303.
[94] For John see *LSJ* 2/26/1926 and for Viola see *DFP* 3/27/1926.

FREDERICK M. POSSELL RESIDENCE

922 E. Jefferson Boulevard, South Bend, IN.
Note the simple bump out on the second-floor driveway side, just behind the tower. This was Bailey's first residential commission. Image from 2015.

"R.A. Bailey, Jr., went to Chicago to make drawings for a $4,000 residence for Fred Possell of South Bend, Ind" (*SR* 7/5/1892).

"The Capital Lumber Company of this city has the contract for the interior finish for a handsome residence which is being erected in Indiana, under the supervision of Architect R.A. Bailey, Jr. The work is now being turned out, and it is safe to say that not one residence in ten thousand will be finished so elaborately. The portiere between the hall and library is a particularly elaborate affair, consisting of two handsomely arched pedestals of quarter-sawed and curly oak, surmounted with columns extending to the ceiling. The workmanship is perfect, and the design very handsome. The Capital Lumber Company is turning out a good deal of this kind of work in competition with the leading lumber houses of the west" (*LJW* 5/19/1893). I have assumed that the article is referring to the Frederick M. Possell home in South Bend, Indiana.

Frederick M. Possell home in South Bend. In many ways the home seems off balance, but when seen from the street presents an imposing structure.

Frederick [Fred] M. and Margaret S. Possell purchase a portion of Lot 7, of the Adam Barman's Addition in June 1890 for $500. Later in that same year the couple purchased Lot 8 from John Mohler Studebaker for $900. Fred was a buyer for the Shafer Brother's Lumber Company of South Bend when he purchased the property. In 1898, the Possell's sold the home to Cyrus M. Shafer the owner of Shafer Brother's Lumber Company.

The residence that Bailey planned for Possell was the first residence that he designed. The home is in the Queen Anne style and quite a departure from his later work. On the front closed gable, there seems to be a Palladian style window; however this is a visual deception. It is not a Palladian window but rather a triple window with a sunburst detail over the center window. Notice how the front gable shingles match those on the side gable presenting a two-tone color scheme to the home differentiating the third floor from the rest of the structure. The tower has a Witch's Cap roof and next to the tower there is a small side porch on the second floor with bowed facing which is a remarkable feature that can be seen in the following image. The home is still standing in 2019.

Frederick M. Possell's birth location is somewhat of a mystery. He was either born in the state of New York as his obituary states, in France as his death certificate asserts or in Germany as the United States Census listed. His parents were Joseph and Charlotte Possell of Buffalo, New York. Frederick began working in local lumberyards at an early age and learned the lumber business from the ground up.

149

A close-up of the tower on the Possell home. Note the intricate scrollwork detail above the cross-hatch feature on the transom windows in the tower.

He married Margaret and the couple had four children, Ellen [Ella], George, Sarah and Frederick. The family left Buffalo for South Bend, Indiana where Frederick worked in the lumber department for the Studebaker Brothers Manufacturing Company and the Shafer Brother's Lumber Company for 17 years. The family moved to Cincinnati in 1900 where Frederick was co-owner of the Gage & Possell Lumber Company; he later sold his interests to James B. King and C.C. Trimble in 1908. By early 1907 the family was back in Buffalo. It seems that in November 1907, Frederick deserted his wife and children and refused to live with them or pay for their support. In April 1911, Margaret sued for divorce in the state of Nevada and her request was granted on June 28, 1911.[95] In June of 1914, Frederick traveled to St. Louis, Missouri on business for a lumber company based in Quincy, Illinois. The temperature in St. Louis on June 26 hit 101° and on June 27, the temperature was 97°. A chambermaid entered Frederick's room on June 26 and observed Frederick asleep across the foot of the bed, so she left. On June 27, 1914 Frederick was found dead in his room at the American Hotel, the cause of death insolation, or as it is more commonly known, heat stroke.[96]

---

[95] See *NSJ* 4/12/1911 and *NSJ* 6/29/1911.
[96] See Death Certificate, *SLPD* 6/27/1914 and *South Bend Tribune* 7/3/1914. Frederick was one of

MISS BENNETT'S STORES

318-326 N. Washington, Lansing, MI.
Notice the recessed brick panels on the parapet. Each business block is differentiated by the small
finial and ball on the facade. (CADL/FPLA)

"Mr. Bailey is also making plans for a brick block to be erected by Miss Bennett on the old Seager property, Washington avenue north. It will contain six stores, 20x60 feet, and will be completed about September 1" (*SR* 7/5/1892).

"The contract for the masonry on the block of six new stores which Miss Bennett will erect on Washington avenue north, has been let to Chittenden & Clark. The carpenter work was let to William Sullivan. The work will be commenced at once and the building will be pushed rapidly to completion" (*SR* 7/21/1892).

The stores Bailey designed for Bennett were six separate blocks all in the same style. At first glance, there is not much to see, but if you look up you will notice the small ball and column detail on the parapet separating each of the business blocks, they are finials. There was also a series of recessed panels placed within a larger recessed panel. These panels followed the pattern of a rectangle, with a raised rectangle insert, followed by a square recessed panel with a square insert followed by a repeat of the rectangular insert. These were simple with relatively inexpensive architectural details that enhanced the appearance of the building at almost no cost, but which spoke to the skill of the masons who constructed the buildings. The building were torn down in August 1967.

---

seven people who died of heat stroke in St. Louis on June 27. *SLPD* 6/28/1917.

318-326 N. Washington, Lansing, MI.
The Bennett blocks can in some ways be considered the Meijer's of their time. All one needed to do was walk along the sidewalk and chose what store to enter. There were butchers, grocers, tailors, shoe and hardware stores which served the needs of the community. (CADL/FPLA)

Just who Miss Bennett was is a bit of a mystery. A search of the property records for this time revealed no Miss Bennett owning property on North Washington. In fact the property on Lot 67 was owned by a Mrs. Alice Bennett, the wife of William G. Bennett. It is possible that the reporter for the *State Republican* was confused regarding Alice's marital status. She may have been engaged to William in 1892 hence the confusion. Born Alice J. Tilden in 1866, in Lenawee, Michigan, Alice was the daughter of Joseph and Abigail Tilden. On July 24, 1894, Alice married William G. Bennett in Tecumseh, Michigan. William worked as a clerk at Mapes Clothing Company and later managed the company after the death of its owner, James D. Derby in 1906. After Mapes Clothing Company was sold, William opened his own men's furnishings store, Bennett & Throop at 1208 S. Washington. William died at his home on Saturday, December 30, 1933. Alice Bennett died on January 11, 1950 at the age of 84, there was no obituary which was odd considering her previous position in the community and the role she played in the development of North Washington Avenue (*LSJ* 1/13/1950).

JAMES URQUHART'S HOME

414 (408) S. Grand, Lansing, MI. (1895)
No other image has been discovered of the Urquhart's home. Note how each floor is separated by flaring of the shingles or a pent roof.

"Arthur Bailey is drawing plans for $3,000 worth of alterations on the home of James Urquhart, Grand street south" (*SR* 8/27/1892)

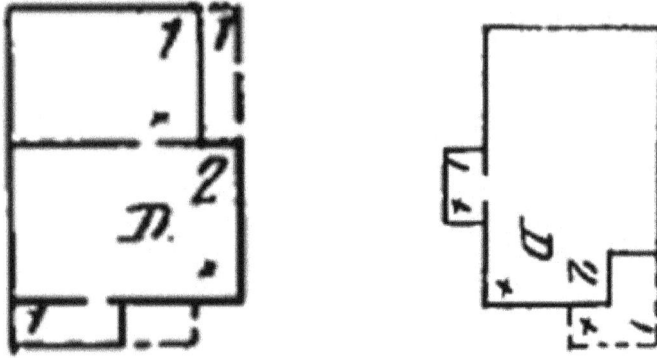

Two views of the Urquhart residence. The first image at the left is from the 1892 Sanborn. The second image at the right is from the 1898 Sanborn maps. As you can see, the footprint of the home changed.

Just what work Bailey was commissioned to complete on the Urquhart home is unclear. He may have been employed to renovate the interior of the home, but based upon the photograph from 1895, it seems that Bailey's work was a complete reconstruction. This is based upon the changes to the structure at 414 S. Grand between the 1892 Lansing Sanborn map and the 1898 Lansing Sanborn map. The residence seems to have been completely rebuilt from two-story front with one-story rear structure, to a two and a half story residence. Another factor to be considered was that Urquhart was spending about $75,000 in today's money on his residence, which is quite a bit of money for just interior renovation. So, it is reasonable to conclude that Bailey redesigned both the interior and exterior of the home. The residence was a Queen Anne style house; notice the flaring of the siding between the floors. The porch extended from the home and wrapped around the home just slightly and was recessed into the structure on the north side. The side porch which replaced the porch at the rear of the structure is barely visible to the left in the first image. The repositioning of this porch seems to lend credence that Bailey redesigned both the interior and exterior of the structure. Anyone who has engaged in any type of remodeling of a home understands that relocating a porch means a redesign of the interior of a structure. Finally, the three-pane set of windows above the second floor, on the front gable, may have been recessed; the quality of the image prevents a clear statement upon this feature. Since this was a redesign of the home, it is odd Bailey did not reconfigure the windows on the facade. The peculiar pattern created an unbalanced view from the street and takes away from the home's appearance. The home was torn down in 1940.

James A. Urquhart 1857-1938

James A. Urquhart was born in Toronto, Canada in 1857, to Hector and Christina (née Mitchell) Urquhart. James spent his early years in Toronto, where his father managed a hardware store. In 1887 Hector and his family moved to Lansing, Michigan where Hector and James established the Urquhart Brothers Cracker Factory at 309-311 N. Washington Avenue. The factory produced the 'U' cracker and other bake goods. In 1893, Hector and James sold the factory to the United States Baking Company, later part of the National Baking Company. Both father and son managed the Lansing factory. James served four terms as a Lansing alderman and received many accolades for his public service. In 1896, Hector moved to Springfield, Ohio to assume management of a National Baking Company Plant. Hector purchased the plant in Springfield in 1905 and formed the Springfield Baking Company. James continued to manage the Lansing plant until he moved to St. Louis, Missouri, where he managed the National Baking Company's facility.

On February 7, 1877, James married Miss Elizabeth Maretta Barrie, in Markham, York County, Ontario, Canada; the couple had three children; Ethel G., Merle A., and Vera B. Urquhart. Elizabeth died on February 3, 1905 in St. Louis, Missouri, after surgery to remove a tumor (*SLPD* 2/4/1905). James remarried on August 8, 1906, to Eleanor P. Smith-Fields in Lansing, Michigan, the couple decided to make their home in St Louis, Missouri, where they lived until James' retirement. After his retirement the couple moved to Daytona Beach, Florida in 1923 to enjoy the benefits of the Sunshine State. Eleanor Urquhart passed away in Florida on May 12, 1932, James died six years later while visiting his daughter in Toronto on September 5, 1938.[97]

---

[97] The above information has been compiled from census records, the Archives of Canada Registration of Deaths, 1869-1938, *SLPD* 9/6/1938 and from Price 252-253. For Eleanor (Nellie) death see *LSJ* 5/14/1931.

BEMENT AGRICULTURAL IMPLEMENT FACTORY

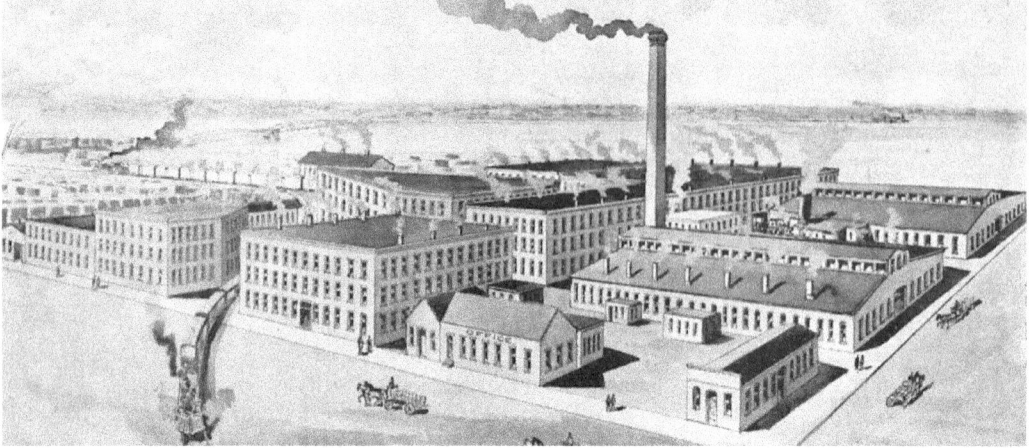

200-332 N. Grand, Lansing, MI.
The Bement factory was an immense industrial complex that grew slowly over the years.

A STEP FORWARD
E. BEMENT & SONS BREAK GROUND FOR A BIG ADDITION
They will Greatly Increase Their Capacity for Manufacturing Stoves—100 More Hands to be Employed.

"The erection of a new foundry which will be entirely devoted to the manufacture of stoves, will begin tomorrow, weather permitting. The building will be three stories high, built of brick, the dimensions being 120x80 feet. It will be situated on the north section of the present foundry. It will, of course, be impossible to suspend work in the foundry, so the old walls will not be torn down until the new walls are up, and the work can be carried on to some degree in the new building. The second and third floors will be used for stove fittings entirely, the first floor containing the molding room. An elevator will carry the castings from the first to the second floor for cleaning, and thence to the third for mounting. All the latest mechanical appliances will be procured, and special care will be made to get rid of dirt and dust and keep the new shop clean.

"The new addition will increase the stove capacity of the establishment to 4,000 per annum. The capacity of help will be increased; twenty new molders being required and fifteen mounters. This will bring the molding force to over one hundred men. The new building will make the work of the establishment run smoother, as the implement and stove departments will be separate. As it is now, the work being done together, is somewhat confusing. The architect, Arthur Bailey, says the building is a good one and will be a great improvement on the present arrangements" (SR 11/1/1892).

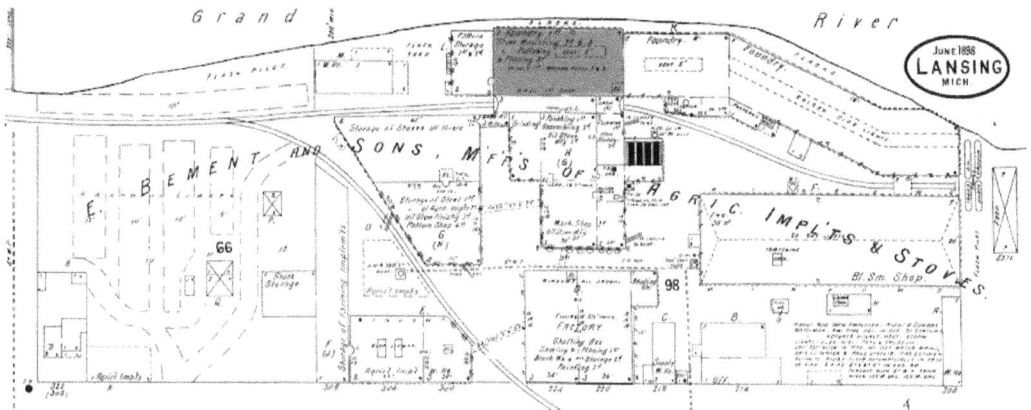

Bement Agricultural Implement and Stove Plant in 1898, the size of the plant is impressive. Bailey's work is shaded in grey. (Sanborn Map)

Edwin Bement and his son Arthur Orin Bement came to Lansing from Fostoria, Ohio in 1869. They purchased property along Grand Avenue but did not have the funds to build a foundry. Father and son formed E. & A. O. Bement Company and began to melt iron at a shop at the foot of Lenawee and River streets at the site of the old Houghton Foundry, while attempting to raise funds to build a new plant on the North Grand Avenue property they owned. At this time, the company produced plows, sleigh shoes and caldron pots. In July of 1870 the company received the capital needed to build a plant on North Grand Avenue.

George Willis Bement, Arthur's brother joined the company and the firm's name was changed to E. Bement & Sons; in 1878 Clarence Edwin Bement joined the firm. In 1886 the business incorporated with Arthur O. Bement, President; Cornelius A. Gower, Vice President; George W. Bement, Secretary and Treasurer; Clarence E. Bement, Superintendent; and Augustus S. Bement, Assistant Superintendent.

A panoramic view of the Bement Factory complex, situated between Ottawa and Shiawassee and Streets, east of Grand Avenue.

Before the advent of the automobile industry, E. Bement & Sons Company was the largest manufacturing concern in Lansing. The company's plant on North Grand Avenue stretched from Ottawa Street to Shiawassee Street and the firm produced a variety of farm implements. The best-known piece of equipment the company manufactured was a spring tooth harrow, which was sold throughout the United States. Oddly enough the company also built a range of bobsleds. In 1878, Bement & Sons began manufacturing a line of stoves for which the Bement name became synonymous. The company's finest stove was the Bement Palace Oak stove.

Workers at the Bement Foundry circa 1890. (CADL/FPLA)

Following the recession of 1902-1903 the company was in placed in receivership in 1905-1906, under the control of the Detroit Trust Company. At an auction in May of 1906 the assets of E. Bement & Sons were broken up and sold to several bidders for over $900,000. The highest bidders were Harris E. Thomas, later President of Auto Body, Cabe & McKinney of Chicago and W.L. Kinney of Marion, Michigan. It is important to remember that with the failure of E. Bement & Sons over 500 highly skilled workers were released to help fuel the explosive growth in the automobile industry in Lansing.[98] Both the Olds Motor Car Company and R.E.O. Company could utilize this well trained and professional workforce.[99] No buildings survived from the Bement industrial complex.

---

[98] There are many examples of Bement employees moving into the automobile industry. Charles Czich moved from Bement in 1904 to the Olds Motor Works by 1908 as well as his son Valentine. There are many others including John Daman (Olds), Eugene Davis (REO), Otto C. Derk (REO), Clyde Donaldson (Olds) etc.
[99] *SR* 8/10/1891, *LJ* 5/22/1906 and *SR* 5/22/1906.

THE BEMENT FAMILY

Edwin Bement 1811-1880 (CADL/FPLA)

The Bement family was crucial to the industrial development of Lansing and the following biographies of Edwin and his sons help to outline their importance to Lansing.

Edwin Bement was born in Westfield, Massachusetts on August 26, 1811, the son of Rueben and Miriam (née Owen) Bement. In 1820, his parents with their four children left their home in Massachusetts and traveled by wagon to Randolph, Portage County, Ohio. Edwin spent his boyhood serving an apprenticeship as a millwright, and in 1837 at the age of 26, he moved to Fremont, Ohio where he and his brother Orson erected a grist mill and a separate oil mill. Two years later, Edwin married Miss Maria L. Roberts and the couple had four children, Ansel R., Arthur O., George W. and Clarence E. Bement.[100] In 1843 Edwin moved to Risden, where, with his brother, Augustus erected the first grist mill in that area; the brothers also purchased a small foundry.[101] Edwin lived in Fostoria for 26 years, 10 years of which he was engaged in the stove and hardware trade. In 1869, he sold his business in Fostoria and moved to Lansing to establish a foundry with his son Arthur and brother Augustus. On Monday, March 8, 1880 after Edwin unhitched his team of horses in the barn, he suffered a stroke and passed away shortly afterward at his home.[102]

---

[100] Ansel R. Bement died of typhoid pneumonia while serving in the Ohio Volunteer Infantry Regiment, Company F. in the Civil War, *Fremont Journal* 12/6/1861.
[101] Risden and Rome were afterwards consolidated and formed the present city of Fostoria.
[102] *LJ* 3/8/1880

Lieutenant Colonel Augustus Sherwin Bement 1824-1893.
Image courtesy of Brad & Donna Pruden Collection.

Augustus S. Bement was born in Portage County, Ohio on May 16, 1824. The early part of his life was spent in DeKalb County, Indiana where he remained until age 18. Augustus returned to Fostoria where he established a foundry with his brother Edwin. With the outbreak of the Civil War, Augustus enlisted in 55th Ohio Infantry Regiment, Company B where he served as Captain. The campaigns took a toll on Augustus' health, and sickness forced him to resign his commission. Eventually he returned home to Fostoria. After[/] recovering from his illness, Augustus reenlisted and served with the 164th Regiment Ohio Volunteer Infantry as their Lieutenant Colonel. The regiment fought at the Battle of Monocacy and against Mosby's Confederate raiders in Northern Virginia. Ill health again forced Augustus to resign his commission and retire to Fostoria where he remained until 1877. After the death of his brother Orson Bestor Bement in 1848, August married Orson's widow, Margaret in 1849; the couple had three children all of whom predeceased their father. Augustus moved to Lansing in 1878 to work with his brother Edwin as the Assistant Superintendent at the Bement Plant. In May of 1893, after he finished his work at the plant, Augustus began to walk toward his home at 503 Seymour Street. On the walk to his house, Augustus suffered a heart attack near the high school. He was helped to the storm house by a passersby where he expired; Colonel Augustus Sherwin Bement was 69 years old (SR 5/13/1893).

Arthur Orin Bement 1847-1915

Arthur Orin Bement was born in Fostoria, Seneca County, Ohio on May 22, 1847. In 1869, he came to Lansing from Fostoria with his father, Edwin. Father and son created one of the largest manufacturing complexes in Michigan before the advent of the automotive industry. E. Bement & Sons not only produced farm implements, but bobsleds and stoves. In 1889, Arthur purchased the capital stock of the old Lansing Wheelbarrow Company. He expanded and reorganized the business which he named the Lansing Company. Arthur also helped to finance Lansing Wagon Works and under his management established the business as a leading industry in the city. In 1892 Arthur Bement was elected mayor of Lansing and reelected to a second term in 1893.[103] During his administration, the city purchased the Electric Lighting Plant and the Water Works Plant. On October 9, 1873, Arthur married Miss Alice Jenison of Eagle, Michigan; the couple had one child, Edwin. Tragically Alice passed away on July 22, 1884 of heart disease. Three years later Arthur married Miss Vina Mosher on July 6, 1887 and the couple had two children, Dorothy and Rosalind. Arthur Orin Bement, one of Lansing's leading citizens, died at his home at 1617 Jerome Street on Tuesday January 26, 1915.[104]

---

[103] At that time Lansing Mayors served for one year.
[104] *LSJ* 1/27/1915 and *LEP* 1/27/1915.

George Willis Bement 1850-1903

George Willis Bement was born in Fostoria, Ohio on November 9, 1850. George spent his summer vacations working at his father's plant where he became a skilled moulder. After teaching a year at a small school near Fostoria, George moved to Tiffin, Ohio to work as a moulder at the Loomis & Nyman factory. He later worked at several other manufacturing plants in the Midwest, finally settling in Battle Creek, Michigan to work at Shepherd & Nichols factory. Eventually George retuned to Fostoria, where he accepted a position at Charles Foster's store. Foster would later be elected Governor of the state of Ohio in 1880. George left Fostoria in 1870 for Lansing, to work in his father's plant. During the day, he labored on the shop floor and at night George kept the company's accounts. He later became Secretary and Treasurer of E. Bement & Sons Company. In 1893 George was appointed to the Board of Control of the Michigan School for the Blind and he was selected treasurer of the board, a position he held until his death. Between 1895 and 1899 George served on the Lansing City Council.

On June 13, 1872 George married Miss Rillie Finsthwait and the couple had two children: Howard and Frank Bement. On Friday, April 17, 1903 while George was addressing the Knights Templar at their banquet, he suffered a stroke. Medical aid was immediate and George was taken to his home where he lingered for two days, suffering a further series of strokes. On Sunday, April 19, 1903 George Willis Bement died in the home that he loved. To honor George's memory all factories in Lansing were closed on April 21, 1903 to show respect for George W. Bement, a remarkable tribute.[105]

---

[105] *LJ* 4/20/1903 and *SR* 4/20/1903.

Clarence E. Bement 1856-1935

Clarence E. Bement, a fixture of Lansing's social and industrial society for many years, passed away on Sunday night June 9, 1935 at his home at 505 Seymour Avenue. Clarence was born in Fostoria, Ohio in 1856. At the age of 13 he moved to Lansing with his parents and attended the city schools. In 1874 Clarence was one of the first graduates from the new Lansing high school and in the fall of 1876 he entered the University of Michigan where he graduated in 1880. After he completed his studies, Clarence worked for his father at the factory and learned the business by working on the shop floor. When the company went into receivership in 1904, Clarence acquired the parts department of the company, which he later sold to a Chicago company. On November 16, 1907 Clarence purchased the Hildreth Manufacturing Company in North Lansing. Two years later the Hildreth Company was renamed the Novo Engine Company. After Clarence acquired the old Schultz Stave & Barrel Factory property, the Novo Engine Company expanded its industrial footprint, the old Hildreth plant was torn down and a new factory was built. The Novo Engine Company grew to be one of the largest manufactures of lubricating engines in the United States, between the years 1907 and 1932. At its peak the company employed over 500 men. In 1932, Edward Teel succeeded Clarence as president, while his nephew Edwin J. Bement was Vice President, Clarence's son, Robert E. Bement, became Assistant Factory Superintendent. The Novo Engine Company ended production in 1953.[106]

Clarence also served as a member of the Lansing School Board from 1898 until 1910. He was President of the Michigan Manufacturers Association and the Lansing Chamber of Commerce. Aside from these commitments he also served as Vice President of Federal Drop Forge and for 15 years was Director of the American Savings Bank. Clarence was

---

[106] See *LSJ* 12/31/1953.

the last charter member of the U&I Club, an organization that was formed in 1885 and was President of the Michigan Pioneer & Historical Society. As a side note, Clarence collected books, including first editions, creating one of the finest libraries in Michigan. On November 24, 1880 Clarence married Miss Carrie Roberts of Cleveland, Ohio, in Lansing Michigan. The couple had two children: Robert S. and Constance Bement.[107]

JONES & PORTER FLATS

812-818 Eureka, Lansing, MI.
The flats designed by Bailey were symmetrical in their appearance. Note the intricate brickwork surrounding the windows. (CADL/FPLA)

"Arthur Bailey is preparing plans and specifications for a row of eight flats on the Green Oak addition by Jones & Porter during the coming spring" (*SR* 3/22/1893). The Green Oaks Addition was south of Michigan Avenue, west of Holmes Street and east of the railroad tracks.

Viewed from the street, it may seem that there were only four units at 812-818 Eureka Street, but there were four more apartments located at the rear of the building. Their address was 812 A, 814 A etc. The field stone facings of the building are interesting, but it is important to remember when these row houses were constructed field stone was a common building component. Notice that the sides of the building were constructed with brick and all the expensive architectural features face the street, saving the developer money. The field stone was only meant to face the street and implies a sense of permanence to the structure. These were apartments you wanted to live in during late 19th Century society; in today's parlance it was classy and fashionable. The stone work on the

---

[107] *LSJ* 6/10/1935. For more on the Bement family see Leach 1928.

building is striking, including the faux mansard roof facing the street and the porte-cochere which is visible in the next image. Interestingly the porte-cochere also functions as a porch for two of the side units. Observe how the front porch's roof mimics the main roofline with the flaring. Overall the building has stood the test of time, although by modern standards the structure may project an air of heaviness. The design by Bailey is a gem. The apartments are still standing in 2019.

Notice the trellis and formal gardens to the right in the image. In its day, this was one of the most desirable places to live in the city. (CADL/FPLA)

Nelson Bradley Jones was born in New York City on October 22, 1835 to Elisha and Eliza (née Bradley) Jones. Soon after his birth, Nelson's father passed away and his mother Eliza moved to Jackson, Michigan. As a boy, Nelson worked as messenger in the Michigan House of Representatives. In 1850 Nelson apprenticed as a printer under James O'Donnell, and found employment, in Indiana with the *Knox County Republican* in 1856. Two years later he returned to Michigan where he started the *Cass County Republican* newspaper in Dowagiac. Nelson sold the paper and returned to Lansing and became foreman and local editor of the *Lansing Republican*, where he worked under the guidance of John A. Kerr. In 1861, Nelson was appointed assistant clerk of the Michigan House of Representatives, and later he was elected chief clerk, a position he held until 1871. Nelson also served as a member of the Lansing Common Council, where he was instrumental in the establishment of Mt. Hope Cemetery.

In 1867 he formed a partnership with James B. Porter and established the real estate firm of Jones & Porter, a firm that survived for 27 years and helped to plan the development of the city of Lansing. On May 9, 1865, Nelson married Miss Irma Theoda Andrews, a niece of John A. Kerr. There were five children from the marriage, four sons; Roy G., Dana T., Carl S., Perley B., and a daughter Neenah E. who married James P. Edmonds. Nelson was a founding member of Plymouth Congregational Church, the Central Michigan Agricultural Society, and YMCA. He was also involved in many fraternal organizations, the Knights Templar, the Odd Fellows and Blue Goose International. When the real estate business of Jones & Porter was dissolved, Nelson moved to Detroit where he represented the Insurance Company of the State of Pennsylvania. Nelson Bradley Jones died at his home at 65 Leicester Court on February 3, 1914.[108]

James B. Porter was born in Marcellus, New York on September 7, 1824, the son of the Reverend Seth J. Porter and Cynthia M. (née Haines) Porter. His father moved the family to Michigan in the fall of 1833. Unfortunately Reverend Seth Porter died unexpectedly in 1834, leaving Cynthia Porter to raise three children. James attended Allegan Seminary School and studied under Elisha Bassett, paying his fees and board by working at the local dry goods store. Upon graduation James established a business partnership with Rolin C. Denison in 1845 and opened a general dry goods store in Otsego, Michigan. The business survived until 1853 when Denison left the firm and a new partner with Orsmus Eaton joined James in the business. His new business partner was a disaster. Eaton embezzled funds from the company, then fled Michigan, leaving the firm $14,000 in debt, which James Porter assumed and paid off. In 1850 James was elected Register of Deeds and County Clerk for Allegan County, a position he held for ten years. James was one of the founders of the Republican Party in Jackson, Michigan 'Under the Oaks' in 1854. In the election of 1860, James was voted Secretary of State as a Republican and served in that position in the Blair administration throughout the Civil War, leaving office in 1867. On August 17, 1845 James married Miss Eunice J. House in Otsego, the couple had two sons; Edgar S., and William J. Porter. In 1866 James moved his family to Lansing and after leaving public office formed a real estate and insurance business with Nelson B. Jones, the firm was known as Jones & Porter. After the real estate firm disbanded in early 1894, James entered into a short working partnership with his brother Edwin H. Porter, and the firm of Porter & Porter was formed. His sister-in-law, Emily Porter, later bought out James' interest in the company on May 1, 1894, becoming Lansing's first husband and wife real estate firm.

James was preparing to attend church on a Sunday morning in March, when he was informed that the pipes at his building at 303 S. Washington were frozen.[109] While overseeing repairs James began to suffer chest pains and decided to return to his home. His son William spotted his father in distress and rushed to his aid. James was brought to his home at 215 N. Capitol Avenue where Dr. Ranney was summoned. At 1:30 pm on Sunday March 7, 1897, James B. Porter a former Secretary of State of Michigan and one of the founding members of the Republican Party passed away.[110]

---

[108] LSJ 2/6/1914 and Bernard 43.
[109] The Porter building stands today at 303 S. Washington; the building was constructed in 1892 and designed by Fred W. Hollister of Saginaw Michigan who also designed the Hollister Building in Lansing for Harry L. Hollister, no relation.
[110] *SR* 3/8/1897, *LJ* 3/8/1897 and Portrait 420.

JOHN HERRMANN HOME

520 N. Capitol, Lansing, MI.
One of the iconic residences in Lansing. Lansing Community College should be commended for their preservation efforts. Image from 1978. (CADL/FPLA)

"Architect J. Arthur Bailey is engaged in drafting plans for the erection of a handsome residence to be built in the spring for John Herrmann. The new house, which is expected to cost about $5,000, will be located on Capital avenue, between Genesee and Lapeer streets. It will be built of brick and contain all the modern conveniences" (*SR* 11/17/1893).

"Saturday afternoon and this afternoon the new Herrmann residence on Capitol avenue north was inspected by a large number of people, upon invitation of Architect Bailey. The new house is one of the most elegant in the city, and full of the latest conveniences" (*SR* 1/28/1895).

Observe the intricate scrollwork in the parapet of the two-story, canted bay windows at the front of the building. The scrollwork is repeated again above the bowed side window.

What can be said of the Herrmann house? Compare the architectural styles of the Herrmann residence to the Rogers Carrier home, which is located just to the north of the Herrmann house. The Rogers Carrier home was designed by Darius B. Moon, just three years previous to the construction of the Herrmann home. When you compare the styles of the two structures, the Rogers Carrier residence seems to be the last gasp of Victorian architecture in Lansing while the Herrmann house represented the contemporary style of architecture that had developed in the Midwest in the middle years of the 1890s.

It is interesting to consider what impact Bailey's apprenticeship in Detroit with Gordon W. Lloyd and the architectural firm of Mason & Rice had on his design style. Just a year previous, Bailey planned a typical Queen Anne residence for Frederick Possell. The Herrmann house was quite a departure from the Possell home. The Detroit architect Gordon Lloyd, specialized in religious architecture, he developed the plans for Christ Church and Central United Methodist, both in Detroit and St. James Episcopal Church in Milwaukee.

The Herrmann House located on the campus of Lansing Community College is well worth a visit. Viewing the home is best in the evening as the soft light accentuates the color of the brickwork; visitors can also tour the Shigematsu Memorial Garden adjacent to the home.

Lloyd is remembered in Detroit for his design on the David Whitney Mansion, a massive 21,000 square foot residence, built in the Romanesque Revival style. It seems likely that Bailey's architectural style was shaped by the time he spent at Mason & Rice in Detroit. The Detroit firm of George Mason and Zachariah Rice were known for their work in a variety of architectural styles. George D. Mason was described by historian Clarence M. Burton as "the Dean of Detroit architects" (Burton 3: 696). While Bailey was working for the firm, their major project was the First Presbyterian Church in Detroit, a massive Richardsonian Romanesque style building of red sandstone. The brickwork on the Herrmann House mimics the type of building material used in the construction of the church at only a fraction of the cost of using sandstone. Mason & Rice also designed a series of homes and businesses in Walkerville, Ontario, in the Tudor Revival style, that strongly resemble Bailey's design of the Herrmann house. Undoubtedly, Bailey was influenced by his time at Mason & Rice and it can be seen in Bailey's later architectural work. Bailey knew Albert Kahn as they apprenticed together at Mason & Rice. One might speculate whether Bailey and Kahn ever discussed architectural styles and design. The Herrmann house is in the Tudor Revival style. Notice the gables in any of the images and how they extend above the roofline, a feature I have not seen before. The lintels on the triple windows on the front and south side separate the window from the transom above, strangely the north side of the home only has a pair of windows in that position. The small arched windows on the second floor, a triple bank on the north side and a double set on the front add elegance to the home; these were costly additions. The two-story canted bay window on the facade with the elegant upper porch and the smaller bowed bay window on the south side of the structure, help to make the Herrmann home one of the most graceful residences in Lansing. In 2013-2014 the home went through a $1,000,000 renovation to serve the needs of Lansing Community College's President Brent Knight (*Lansing City Pulse* 1/30/2013). The cost may shock people, but it was money well spent to preserve one of the few architectural treasures in Lansing. The home is still standing in 2019.

John T. Herrmann 1837-1898

John Theodore Herrmann was born in Darmstadt, Germany, on September 9, 1837. Like his father, John worked as a tailor, before coming to Lansing in May of 1872. For six years, he labored as a tailor in the employ of Lemley & Westcott, then in 1878 John opened his own business on North Washington Avenue. His store was known for the lines of fine clothing he sold and had a reputation for producing fashionable garments. John was a member of the Arbieter and Liederkranz Societies. John was married to Miss Katherine Dorothea Krieger in Germany; the couple had six children: Henry, Christian, Charles, Elizabeth, Katherine and Marie Herrmann. John Theodore Herrmann passed away at his home at 12:50 pm on June 24, 1898 (*SR* 6/24/1898).

HENRY B. KEBLER HOME

1034 N. Washington, Lansing, MI.
There is no record that Bailey designed this home, but the similarities in architectural style of the Kebler residence to that of the Herrmann house are remarkable. (CADL/FPLA)

Over the many years of researching Lansing History I have seldom encountered unexplained enigmas. However, the Kebler house is just such an anomaly. When I came across these images I was sure they were misfiled as the resemblance to the Herrmann house was so striking. The clue to help solve the mystery is the car parked on the street, which can be observed in the second image. There was no way this could be the Herrmann house because there were two other homes between the Herrmann house and Lapeer Street. It is dangerous territory when one enters into the speculation of who designed what structure because it resembles a structure that an architect previously designed. In this case, it is justified. The Kebler residence on North Washington Avenue was almost an exact copy of the Herrmann house, located on the campus of Lansing Community College. The only real difference between the Kebler house and the Herrmann residence was the style of the windows on the third floor. There were just two on the north and south side and all including the front, lacked the lintel that separated the upper and lower windows. The home also was missing the small double arched windows on the second-floor facade.

Compare this image of the Kebler home to the north side view of the Herrmann house and you can observe many similarities and several slight differences, mainly the style of windows.
(CADL/FPLA)

Lot 13, Block 42 was originally owned by Frank I. Moore, who sold/gifted the property to his son Benjamin who in turn sold the lot in 1903 to Henry Kebler for $1,500. There was only a brief mention of the home's construction in the newspaper. It is unknown if Bailey designed the residence, but is seems quite probable that he did, or he sold the plans for the home to Kebler. This was not an uncommon practice; architects resold designs all the time. Just compare the structure of the eaves and the downspout over the porch on the Kebler home and the Herrmann house, they are the same. It is doubtful that any architect could be so bold as to make such a detailed copy of a home and sell it in the same city as the original. Although copyright was not extended to architectural drawings until 1909 it is highly unlikely that an architect would risk his reputation in that manner. The Kebler home was torn down in 1957.

The following is the only reference I have discover regarding the home.

"H.B. Kebler will erect a brick dwelling on Washington avenue near Maple street, work to commence immediately" (*LJ* 6/3/1903).

Henry and Edith Kebler in front of their home. Although the house lacked certain architectural details that are present in the Herrmann home, it does have the identical dentil brickwork pattern under the porch atop the two-story canted bay window.

Henry B. Kebler was born in Eagle Township, Clinton County, Michigan on November 23, 1869, the son of Christian and Elizabeth (née Schlee) Kebler. On February 4, 1892 Henry married Miss Edith M. Christopher, the daughter of Burroughs P. and Josephine (née Ten Eyck) Christopher. Henry and Edith did not have children. Henry owned a Boot & Shoe Store at 123 East Franklin [Grand River] Avenue for fifty years; he retired in 1945 after the death of his wife.[111] Henry continued to reside in Lansing after the death of Edith. Henry passed away while on vacation with his brother Fred in Bradenton, Florida, on October 30, 1952.[112]

---

[111] Edith M. Kebler died on June 18, 1945. She had been a resident of Lansing her entire life and was a member of the Lansing Federation of Women's Clubs.

[112] For Henry's death see the *LSJ* 10/31/1952; for Edith see the *LSJ* 6/18/1945.

JUDGE MCPEEK HOUSE

416 Lawrence, Charlotte, MI.
Observe the simple diamond shaped inlay at the peaks of the dormer and gable ends, an inexpensive but pleasing addition to the home.

"Judge McPeek of Charlotte was in city yesterday and left an order with Architect Bailey for plans for a new $3,000 residence" (*SR* 3/9/1894).

The McPeek home is a wonderful Queen Anne style residence. Notice the front gable with the upper closed gable, which combines the elements of scrollwork below the small ornamental closed gable near the peak with the diamond inlay. This component is repeated on the other gables and the wonderful smaller open dormers. The fish scale siding is present above the window and each of the gable ends. The McPeek home was such a departure from the Herrmann home and demonstrates Bailey's architectural range. The home is still standing in 2019.

The carriage house can be seen behind the home and except for the added garage door the structure is almost original. Carriage houses are a piece of American architecture that are quickly disappearing from the American landscape.

Jacob L. McPeek was born on May 4, 1848 in Madison, Ohio, to Samuel and Mary (née Gartrell) McPeek. In 1852, his father purchased a farm in Onieda Township, Eaton County and moved his family to Michigan. Jacob attended school in Leoni Township and later Lansing. In 1871, he opened a real estate business in Grand Ledge, Michigan and became editor of the *Grand Ledge Independent*. In addition to his other positions, Jacob began to study law, a subject at which he excelled. In 1875, he was admitted to the bar and served as Trustee, Justice of the Peace and Recorder for city of Grand Ledge. Jacob was elected State Senator for Barry and Eaton Counties in 1876 and stayed one term, he was elected Probate Judge for Eaton County in 1888 and served for eight years, losing the election in 1896. In 1874 Jacob married Miss Inez DeGroff of Huron County, Ohio; the couple had one child, Roy. On Friday, January 21, 1898 Judge Jacob L. McPeek passed away at his home on Lawrence Street in Charlotte, Michigan.[113]

---

[113] *Charlotte Tribune* 1/26/1898 and the *DFP* 1/22/1898.

GERMAN METHODIST EPISCOPAL CHURCH

The Five Corners at Holt, Michigan. The design of the German Methodist Episcopal Church is in many ways a modestly designed structure. Observe the ornate spindle work along the top of the entrance porch and the paintwork on shingles and tower. Bailey designed a simple but attractive structure for the church members.

German M.E. Church Dedicated

"The new German M.E. church at Holt was dedicated under the fine auspices last Sunday. The ministers present were Rev. L. Allinger, presiding elder, of Detroit; Rev. Geo. Wahl, preacher in charge; Rev. C. Baumer, of Lansing; Rev. A. Mayer and Rev. C. Heitmire of DeWitt, and Rev. Wm. Folkner, professor of German, Wallace College, Berea, Ohio. The latter preached the German sermon in the morning and in the afternoon Rev. Washington Gardner preached the sermon in English.

"The church has a seating capacity of 350. By placing chairs in the aisles, it would hold 450. Yet in the afternoon all space was filled and many turned away. The cost of the building was $4,100, all but $800 of which had been paid or secured by subscription before dedication. The remaining $800 was easily raised at the Sunday services, leaving the organization free from debt. The structure was designed by Arthur Bailey of Lansing, the carpenter work done by A. Douglass of Holt, mason work by Wm. Demon of Lansing and the frescoing by J.C. Hawes of Lansing. The seats were placed by the Globe Furniture Co. of Northville and the pulpit chairs by Stroud of Mason. It is heated with a Peninsular furnace, the setting up and tin work being done by Earle of Mason. The 21-light chandelier is from Fink of New York. The congregation are very proud of the structure, as they have reason to be, for it is without doubt one of the finest if not the finest church in the county outside of the cities. Sincere thanks are extended by the trustees to all who aided in the work, donations, etc." (*ICN* 10/11/1894).

The church was located on the Five Corners in Holt, now the site of the Holt United Methodist Church's parking lot. It is unknown what happened to the fantastic stained-glass window that appeared in the first image. (CADL/FPLA)

The German Methodist Episcopal Church was a Steepled Ell design which incorporated the entrance into the steeple. The steeple was broader than the traditional church steeple, with an enclosed belfry capped with a four-side spire. The bold placement of the large three section Gothic headed stained glass window, as seen in the first image, completed the facade. The only embellishment was the scroll work on the front gable. This was not meant to be an ornate church, it reflected the principles of the religious community that it served. The structure later served as the home of the Holt/Delhi Public Library and was torn down circa 1979-1980.

UNION SCHOOL

Union School, Manistee, MI.

"R. Arthur Bailey has received the contract for the plans and specifications for the new union school house at Manistee" (*SR* 6/8/1894).

The Union schoolhouse in Manistee was built on the southwest corner of First and Oak Streets in 1866, the building was enlarged to meet the needs of the growing community in 1870. On April 30, 1886, the school was destroyed by fire.[114] Two weeks later Fred W. Hollister the well-known Saginaw architect, was commissioned to design a new school. Hollister was in Manistee at the time of the fire, overseeing the construction of the new fire hall that he designed for the city. On July 6, 1886, the contract for building the school was awarded to L.B. Long & Company.[115] The *State Republican* article stated that Bailey "received the contract for the plans and specifications for the new union school house at Manistee". It is doubtful that the Manistee school board was considering replacing a school that was less than ten years old. The board may have been investigating the expansion of the school district by adding an elementary school, although a review of the 1893 *Manistee City Directory* and the 1902 *Manistee City Directory* show no additional school had been added between these dates. No documentation has been found to substantiate the *State Republican* article.

---

[114] There seems some confusion regarding when the fire occurred. The *Owosso Times* on April 30, 1886 mentioned the fire, while Steve Harold in the *History of Manistee Area Public Schools* gives the date as May 1 (Harold 8).

[115] See *Manistee Democrat* 5/1/1886, *Manistee Democrat* 7/8/1886, the *Manistee Weekly Times* 7/9/1886, *Manistee Advocate* 7/10/1886 and the *Manistee Sentinel* 7/10/1886.

ISER CLUBHOUSE

The Iser Clubhouse, Pine Lake [Lake Lansing], Haslett, MI.

The Iser Club
ITS MEMBERS WILL BUILD A HANDSOME HOME AT PINE LAKE
It will be Located Out in the lake and Tis Expected that Twill be a Thing of Beauty and a
Joy Forever

"Lansing is known all over the state as a city of clubs, the social kind, and it is certainly true that she sustains the name right bravely. Another has been added to the long list, and this last acquisition will no doubt prove to be among the most club-like of the lot. It will be known as the 'Iser outing club' and judging from the make-up of the membership there will be no lack of mode of enjoyment which appeals in a peculiar manner to the male side of humanity. For the past few weeks a number of the prominent business and professional men of the city, who are lovers of legitimate sport in its varied forms, have been holding meetings and the "Iser club" is the outcome. A *Republican* reporter came across a few of them in the office of Architect R.A. Bailey looking over plans of what appeared to be an elegant club house. "Just a little scheme," was the answer to the reporter's query, but since then the scheme has developed into a reality. Pine lake has been a steadily growing attraction for this city and within the past year particularly plans for new buildings and resorts have been contemplated. It has also been a favorite place for duck shooting and fishing and on this account, has caught the eye of the "Iser club". Near the middle of the lake there is a sandbar, at which point the water is very shallow. These points have helped toward the formation of the club. The plans are these: The club will consist of twelve members, who shall subscribe to begin with $100 each to the general fund; a club house costing about $1,500 will be erected on the sandbar in the middle of the lake, and then good times galore will follow as a matter of course. There was little trouble in completing the membership and there are already twenty names of application on file. The members at present are R.B. Shank, Charles Broas, R.A. Montgomery, J.P. Lee, Charles P. Downey, A.H. Whitehead, R.C. Ostrander, Guy W. Renyx, Fred Moliter, Fred North and two undecided. R.B. Shank has been the moving spirit in the scheme and is looking after the completion of affairs.

"The club house will be a beauty both in appearance, convenience and comfort. A look at the plans prepared by R. Arthur Bailey, makes one wish he was a member in anticipation of the jolly times to be had after its completion. The house will, of course, be frame and rest on piles. It will be forty by forty feet and two stories high, with a cupola. The cupola will be surrounded with a balcony, and the interior will be so arranged as to serve as a shooting box. The second floor will be fitted up with twelve sleeping rooms with a gallery running around in front of the entrances, as the interior will be built on the plan of the capitol rotunda, having an open court from the first floor to the cupola. It is understood the members will furnish their own sleeping apartments to suit their own tastes. The first floor will be devoted to a reception room 25 by 40 feet, having a fireplace large enough to burn four foot logs; a dining room 15 by 25 feet, a kitchen, and butler's room. The ceiling of the reception and dining rooms will be beamed, and the floor made of hard wood. Surrounding the entire club house will be a 10-foot veranda. Work will be commenced just as soon as the ice on the lake will permit of work, and everything will be in readiness for next season's pleasures.

"The name of the club is rather a unique one, but when understood fully demonstrates the feeling of the club. It is said that a farmer once wished to purchase a good horse, and with this end in view visited a well-known stable. He was first shown a colt; whose pedigree was long enough and of whom great things were expected. Next he was shown a beautiful animal, whose last year's record was 2:15. Said the old farmer; 'Them animals may be all right, but I don't want no may bes or has beens. I tell you I want an iser.' There are no 'has beens ' or 'going to bes' in the present club. Every member is an 'iser'" (*SR* 11/14/1894).[116]

---

[116] There is an alternative story in regard to the club's name. The *Lansing State Journal* in 1951

"Architect R. Arthur Bailey has nearly completed the plans for the club house of the Iser club, to be erected at Pine lake. An addition has been made to the original plans, being a 26x36 feet boat house to shelter the two launches and the yacht. Work will be commenced on the building next week" (*SR* 1/4/1895).

In the above image, you can observe the boathouse, which was attached to the rear of the structure. Bailey designing the structure to sit on pylons in the middle of a lake is a testament to his architectural skills.

The Iser or Izzer Club (accounts about the club appear under both names) was established in 1895 and there are different versions of the source of the name. One is the explanation as outlined above, the second comes from the *Lansing Capital News,* which stated that the club was named after the yacht Izzer, which was purchased by Charles P. Downey and other members of the club from its owner and brought to Pine Lake. It was said that the Izzer was one of the fastest boats on the Detroit River and captured Downey's attention there during a race. The Izzer was reported to be very fast but a demanding boat to handle, at one time it 'busted loose' almost splitting the club house in two, destroying the porch, and depositing members of the club in the lake. In 1917 the building was moved off its pylons because they had rotted and shifted over to new pylons. Oddly the Club never owned the land that the clubhouse was built upon, the liquid lot where the clubhouse was located was owned by the state of Michigan. (*LSJ* 5/21/1937) After the club disbanded, Charles Downey maintained the property and paid the taxes. The Downey family occasionally used the club house for social events. Charles Downey preserved the building because he enjoyed the times he spent at the club when he was

relates a shortened version of the same story only Izzer is used not Iser (*LSJ* 8/1/1951).

young. In 1922 after the death of Downey the only surviving member of the club was William C. Durant.

Michigan Agricultural College (MAC) 1914 Football Team that went 5-2 and lost to Michigan, 3-0 at College Field in East Lansing.

One of the last uses for the old clubhouse was as a training headquarters for the Michigan Agricultural College (MAC) Football team under Coach John Macklin. Charles P. Downey was an enthusiastic supporter of the M.A.C. Football team and the team responded to their time at Pine Lake by beating University of Michigan in 1913 and in 1915.[117] Charles P. Downey passed away in 1921. Before her death in 1937, Margaret T. Downey, Charles' mother donated the clubhouse to the Lansing Boy's Maritime Corporation, the local Sea Scouts Organization who maintained the site. Unfortunately, in early 1940 the clubhouse was ravaged by vandals who stripped and wrecked the structure. The building was removed in January of 1940 by the Capitol Wrecking Company with some of the wood used to build a new boathouse on shore for the Sea Scouts.[118] What can be said about this structure? It is a unique design, a structure that must have been fantastic to see in person. In many ways, the structure resembled an east coast shoal lighthouse.

---

[117] Oddly the club house was offered to the University of Michigan in 1904 as a dormitory for the football team so they could have their summer training at the park (*DFP* 6/26/1904).

[118] See the *LSJ* 10/10/1937, *LSJ* 1/15/1940 and *LSJ* 1/21/1940. The newspaper accounts are confusing, one states that the property was donated by Mrs. Margaret T. Downey, Charles' mother, the other by Mrs. Harriet P. Downey, Charles' wife.

FRED ROW RESIDENCE

116 (112) W. Hillsdale, Lansing, MI. (CADL/FPLA)

"Work was commenced this morning on the new $3,500 residence for Frank Row on Hillsdale street west, between Capital and Washington avenues. R.A. Bailey is the architect" (*SR* 4/25/1895).

The Row home was a bizarre mixture of architectural styles. The third-floor windows on the gable end resemble those on the Herrmann house with a lintel at the top of the window creating an arched transom window above. At the front of the third floor there was an eyebrow dormer, an agreeable feature. On the second-floor there was a sleeping porch that extended over the back of the structure. The four small arched windows over the first-floor bay window may have provided light for the third-floor staircase. Notice the oriel window on the front side of the house on the second floor. The small oval window just off the front porch completes the interesting exterior features of the home. Frankly there is too much going on here with Bailey's plan. He seems to be trying to incorporate as many different architectural elements into the home as possible. One example is the way the structure overwhelms the small front porch. A second example is the lack of symmetry in the way Bailey stacked the windows of the home. It is a jumbled mess when compared to the design of the Herrmann residence. Although impressive, this was not one of Bailey's best designs.

Frank G. Row was born in Lansing, Michigan on November 11, 1866, the son of Samuel H. and Elizabeth (née Wilson) Row. Frank's father worked for the Michigan Secretary of State and received an appointment as the first Insurance Commissioner for the state of Michigan. Frank attended public school in Lansing and left school at the age of 14 to work as an assistant at a local drug store. Frank moved from Lansing to Chicago, in July of 1885, to work as a clerk in the insurance office of Fred S. James & Company. Three years later, Frank returned to Lansing where he served as the agent for the Springfield Fire & Marine Insurance Company of Massachusetts. On November 25, 1891, Frank married Miss Louise B. Chaney of Lansing, the couple had two children: Frank Damon and Rosina Row. Frank moved his family in 1905 to Grand Rapids where he partnered with Charles L. Grinnell and established the Grinnell-Row Insurance Company. Frank G. Row passed away at the age of 85 in Grand Rapids on November 26, 1951.[119]

---

[119] *Grand Rapids Press* 11/27/1951 and Fisher 140.

FIRST UNIVERSALIST CHURCH

128 W. Ottawa, Lansing, MI.
Notice the telephone poles and how low the wires were.(CADL/FPLA)

The description which follows is of the design that Bailey submitted, it in no way matches the church that was finally built by the Universalist Society.

Modest but Pretty
WILL BE THE NEW UNIVERSALIST CHURCH
Architect Bailey has Plans Completed for the New $15,000 Edifice at the Corner of Capitol Avenue and Ottawa Street.

"The design and plans of Architect R. Arthur Bailey for the new Universalist church at the corner of Capitol avenue and Ottawa street has been accepted by the building committee of the church. The new edifice, as shown on paper, is a very beautiful and artistic structure. The architecture is of the modern gothic style, while the detail is ancient gothic. The material to be used is pressed brick with stone trimmings. The church will have three entrances, the main entrance will be at the base of the tower, which will be situated at the southwest corner of the building, the gallery and Sunday school entrance will be at the northwest corner, and the pastor's entrance at the southeast corner. There are two smaller towers, which, with the 100 foot main tower, and the four gables and domed roof, make a very picturesque building. The seating capacity of the church will be 600. The main auditorium is built on the plan of an octagon and is lighted by four oriel windows and also from the dome. A gallery runs across the west end, the pulpit and choir loft being in the east. The choir will have seating capacity for twenty-five singers. The pastor's study is situated over the Ottawa street entrance. The interior will be finished in hard wood and handsomely decorated. In the basement will be the Sunday school room, with class rooms and library, and the kitchen and ladies' parlor. It is expected that the completed church will cost $15,000 and work will be commenced as soon as the working plans are completed" (*SR* 6/3/1895).

"At a meeting held on Wednesday evening by the building committee of the Universalist church the plans of Earl H. Mead were finally accepted and adopted. The church will be built of fine stock of compressed brick with stone trimmings. The exterior is not elaborately decorated, but presents a very substantial appearance" (*SR* 6/20/1895).

However, Bailey was not awarded the contract to design the church. Seven days later the building committee selected the plans of Earl H. Mead, a respected Lansing architect. Why the change? The reason Bailey lost the contract for the church is never explained in church documents. It may be that the church members felt Bailey's design for the church was simply too extravagant given the principles of the church. If you compare the description of the church building that Bailey proposed to the structure that was built you can see that the design of Earl Mead is much more subdued. The building committee's choice of Earl Mead's design may have been a contributing factor in Bailey's decision to move to Detroit. The building was dedicated as the Church of Our Father in 1897.[120] The Universalist Church was incorporated on March 16, 1849, although meetings had been held in 1848. The earliest meetings were conducted in the State Senate Chamber, led by Reverend John H. Sanford of Ann Arbor. Sanford continued to hold services at intervals until 1852, when the Reverend Chauncey W. Knickerbocker came to serve the Universalist Church as minister. At a meeting in Lansing on October 24, 1852 a Constitution and By-Laws were adopted and signed by Daniel Johnson, C.P. Cowles, Alanson Ward, George Parsons and C.C. Crane. In 1852, the church had about 65 members. When access to the Capitol was denied to the organization for services, the schoolhouse in District 4 was engaged for meetings until 1859, when the state again allowed religious services to be held in the Capitol.[121] The members of the church arranged with the city of Lansing to purchase property on Grand Avenue at the foot of Allegan Street to build a church, for a consideration of one dollar.

In the late 1930s the Lansing Universalist Society fell into financial difficulties and the Universalist General Convention assumed the note on the property. Then in 1941 the Universalist General Convention sold the structure to Lee Cahill, a Lansing businessman, who converted the structure into an office building and managed the business until it was torn down in 1960. This is a wonderful example of a plain Romanesque style church and will be discussed in the forthcoming book on architect Earl H. Mead.

---

[120] See *SR* 9/4/1897, *SR* 9/11/1897 and *SR* 9/13/1897.
[121] The school where the Universalist Church held their services may have been at Fractional District #4, located on the southwest corner of Waverly and St. Joseph. There was no 4th Ward school in Lansing prior to 1868.

MONTGOMERY HOME

615 S. Washington, Lansing, MI. (CADL/FPLA)

"R.A. Bailey is at work on plans for quite an extensive addition, and alterations on R.A. Montgomery's residence, Washington avenue south. The changes will cost $2,000" (*SR* 6/3/1895).

Darius B. Moon originally designed the home at 615 S. Washington in 1891 for Alonzo Miles Henry, co-owner of the Lansing Artificial Stone. It is interesting that Montgomery spent $2,000, well over $55,000 in today's money on renovating a home that was built just four years previously Montgomery paid over $5,500 then to acquire the home.[122] The $2,000 spent on an addition and improvements may have included building on to the rear of the house, rewiring the structure for incandescent lights, updating the bathroom with a bathtub and hot and cold running water, or modernizing the kitchen. Many of these advancements occurred in middle class domestic life during the mid-1890s. The residence was in the fashionable Queen Anne style, with the usual variations in the roofline, the multiple chimneys and if you look closely you can see some interesting features over the windows. The pediment over the porch displays a sunburst motif while over the front second floor window is another sunburst motif in the triangle above the window. The residence is no longer standing and the site is now a parking lot.

---

[122] Measuring the value of a dollar is based upon multiplying $2,000 by the percentage increase in the CPI from 1895 to 2015. See www.measuringworth.com.

Richard A. Montgomery 1845-1902

Richard A. Montgomery was born in Eaton Rapids, Michigan on October 20, 1845, the son of William and Harriett (née Bryant) Montgomery. After he graduated from Eaton Rapids High School, Richard studied law at the firm of Crane & Montgomery in Eaton Rapids. Under the guidance of the partners, Isaac M. Crane and Martin V. Montgomery, Richard was admitted to the Michigan Bar in 1871. Richard then moved to Pentwater, Michigan where he formed a law firm with his cousin, Robert M. Montgomery. In 1875, Richard moved to Lansing where, with his brother Martin they established the M.V. & R.A. Montgomery Law Firm. The practice was for many years one of the best-known legal firms in Central Michigan. President Grover Cleveland appointed Martin Montgomery to the United States District Court for the District of Columbia in 1888; Martin resigned from the District Court in 1892. Martin passed away at the age of 58 in 1898 and Richard continued the firm's practice alone. In marked contrast to his brother Martin, Richard did not seek public office but agreed to serve as City Attorney on several occasions.

Richard was married to Miss Arrietta Ann Gale, the daughter of John C. and Caroline (née Correll) Gale. Richard and Arrietta had one child Julia who later married Clarence D Clark. Richard A. Montgomery passed away at the age of 57 on August 22, 1902 due to chronic inflammation of the stomach, likely stomach cancer. Arrietta had moved to Arizona to care for her ill granddaughter; Arrietta died in Prescott, Arizona on April 16, 1912.

GEORGE E. RANNEY HOME

418 W. Allegan, Lansing, MI.

"Architect Bailey is working on plans to remodel and modernize the residence of Dr. Ranney on Allegan street west. It is the doctor's intention to make of his property one of the handsomest residences in the city" (*SR* 6/19/1895).

No image of 418 W. Allegan has been located, what we do have is an 1898 Sanborn map footprint of the home and a 1948 aerial photograph of the house. What we can determine from these resources is the home was two stories with a hipped roof with a small flat section at the center. There were two one story structures attached to the rear of the home, one of which may have functioned as Doctor Ranney's private surgery. Based upon these limited resources there is little else that can be said about the home.

Dr. George Emery Ranney, a respected Lansing resident, was born in Batavia, New York on June 13, 1839, to Joel and Elizabeth (née Champlain) Ranney. His family would later move to Sheridan Township, Calhoun County, Michigan. After attending the Stafford Academy and Rushford Academy, George enrolled at the University of Michigan to study medicine. When the Civil War began he enlisted in the Second Michigan Cavalry in September of 1861. Overwork forced his retirement from the service in 1863 and he returned to the University of Michigan to complete his studies in medicine. After graduation, Ranney returned to his old regiment as a surgeon. He was taken prisoner at the Battle of Chickamauga and was sent to Libby prison for 44 days. In 1901, he was awarded the Medal of Honor for, as the citation reads, "At great personal risk, went to the aid of a wounded soldier, Pvt. Charles W. Baker, lying under heavy fire between the lines, and with the aid of an orderly carried him to a place of safety."

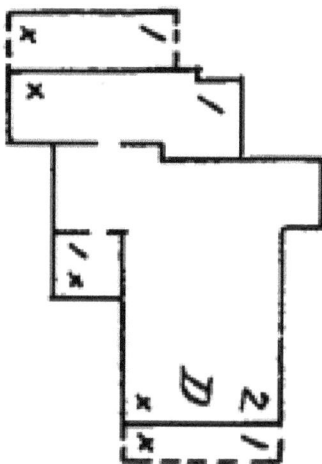

418 W. Allegan in 1898, from the Sanborn maps

He mustered out of the army in 1866 and settled in Lansing to practice medicine. Ranney was well known as a researcher; the first physician to discover the link between bad water and typhoid, diphtheria and other waterborne diseases. He worked tirelessly to make municipal water supplies safe, and had an international reputation for his work in this area. He was a member of the American Medical Association, the British Medical Association, a fellow of the British Gynecological Association and the Superintendent of Lansing City Hospital along with many other honors and awards. The citizens of Lansing are indebted to him for his work to have 11,000 trees planted in the city to improve its appearance.

On September 15, 1869 Dr. Ranney married Isabella E. Sparrow; they had two children, Ralph S and Florence, both who predeceased their parents. Following the death of his wife Isabella on October 17, 1906, Dr. Ranney lived alone above the Ranney Block. After the death of his friend Dr. Julius A. Post on October 28, 1915, Dr. Ranney accompanied the body east to Bethany, New York. The strain of losing a lifelong friend and Civil War comrade overwhelmed Dr. Ranney; he died after suffering a stroke in his office on November 10, 1915. [123]

---

[123] *LSJ* 11/10/1915.

MARSHALL RUMSEY HOME

1619 E. Michigan, Lansing, MI.
Observe the recessed porch on the gambrel gable and the oval windows on the second floor with their cross accents.

"Marshall E. Rumsey of Leslie is contemplating the building of an $8,000 residence on his addition on Michigan avenue east. Architect Bailey has prepared the plans" (*ICN* 8/29/1895).

A HANDSOME HOME
M.E. Rumsey Has Accepted Architect Bailey's Plans for an $8,000 Residence

"The handsome plans of Architect R. Arthur Bailey for the new residence of Hon. M.E. Rumsey to be erected on the Rumsey addition on Michigan avenue east, have been completed and accepted, and work commenced on the foundation. The residence will cost about $8,000. Mr. Rumsey has long contemplated removing from Leslie to the city, and his beautiful grove could hardly be bettered for a splendid residence. The location selected gives a frontage on Michigan avenue of about 150 feet and continues through the block with a full frontage on Rumsey [Marshall] avenue. The large grounds will be fitted up to suit the residence, and will be laid out as a park, with fountains and gardens for flowers and fancy shrubbery, in fact, an ideal home. The house will be in the style of a modern suburban residence, of colonial detail, and will be three stories high. On the front, will be a beautiful stone terrace with stone floor, and the main entrance, which is on the east side, will be accessible through a stone veranda and a handsome porte-cochere.

1619 E. Michigan, in the early 1970s; notice the small dormer that was obscured in the first image. (CADL/FPLA)

"On the first floor will be a large vestibule, reception hall, library, sitting room, drawing room, and a dining room, with a butler's pantry and a modern equipped kitchen. The entire first story will be finished in native hard woods. The second floor will have four large sleeping apartments and a bath room, all of which are accessible from the main staircase hall. On the third floor will be two pleasant sleeping rooms, a large store room and an artistically decorated billiard room. The house will be heated with hot water, and lighted with both gas and electricity, and will be handsomely decorated throughout. Mr. Rumsey expects that the house will be ready for occupancy in early spring" (*SR* 9/14/1895).

The rear of the Marshall Rumsey Home, note the larger gambrel gable with the flared shingles which gives the appearance of a partially closed gable. (CADL/FPLA)

The Rumsey home is a difficult home to describe due to the lack of clear photographs. The home was an interesting structure that mixed elements of different architectural styles and was a far more pleasing design than the Row residence, with a porte-cochere and an elegant porch above the first floor. The gambrel gable on the front of the home with the striking inset porch on the third floor is matched by the small dormer with its flared roof and sides. Notice the flaring of the siding at the transition between the floors and the offset entrance porch, all elements that provided for an elegant facade. What is odd is the placement of the windows on the facade, they are not symmetrical and it begs the question, did Bailey have difficulty in the placement of windows early in his career? It is unfortunate that there is not an image of either side of the structure. The back of the home is overwhelmed by the large gambrel gable and the windows on the rear may have been moved with the conversion of the residence in to apartments. The home is no longer standing; the date of its demise is unknown.

Marshall E. Rumsey 1840-1900

Marshall E. Rumsey was born in the village of Bethany, Genesee County, New York on January 17, 1840 to George W. and Fannie M. (née Canfield) Rumsey. He attended the Academy at Bethany Center and high school at Genesee, New York. At the age of 17, Marshall taught at the district school during the winter and in the summer worked as a farm hand. In 1862 Marshall moved west to Illinois and was engaged in business in Chicago until 1867. There is no listing in the 1866 *Chicago City Directory* for a Marshall Rumsey. After leaving Chicago, Marshall settled in Leslie, Michigan where he purchased a farm. In Leslie, Marshall invested in a variety of local businesses; he was president of the First National Bank of Leslie and later the People's Bank of Leslie, owned a lumber yard and had a thriving real estate business. Marshall was a member of the Leslie Village Council, the school board and twice represented Ingham County's Second District in the Michigan State House in 1885 and 1887. On May 15, 1865 Marshall married Miss Hattie Wickwire, the daughter of Rensselaer and Sarah (née Whipple) Wickwire. Marshall and Sarah had two children, Edward M., who died at the age of 17 and Fannie M., who later married Fred Haynes of Leslie. Marshall E. Rumsey passed away on December 3, 1900 at his home in Lansing.[124]

---

[124] *SR* 12/4/1900, *LR* 12/4/1900, *Leslie Local Republican* 12/7/1900 and *Portrait and Biographical Album of Ingham and Livingston Counties, Michigan* p 291.

DR. RALPH W. MORSE HOME

216 W. St. Joseph, Lansing, MI.

The Morse house was a massive structure, note the gambrel gables and the shingle work above the third floor windows that form an arch key pediment, a detail usually seen in brick homes. (CADL/FPLA)

"R.A. Bailey, Jr., returned to Detroit today. Mr. Bailey is preparing plans for a new residence which Dr. R.W. Morse is preparing to build on Main street west" (*SR* 3/6/1896). The State Republican article from March 6, 1896 was incorrect in stating that Dr. Morse new house was to be built on West Main Street, Dr. Morse only owned property on West St. Joseph, Block 159, Lot 5 or 216 W. St Joseph.

In many ways, the Morse home resembled the Rumsey house on East Michigan Avenue. The facade of the Morse residence had a gambrel front gable with a small offset dormer but that is where the similarities end. To start with, the Morse home had a notable side porch that is barely visible in the second image, which extended on the east side of the home under the second floor. There is a small front entrance porch but the structure does not overwhelm the porch as in the Row residence. The structure seems to absorb the porch, which is offset by the small side porch. There is a balanced element to the house that was not present in the Row home, the windows follow a symmetrical pattern between the floors. Notice the flaring between the first and second floor, not only does it present a pleasing architectural feature, it offers the practical aspect of shedding water away from the foundation. In 1934, the home was heavily damaged by fire, which started in the barn, just to the rear of the home, and quickly spread to the house. The damage to the home was recorded at $4,000 (*LSJ* 4/18/1934). The home later served as McLaughlin Hospital and as a U.A.W. Regional headquarters. In 2019, the site of the home is now a parking lot.

The side porch detail at 216 W. St. Joseph.

Ralph W. Morse was born in 1861 to Doctor Marcus F. and Elizabeth (née Gail) Morse in Angola, Indiana. Ralph attended the University of Chicago, College of Dentistry and began his practice in Lansing in 1888. That same year Ralph married Adelia Hough Gibson on September 18 and the couple had three children; Robert M., Laura E., and Marian Morse. Ralph was an active member of the Lansing School Board for several years and was elected the President of the Central Michigan Dental Society. On July 18, 1945 Doctor Ralph W. Morse died at his home in Lansing at the age of 85. Adelia Morse passed away at the Midland Hospital on November 7, 1956 at the age of 97. Adelia was born in Tiffin, Ohio in January of 1858.[125]

---

[125] For Ralph see *LSJ* 7/18/1945 for Adelia the *LSJ* 11/9/1956. Adelia's date of birth may have been July 1, 1859; the records are unclear.

CITY NATIONAL BANK

101-103 N. Washington, Lansing, MI.
Bailey supplied the interior decorations for the renovation of the bank. In 1896 Bailey operated a
company that specialized in providing building materials and artistic furnishings.

Modern New Home
CITY NATIONAL BANK TO HAVE ONE SOON
Work Has Been Commenced on Remodeling the Old Central Michigan Bank Property—
Will be Handsome and up to Date—Ready January 1.

"Active work has begun on the old Central Michigan savings bank building, now the property of the City National bank, which will transform it into an elegant modern bank and office building. The front, up to the second floor, will be of Amherst stone. The entrance will be at the northeast corner, and the first floor, which will be raised a little above the level of the walk, will be reached by stone steps. The front door will be guarded by an elegant iron gate. Inside the gate will be a threshold of Tennessee marble and the door. The bank office will be thirty-seven feet long. One large plate glass window will take up most of the front and another of the same size will open on Michigan avenue. The stone trimmings about the windows will be recut, and new sash and plate glass will be put in. New vaults will be put in, extending from the basement to the second floor. The vault in the bank will have two stories (*SR* 9/28/1896).

"R. Arthur Bailey of Detroit has secured the contract for the interior decorations in the new City National bank building" (*SR* 4/12/1897).

The City National Bank of Lansing received an Office of the Comptroller of the Currency charter under the National Banking Law on June 1, 1886. The early history of the City National Bank is intriguing. On July 31, 1884, the Second National Bank of Lansing surrendered its Federal Charter and became the Longyear's Bank, a private financial institution. City National Bank was established on January 1, 1886 after Edward Sparrow acquired control of the Longyear's Bank. The new bank opened with $100,000 in capital, the equivalent of $23,000,000 in today's money. The bank received its Federal Charter that same year. On Tuesday March 1, 1931 workers from the H.G. Christman Company began the dismantling of the City National Bank building located on the northwest corner of Washington and Michigan Avenues to prepare the site for the new City National Bank building.

Residents of Lansing know this building today as the Comerica Bank building at 101 North Washington Square, or the building with the elephants above the entrance. The building committee for the new banking tower consisted of, B.F. Davis Chairman of the Board of Directors; Harry E. Moore, Vice Chairman; Richard H. Scott, President; John W. Haarer, Executive Vice President; J.W. Knapp, Vice President, and John T. Watkins a member of the Board of Directors of the City National Bank of Lansing. They oversaw the construction of a fifteen story Art Deco bank and office building designed by the Black & Black architectural firm, Lee and Kenneth C. Black.

On December 22, 1931, as a result of the Great Depression, there was a run on the American State Savings Bank, located kitty corner from the City National Bank of Lansing. Four days later it was announced that the Capital National Bank, a part of the Guardian Detroit Union Bank group, had purchased the City National Bank of Lansing. The result of this merger stabilized the banks in Lansing, however the construction of the City National Bank building was delayed. Lansing residents approved of the merger and over $1,000,000 in deposits flowed into the coffers of the new bank conglomerate. The officers of the new financial institution were R.E. Olds, President; Arthur C. Stebbins, Vice President; Frank Gorman, Executive Vice President; Albert A. Elsesser, Vice President and Cashier; Charles Bryan, Vice President; Marshall Westfall, Miles D. Grant and George Goodell assistant cashiers. The new Board of Directors was a who's who of Lansing businessmen: F.N. Arbaugh, Bruce E. Anderson, Arthur D. Baker, Byron L. Ballard, E.I. Cooley, Ernest I. Dail, D.S. Eddins, Albert A. Elsesser, Frank E. Gorman, A.B.C. Hardy, N.P. Hull, R.E. Olds, Drury L. Porter, Ray Potter, I.J. Reutter, C.J. Rouser, A.C. Stebbins, Frank A. Stolte and Smith G. Young. Control of the bank was placed in the hands of prominent Lansing businessmen who were determined to see to its success.[126]

There is little that can be said regarding Bailey's work on the City National Bank building since no interior images of the bank have been located. With many older buildings, there is some remorse when they are torn down; in this case, the City National Bank building was replaced by a far more elegant structure.

---

[126] *LSJ* 3/3/1931 and *LSJ* 1/1/1932.

GEORGE E. LANE HOME

116 (60) Delaware Street, Detroit, MI. From the *Detroit News*.

"Building Permits R.A. Bailey, 2 story brick dwelling, No. 60 Delaware $5,000" (*DFP* 2/21/1897).

The difficulty with the above citation is that we do not know if Bailey was acting as a contractor or the architect for the home. It is far more likely that Bailey was the architect as he had limited experience as a contractor. Based upon a review of the Detroit City Directories and Sanborn maps the home at 60 Delaware Street is the only structure whose footprint and location fits the criteria based upon what was presented in the architectural drawing published in the *Detroit News* on February 21, 1897. The front entrance is recessed into the home which can be seen in the following Sanborn image of the home at 116 (60) Delaware Street, although it does not show a front porch. The home was two and a half stories, there were no three-story homes on Delaware Street, between Woodward and Second Avenues. The final piece to be considered is the placement of the tower and the fact that the home had a straight facade. No other home on Delaware Street between Woodward and Second Avenues had a straight facade, they all show a porch being present, however the porch in the first image is recessed. All indications are that this was a striking home when viewed from the street. The masonry arch over the porch, a mixture of large and small stonework (the technical term is voussoir) creates a flow to the building which is carried by the heavy plain lintels over the first-floor windows.[127] Above the entrance is an oriel window, a feature you will see often in Bailey's early designs. Starting at the top there is a hip roof with an ornate balustrade with finials at each corner. The series of third floor dormers are in a standard design while the corner tower with the conical 'witch's hat' roof, adds a whimsical element. The home was a statement, it told the passerby that this was the residence of someone of means. The address of the Lane home changed to 116 Delaware Street in 1921, the site is now an empty lot.

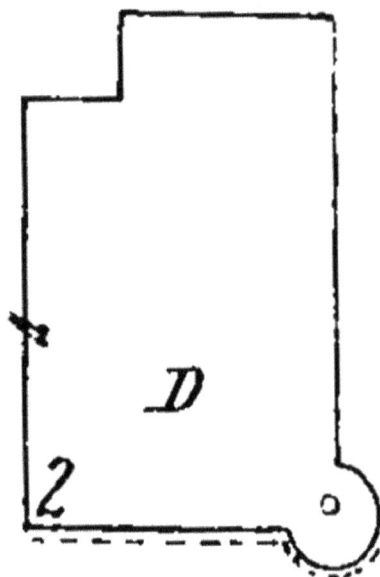

An image of 116 (60) Delaware Street from 1915 Sanborn map. The 1910 Sanborn map shows the home as being 2½ stories. What is important to notice in this image is there was no entrance displayed in the image. If you look at the image of 116 (60) Delaware, the recessed entrance would be where the **2** is in the above image.

In the late 1970s the Detroit Historic Designation Advisory Board proposed a New Center Area Historic District, to be added to the National Register of Historic Places. The projected district encompassed the area north of Lothrop Street to Virginia Park Street, west of Woodward and included the first block on Delaware Street between Woodward and Second Avenues.[128] The report contained a description of the Lane residence at 116 Delaware. The description of the Lane House, was as follows. "Its porch is recessed on the west side of the facade; an arched opening leads to the porch and entrance. Above the entrance on the second story is a bowed oriel window. An oriel window is also on the west elevation. On the east corner of the facade is a two-story tower with a steep conical

---

[127] A voussoir was a wedge-shaped stone used in arches.
[128] The proposed historic district was never established. Instead the report became the basis for the Virginia Park Historic District in 1982.

roof. The first and second stories are divided by a band of brick headers cut on the diagonal. Beneath the cornice is a frieze of decorative brickwork. The main roof of the house is a steep hip with a flat top roof; it has one centrally located dormer projecting from it."[129] The description covered in the proposal matched the architectural rendering of the home that was published in the *Detroit News*. It is unfortunate that it was torn down at some point in the 1980s. The historic district proposal mentioned that the Lane home had many of the characteristics of the Perry McAdow House at 4605 Cass Avenue in Detroit.

Perry McAdow house at 4605 Cass Avenue in Detroit, MI.
A proposal for a New Center Historic District in Detroit described the Lane home as having many of the architectural features present in the McAdow home, shown above, which was designed by the architect, Martin Scholls.

The home at 116 (60) Delaware Street was owned by George E. Lane in 1900. George was the Secretary and Treasurer of Morgan & Whately Company, which manufactured ladies' skirts and wrappers. The firm went bankrupt in 1903 and its assets were sold to J.L. Hudson (*DFP* 5/7/1903). Afterward George became President of the Babbitt-Taylor-Lane

---

[129] Detroit City Council 13.

Company, a business that manufactured women's skirts. George E. Lane was born in Michigan on September 26, 1869, to George M. and Mary (née Edwards) Lane. George married Miss Alice Cherry on October 8, 1895, the couple had two children; Cherry and Minot Edward Lane. George Edwards Lane passed away in Detroit on January 29, 1944, his wife Alice Cherry Lane died as a result of an automobile accident in Washington D.C. on July 13, 1944.[130]

ORIN S. HAWES HOME

628(106) Pingree, Detroit, MI.

"Architect R. Arthur Bailey has prepared plans for a very elegant residence for Orin S. Hawes, manager of the Salling, Hansen & Co. lumber company, to be built on the north side of Pingree avenue a little west of Second avenue. It will be constructed of fieldstone and frame covered with shingles in artistic design, having a frontage of 36 feet by 50 feet in depth and two and a half stories high. The interior finish will be especially fine. The vestibule and reception hall will have oak floors, will be wainscoted to the height of six feet in English oak and decorated in English style. The reception parlor will be finished in white enamel and decorated in Louis XV style. The library will be finished in red curled birch-mahogany finish with wainscoting five feet high and decorated in Empire style. The

---

[130] *DFP* 1/31/1944 and *DFP* 7/18/1944

dining room will be finished in antique quartered oak, wainscoted and decorated in colonial style. On the second floor, there will be a suite of apartments, consisting of chamber, sitting room, dressing room and bath room finished in red curled birch-mahogany finish, and decorated with special designs. Other apartments to be finished in white enamel. Berry Bros' hard oil finish will be used for all the work. The bath tubs will be of heavy white porcelain and all the plumbing pipes will be full nickel plated. The roof will be covered with shingles which with the shingle work of the sides will be colored with Dexter Bros' shingle stains. The house will cost $8,000" (*DN* 4/11/1897).

628(106) Pingree, Detroit, MI.
Notice the fieldstone porch foundation and the arched basement window. Image from 2016.

The Hawes residence was an architecturally conspicuous home, from the eyebrow dormer to the fieldstone porch with the arched basement window. The oriel window over the entrance porch coupled with the corner turret, which resembles a bartizan, gives the home a medieval appearance.[131] If you compare the two images the third-floor front gable window has been changed from a recessed window to a double window. Notice how Bailey incorporated flared siding over the porch to keep the porch dry when it rained, a small feature that added quite a bit to the comfort of the home owners. Finally, observe in the sketch the side gable and notice the brackets underneath, a feature that has been removed from the home and replaced with a solid beam. Overall this is a wonderful home that is still standing in 2019. The owners should be commended for preserving the structure.

A caricature of Oren Hawes.

Oren Star Hawes born in Housatonic, Massachusetts on March 9, 1868, to Stephen Starr and Mary E. (née Bond) Hawes. Oren attended high school in Great Barrington, Massachusetts and after graduation, in 1884, he moved to Manistee, Michigan to work at a hardware store. While in Manistee, Oren studied the lumber trade and in 1895 accepted a position at the Salling & Hanson Company. Throughout his life, Oren worked for a variety of lumber companies, including the Johannesburg Manufacturing Company and the Thomas Forman Company, before founding his own business, the O.S. Hawes Lumber Company. Years later, Oren served as director of the Merchant's National Bank, the Detroit Trust Company and was Secretary of the First Federal Savings & Loan Association. On April 26, 1893, Oren married Miss Susan Elsie Salling, the daughter of Ernest Nelson Salling, a well-respected lumberman and at one time Oren's employer.

---

[131] A bartizan was a corner turret on a castle, church or military structure.

There were no children from the marriage and Susan passed away at the Hawes estate at 17000 Jefferson Avenue on April 24, 1931. Oren married Miss Rachel Robinson on May 25, 1932; Oren was 64 while Rachel was 39 years old (*DFP* 6/5/1932). Oren passed away at his home at 17129 Maumee, Grosse Pointe, Michigan on January 20, 1941.[132]

ARTHUR G. HOLLAND RESIDENCE

748 (168) Seminole, Detroit, MI.
Note the Ionic style of columns on the porch and the Queen Anne style windows on the two dormers. Image from 2016.

"Architect R. Arthur Bailey: for A.G. Holland. Two and one-half story residence of buff pressed brick with cut stone trimmings. Cost $5,000 [1897]" (Synopsis 50).

---

[132] See Burton 3: 349, *DFP* 1/21/1941, and *Grosse Pointe Review* 1/23/1941. Rachel Hawes later married Colonel Jesse Gurney Vincent on November 10, 1943 (*DFP* 11/11/1943). The colonel was an interesting man; he was the co-designer of the Liberty Engine in World War One and during the Second World War helped design the Rolls Royce fighter plane engine and the engine for the U.S. Navy's PT Boats. The colonel was an engineering legend, he passed away on April 20, 1962 at Harper Hospital (*DFP* 5/11/1962). Rachel Vincent was a fixture in Grosse Pointe society and was a philanthropist who supported the Children's Hospital. She passed away on May 10, 1974 at the age of 81 (*DFP* 5/12/1974).

Observe the French doors on the wing and above them, on the second floor a set of four windows, the area on the second-floor wing may have been designed originally as a sleeping porch. (Walter)

Arthur G. Holland died unexpectedly in White Plains, New York on December 18, 1909. While out for a ride on his horse on the afternoon of December 17, Arthur's horse bolted and threw him to the ground which resulted in a fractured skull. Arthur lingered for 24 hours but he never regained consciousness. Arthur G. Holland was born in Staffordshire, England in July 1868, to Ralph and Mary Ann (née Tatler) Holland. Just when Arthur came to the United States is unclear, the first public record that he appeared in is the 1888 *Detroit City Directory* where he is listed as a bookkeeper at the Russell Wheel and Foundry. He later worked as a bookkeeper for a variety of businesses in Detroit.

In 1900, he formed the Arthur G. Holland & Company, a shoe store, which held the exclusive distribution rights for the Dr. Reed Cushioned Shoe. The business was originally located at the corner of Griswold and Clifford Streets but with the firm's success the store moved in 1901 to 79 Woodward Avenue across from the Avenue Theater. The Dr. Reed Cushioned Shoe must have been the Nike of its day because in 1903 Arthur opened a second store at 621 Sixth Avenue in New York City (*DFP* 12/4/1903). On July 7, 1896, Arthur married Miss Alice Maud Paterson, the daughter of Charles J. and Emma (née Goodyear) Paterson. After the marriage, Arthur was listed in the *Detroit City Directory* as living with his father in law, Charles J. Paterson at 168 Seminole. Arthur handled the sale of the property in 1905, which points toward him owning the property as opposed to his father-in-law. [133] The *Detroit Free Press* in 1899 mentioned that Arthur's wife was holding the meeting of Detroit's Sorosis Society at her home at 168 Seminole Avenue. [134]

A rear view of 748 Seminole, notice the French doors on the side porch and the curious placement of the windows on the second-floor corner of the wing and the main structure. (Walter)

Holland's home at 168 Seminole Avenue is an imposing structure. From the front, it looks like a typical American four-square with double dormers on the facade and single dormers on each side and the rear of the home. Notice the two-story bowed widow and the deep and extensive porch with Ionic columns. The sunroom on the south wing has a double set of French doors on the street side and a single set on the rear. Notice how Bailey blended the rear of the main structure by recessing the extension of the home. It is unknown if the rear porch was original or a later addition, although there does seem to be a door to the porch on the second floor. The chimney has circular pots at the top and decorated brickwork.

---

[133] See the *DFP* 11/1/1903, *DFP* 7/9/1905 and *DFP* 12/19/1909.
[134] The Sorosis Society was the first women's professional society for women who were barred from male professional clubs and professional organizations. See *DFP* 2/5/1899.

MRS. CATHERINE RAQUET HOUSE

650 (150) Van Dyke, Detroit, MI.
Note to the right in the image how the home was built to match the contours of the lot.

"Mr. Bailey is also preparing plans for a two and a half story frame residence with brick foundation for Mrs. Catherine Raquet, to be built on the east side of Van Dyke avenue between Champlain street and Agnes avenue, to cost $3,000" (*DN* 4/11/1897).

The Raquet residence was actually a double house, built in a combination of Greek Revival and Colonial styles. The pediment gable is supported by Ionic columns, and created the classic, cornice and frieze by using brackets and dentils, notice how the pattern is carried throughout the gable. The pediment window is interesting as this would have traditionally been a lunette(semi-circular) window. However in its place seems to be a Palladian style window, except that it is missing the arched head to the center window. Was this a design element employed by Bailey to soften the gable or was the window lost and replaced with a wooden insert? The facade of the home is almost symmetrical except that the bay window in the first floor right is not repeated on the left of the home. The second-floor porches are awkward, a result of the type of balustrade that is currently in place. The originals may have been far more elaborate. If you look closely in the above image you can see that the home bends to fit the shape of the lot, which can be seen more clearly in the Sanborn image below. The entire residence was built in a buff color brick that decreases the imposing facade of the home. The building demonstrated Bailey's range and architectural knowledge and his ability to mix styles and structural elements. The home is still standing in 2019. Despite the description provided in the *Detroit News* the Raquet home was not between Champlain Street and Agnes Avenue, rather it was located between Van Dyke Place and Jefferson Avenue; A fact that is verified by the Detroit City Directories, the Sanborn Maps and the Detroit Department of Public Works New House Numbers guide.

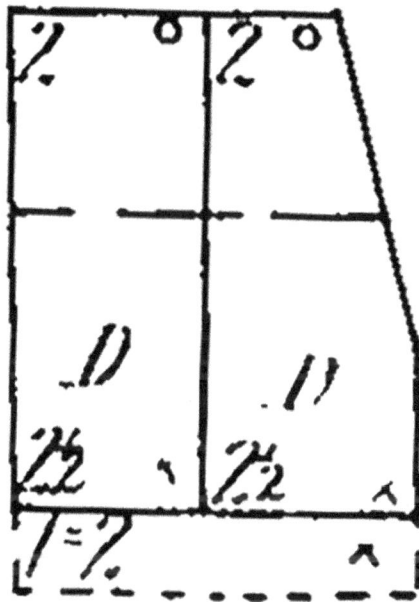

650 (150) Van Dyke, from the 1910 Sanborn Map. Notice how the residence angles toward the rear, now examine the first image, see how the home slants to fit the lot.

Catherine Breithaupt was born in Buffalo, New York on February 18, 1847 to Liborius and Barbara Catharina (née Goetze) Breithaupt. Liborius immigrated from Hesse-Kassel (Germany), in 1844 and settled in Buffalo where he operated a tannery with his son Louis. The business was sold in 1861 by Louis who moved to Berlin (Kitchener), Ontario where he opened a tannery. It was in Buffalo, where Catherine met Jacob Raquet who she married on March 3, 1864, the couple had seven children; William J., Clara M., Edward D., Hatta C., Emilie L., Joseph(Lewis) and a daughter, Anna who died in 1871. Jacob must have had an interesting life; he was born in North Dakota (Missouri Territory) in 1835 and first appears in the 1865 New York Census living in Buffalo with his wife Catherine. The 1865 *Buffalo City Directory* listed Jacob as being a partner in the firm of Ritter, Pauly

& Raquet, Sheep Skin Manufactures. In 1868 Jacob left Buffalo for Detroit where he established a Sheep Skin business at the corner of Michigan and LaSalle Avenues with his brother David. Jacob spent his life as a dealer of skins and hides and passed away on March 11, 1886. Catherine stayed in Detroit and supported her family by operating a boarding house. In 1928, Catherine moved to Santa Monica, California where she lived with her daughter Emilie (Millie). Catherine passed away on October 27, 1933 in California.

JOHN H. SMITH HOME

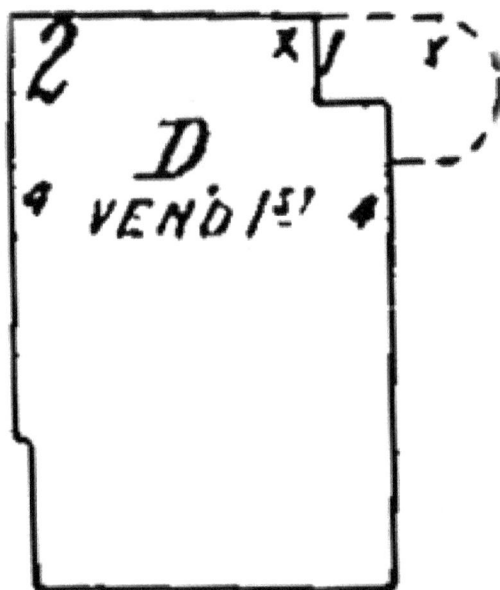

135(67) Delaware, Detroit, MI. From 1910 Sanborn Map.

"Elmer H. Stone has conveyed to Conrad H. Smith and J. Henry Smith 580x104 feet on the south side of Delaware avenue, between Woodward and Second avenues; also, 716x112 feet in depth on the south side of the above avenue [Delaware] between Second and Third avenues, for $40,000" (DFP 4/14/1895). It seems John Henry Smith owned quite a large piece of the south side of Delaware Avenue between Woodward and Third Avenues and was crucial in the development of Delaware Street, which today has some of the finest homes still standing in the city of Detroit.

"Architect R. Arthur Bailey has prepared plans for a fine three-story residence for J. Henry Smith of Peter Smith & Sons, to be built on the south side of Delaware avenue, between Woodward and Second avenues. The foundation will be of stone with superstructure of brick; the upper portion being of frame, covered with shingles, stained with Dexter Bros' shingle stains. It will cost $4,000" (DN 6/6/1897).

"Building Permits R.A. Bailey, two story brick and wood dwelling, No. 67 Delaware avenue $5,000" (*DFP* 7/4/1897). It is likely that the permit Bailey pulled for the home at 67 Delaware Street was the home for J. Henry Smith which was mentioned in *Detroit News* article of June 6, 1897.

John Henry Smith 1868-1940

Unfortunately, the home at 135 (67) Delaware Street was torn down and the site is now a parking lot. There were only three homes standing on the south side of Delaware Street between Woodward and Second Avenues, in 1900, numbers 21, 67 and 71 Delaware Street. The home at 135 (67) Delaware was offered for sale in the fall of 1897 by J. Henry Smith and a short description of the home appeared in the *Detroit Free Press*. "If you want a home in every sense of the word inspect house No 67 Delaware ave. Will be finished in quartered oak, decorated throughout, complete in every way; ready for occupancy October 1. Delaware ave. will be paved this month" (*DFP* 9/12/1897).

John Henry Smith was born on November 19, 1868 to Peter and Frances A. (née Calvert) Smith in Detroit, Michigan. Peter Smith had established a produce business in Detroit in 1859, Peter Smith & Son. John learned the business by working for his father and assumed ownership of the firm in 1904. John expanded the business and opened a branch in Indianapolis, Indiana and renamed the firm Peter Smith & Sons Grocery Company. The wholesale arm of the Peter Smith & Sons Grocery Company was sold to the General Grocer Company in 1912, allowing the Peter Smith & Sons Grocery Company to concentrate on their retail business. (*DFP* 6/30/1912)

The J. Henry Smith Building, located on the southwest corner of State and Griswold Streets, Detroit, Michigan. Although the building has the name Peter Smith on the lower marquee, it was originally named for J. Henry Smith. (LOC)

John was active in Detroit real estate, selling property, obtaining long term leases on land and in one instance built an eleven-story building, the J. Henry Smith Building, on the southwest corner of State and Griswold Streets. The contractor for the J. Henry Smith building was Warren G. Vinton, owner the Vinton Company, for whom Bailey later designed a home. (*DFP* 6/23/1912) John later purchased the Hotel Cadillac that was razed to build the Book-Cadillac Hotel. Essentially John built a real estate empire in Detroit through careful acquisitions and his ability to obtain long term leases on certain properties. On December 30, 1895 John married Mills Mary Adeline Calvert, the couple had three children; Marion C., Grace C., and John Henry Jr. After leaving Detroit, John lived in Manhattan then eventually settled in California, where he passed away in Alameda on August 17, 1940 (Burton 3: 218).

ALBERT A. ROBINSON HOME

220 (76) Chandler, Detroit, MI.
The two-story canted bay was an exceptional element of the Robinson home. Notice the arched windows on both gables and the small oval window. (Walter)

"Architect R. Arthur Bailey is preparing plans for a two and one-half story brick and frame residence for Albert A. Robinson, secretary and treasurer of the Detroit Motor Co., to be built on the south side of Chandler avenue, between Woodward avenue and John R. street. The building will be brick to the top of the first story; above which it will be covered with shingles finished with Dexter Brothers' shingle stain. The interior finish will be exclusively in hard woods. It will cost $4,500" (*DN* 8/8/1897).

Notice the oriel window and the position of the window slightly above and to the left, usually an indication of where a staircase was located in the home. (Walter)

"Architect R. Arthur Bailey… has also let the contracts for a fine residence heretofore reported in the *News-Tribune* for Albert A. Robinson on the south side of Chandler avenue, between Woodward avenue and John R. street. It will be brick-veneered and cost $4,000" (*DN* 11/28/1897).

Albert A. Robinson was listed in the 1899 *Detroit City Directory* as residing at 76 Chandler Avenue. In 1921, the address changed to 220 Chandler with the renumbering of the streets. The residence was located between John R. and Brush streets and not between John R. Street and Woodward Avenue as stated in the preceding articles. The home was built of brick with the third level dormers clad in shingles, again different than what was stated in the *Detroit News* article of August 8, 1897. This is a wonderful example of a Bailey designed home. The structure is asymmetrical with a balanced stacking of the windows. Notice the rusticated stone sills under the windows, an expensive feature, as is the stone banding that stretches across the facade between the first and second floors. On the side of the home, in the above image, there is a simple bay window which may have originally been a simple Chicago style window with a transom window above. The current window mimics this design but is not original. The small dormer next to the chimney is unusual and near the gable end, which can be seen in the next image, a crowded space is created along with a roofer's nightmare.

The rear wooden structure was a later addition to the home. The original rear porch was actually on the side where the one-story structure with the satellite dish is located. Note the dormer next to the chimney which is an extremely odd location.

Albert A. Robinson probably suffered the worst death of all the subjects this writer has researched over the years. On Sunday September 5, 1909, Albert and Sarah Robinson along with Mrs. May C. Tremaine, and her daughter Amy, and the Robinson's chauffeur, Ollie Pike, were out for a drive when their vehicle stalled on the tracks at the Euclid Avenue crossing in Bay City, Michigan. Their car was hit by the Wolverine Flyer, a fast-express train of the Michigan Central Railroad and the collision was devastating. Albert, Sarah and May were killed instantly. All that remained of Albert was his head, Amy was pinned in the vehicle and suffered a skull fracture while Pike was basically unharmed. No one was charged in the accident. Albert A. Robison was born in Michigan in 1861 and his early life is a mystery. On October 29, 1884, Albert married Susie F. Antrobus, the couple did not have children. Suzie wrote under the penname of Suzanne Antrobus and published the novel **The Kings Messenger**. (*DFP* 7/22/1901) The couple divorced on October 10, 1903 and the reason was cruelty and nonsupport. Susie remained at their home on Chandler after the divorce, while Albert moved to 105 Trumbull Avenue. Albert married Sarah E. Marcotte, the daughter of John Israel Marcotte, on June 30, 1906 and there were no children from the marriage. Albert was manager of the Commercial Supply Company of Detroit.[135]

---

[135] *DFP* 9/6/1909 and *DFP* 9/7/1909.

ARCHIE G. ELLAIR HOME

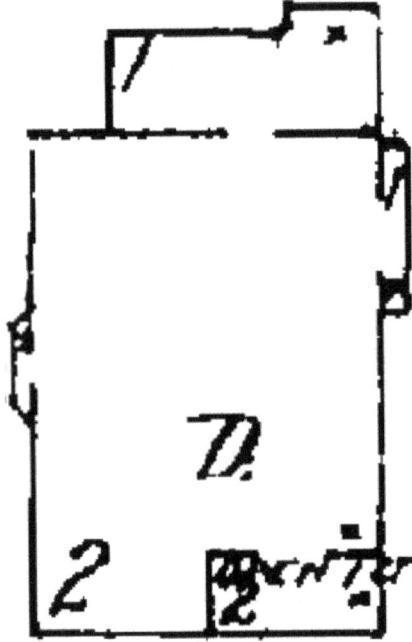

82(40) Hazelwood, Detroit, MI. image from 1915 Sanborn maps. The front of the home is at the bottom of the image.

"Architect R. Arthur Bailey is… Also, preparing plans for a two-story frame residence for Archie G. Ellaire [Ellair], to be built on the north side of Hazelwood avenue, between Woodward and Second avenues. The upper portion and roof will be covered with stained shingles. It will be in the Colonial style of architecture and will cost $3,000" (*DN* 8/8/1897).

The 1900 *Detroit City Directory* listed Archie G. Ellaire [Ellair] as living at 40 Hazelwood Street, the address changed in 1921 to 82 Hazelwood Street. The site is now an empty lot. All that can be said about the home, without an image, is that it seemed to have a two-story entrance porch or that the porch was recessed under the second story.

Archibald MacGregor Ellair was born in England on April 12, 1850 to Peter N. and Annie (née Michie) Ellair. The family moved to Grosse Pointe Township, Michigan when Archibald was an infant. Archibald's father, Peter, was a farmer who wanted a different life for his son, Archibald. At the age of 18, Archibald was apprenticed to George S. Frost, a land dealer. Archibald decided to leave the business and open a produce store with Charles Bray under the name of Ellair & Bray Company. The firm later became Ellair, Bray & Company, grain dealers, with offices in Detroit and Chicago. On May 13, 1872, Archibald married Miss Sarah A. Swartwout of Toronto and the couple had one child,

George who passed away on October 13, 1904 at the age of 31. A year and a half later Sarah died, never recovering from the loss of her son George. Archibald expired on Saturday, May 10, 1914. To give some insight into the personality of Archibald there is a story regarding his interaction with former President Theodore Roosevelt. In 1909, Archibald had booked passage to Europe on a Hamburg-American ocean liner the SS *Hamburg*. Roosevelt was also traveling aboard the liner and requested additional rooms for his party before the ship sailed. The steamship company complied and requested that Archibald surrender his stateroom which adjoined Roosevelt's. Archibald refused and stated, "Roosevelt as president and Roosevelt as a plain citizen are two greatly different persons."[136]

CHARLES T. BRENNAN RESIDENCE

655 Hazelwood Street, Detroit, MI. Once the site of the Brennan home, now the location of the Weber Apartments. (Walter)

"Architect R. Arthur Bailey is…. Also, preparing plans for a two-story frame residence for M.C. Brenhan, to be built on the south side of Hazelwood avenue, between Second and Third avenues. It will cost $2,500" (*DN* 8/8/1897).

---

[136] See the *DFP* 10/15/1904, *DFP* 7/25/1906, *DFP* 5/10/1914 and *NYT* 3/9/1909.

"Architect R. Arthur Bailey has... Also, prepared plans for a two-story frame residence for C.T. Brennan, to be built on the south side of Hazelwood avenue, between Second and Third avenues, to cost $2,500" (*DN* 9/12/1897).

Building Permits "R.A. Bailey, two story frame dwelling, No. 123 Hazelwood ave, $2,500" (*DFP* 8/22/1897). The problem is there was no 123 Hazelwood listed in the 1899 *Detroit City Directory*. Charles T. Brennan, manager Conley & Patterson Restaurant 28-30 W. Congress, owned 121 Hazelwood. All that can be said about the home was that it had a large front porch, and other than that, the home has been lost to history. The Brennan home was torn down in 1926 to build the Weber Apartment Building which currently occupies the site.

A caricature of Charles Brennan.

Charles T. Brennan was one of Detroit's well-known restaurateurs in the late 19th and early 20th centuries. Charles was born in Pittsburgh, Pennsylvania on January 27, 1860 to George and Matilda Brennan.[137] Charles began his career working at the old Island House Hotel in Toledo, first as a bell boy and in the early 1880s as a cashier. He moved to

---

[137] Charles' death certificate recorded his father as Patrick and his mother as unknown. The 1870 Census listed only one 10-year-old child named Charles Brennan in Alleghany County, Pennsylvania, the parents were George and Matilda. There were a lot of Brennans in the coal country of Pennsylvania.

Detroit in 1885 where he accepted a position working as a clerk in the Michigan Central Depot. Investing wisely, Charles slowly began to acquire restaurants. Charles formed a partnership with James Arthur Fitzgerald and Frank W. Sinks establishing the firm of Brennan, Fitzgerald & Sinks. The firm's first venture was the Penobscot Inn, which opened in 1905 in the new Penobscot Building located at 131 W. Fort Street. The company, in 1908, established Detroit's first self-service lunch room, the Majestic Servself in the basement of the Majestic Building, at 1011 Woodward Avenue. A second self-service dining room was opened in 1909, the Avenue Servself at the corner of Larned Street and Woodward Avenue.

THE MAJESTIC SERVSELF, BASEMENT MAJESTIC BUILDING, DETROIT.

The Majestic Servself at 1011 Woodward opened in 1908 and closed in circa 1929. After the closing of the Servself, Brennan, Fitzgerald & Sinks then started another restaurant in the Majestic Building, the Majestic Lunch, located on the ground level at 22 Michigan Avenue.

Charles married Miss Mary Morrison on June 22, 1887 in Toledo, the couple had two children: Vincent M. and a Margaret M. Brennan. Their mother, Mary M. Brennan passed on May 2, 1901. Charles' son Vincent, a graduate of Harvard, worked as a legal advisor to the State of Michigan Labor Department and approved the law limiting restaurant's workers to a 54 hour a week schedule. His father was not impressed. Charles' greatest love was the Detroit Tigers. He never missed a game at Navin Field and many times traveled with the team. This was the era of Ty Cobb's Tigers, so the games were never boring. Charles T. Brennan passed away at Providence Hospital, in Detroit on January 30, 1918.[138]

---

[138] See the *DFP* 5/3/1901, *DFP* 6/5/1904, *DFP* 3/3/1913, and *DFP* 1/31/1918.

Just what was a Servself? Basically it was a cafeteria and what follows is a description of the Servself in the Majestic Building.[139]

The Majestic "Servself."

Detroit's Newest and Greatest Restaurant.

"In the basement of Detroit's magnificent and most central office building—The Majestic—there has opened by Messrs. Brennan, Fitzgerald & Sinks the second of their "Servself" system of restaurants. It is the largest and finest quick-lunch place in the country where one can get the most delicious and appetizing dishes at a modern price of five and ten cents. Here there is no waiting, one is served almost instantly by dainty misses, garbed in black, with spotless white aprons and caps, a la chef. The room is large, and splendidly ventilated by the wash air system. Hundreds of electric lights suspended from Art Noveau chandlers illuminate the room. There are alcoves and corners suitable for little confabs or for families. And speaking of families, here one will see after divine service on Sunday whole families, which for the price of the family roast get a dainty luncheon, besides saving the wife the toil of preparation. No dishes to wash, and away they go, on river, or to park, and mother and wife commence to have some Sunday, too. The Majestic "Servself" is admirably situated in point of location, being in the heart of the city, near the hotels and theaters. People can sojourn at the principal hotels and obtain their meals at the "Servself", with considerable saving of expense. Strong features of this place are delicious coffee, always piping hot, finest clover creamery butter, and rich milk and cream. These as a basis and followed by the fact that all the hot dishes are hot, and the cold really cold, together with dainty pastries and fresh fruit pies, make the Majestic "Servself" appeal to all. Beautiful marble stairways lead down both Michigan and Woodward avenues. Retiring rooms finished in marble and mahogany for both men and women, and reception hall at the foot of Woodward avenue entrance, are other special features. The "Servself" caters to both men and women, and no liquors are sold on premises. The Majestic "Servself" is open day and night" (*DFP* 7/25/1908).

---

[139] On the verso of the postcard is this description of the Majestic Servself. "The Majestic Servself, Detroit's ideally located quick lunch, is the largest, finest and most complete of its kind in America, having a serving capacity of over 1,000 persons an hour. Tempting well-cooked dishes are displayed on large serving counters from which customers select their food. Home cooking, ideal surroundings and the very best of service has made it Detroit's most popular quick lunch. This restaurant appeals particularly to visitors and tourists, street cars from every station and steamboat dock stopping directly in front of the building. The Majestic is only one of the many high-class restaurants operated by Messrs. Brennan, Fitzgerald & Sinks."

HEBERT MALOTT RESIDENCE

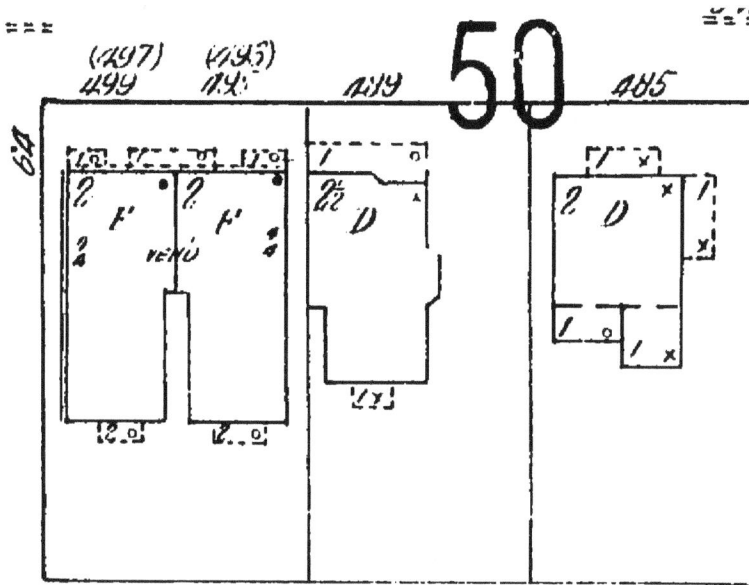

2417(485) Pennsylvania, Detroit, MI.
Image from the 1910 Sanborn Map. All that can be said about the home is that it seemed to have two porches, one on the facade and one on the south side of the house.

"Architect R. Arthur Bailey has prepared plans for a two-story frame cottage for Herbert Malott, to be built on the west side of Pennsylvania avenue, between Jefferson and Sears avenues, at a cost of $2,500" (*DN* 9/12/1897).

"John H. Tigchon has sold for Herbert Malott house and lot 30x105, on the west side of Pennsylvania avenue, north of Kercheval for $4,150" (*DFP* 4/19/1903).

The home on Pennsylvania Avenue is no longer standing, it would have been just south of Vernor Highway on the west side of Pennsylvania Avenue. The confusion arises from the statement in the *Detroit News* that the home was to be erected on Pennsylvania Avenue "between Jefferson and Sears avenues." Sears Avenue only existed for a short period, less than a year, then the name was changed to Agnes Street. The problem is that Agnes Street does not go through to Pennsylvania Avenue and 485 Pennsylvania Avenue is not near Jefferson Avenue, it is closer to Kercheval Avenue. The Detroit City Directories listed Herbert Malott as living at 485 Pennsylvania Avenue from 1898 to 1901.

Herbert was born in Kingsville, Ontario, Canada in 1869 to John Jonas and Hannah (née Iler) Malott. He came to the United States in 1889 where he found employment with John Phillips Case Company as a bookkeeper. Herbert left the company in 1903 and joined the Detroit Show Case Company as the Secretary and Treasurer. In 1907, The Detroit Show Case Company acquired the John Phillips Case Company. The Detroit Show Case

Company manufactured a complete line of show cases and display furniture. The best known national product was the 'Silent Salesman Show Case'. On June 10, 1896, Herbert married Miss Mary Forbes Peden, four children were born to the couple: Forbes I., Jessie P., William H., and Grace P. Malott. The family traveled on a regular basis back to Kingsville, Ontario where the family had a cottage. Herbert died unexpectedly on November 19, 1942, his wife Mary passed away on September 19, 1943.[140]

---

[140] See the *DFP* 5/31/1896, *DFP* 11/20/1942 and *DFP* 9/20/1943.

FREDERICK J. HENNING STORE

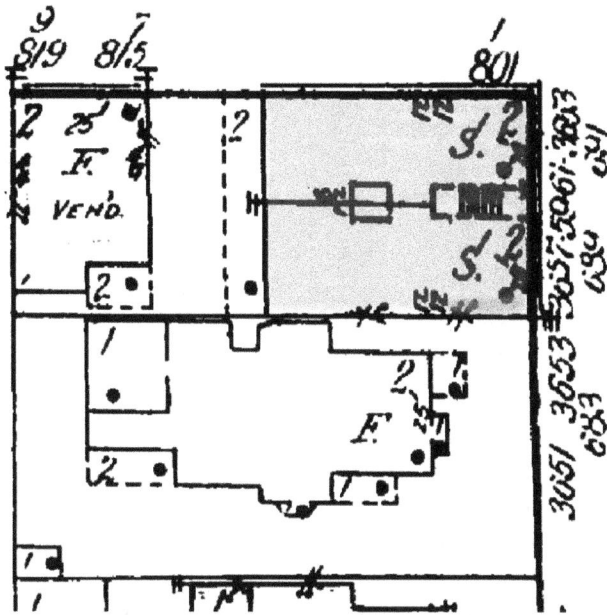

3661(691) Third Avenue, Detroit, MI.
Henning's store shaded in grey. The image is from the 1910 Sanborn map.

"Architect R. Arthur Bailey has... Also, prepared plans for a new and modern front for a drug store occupied by Fred J. Henning, on the west side of Third avenue between Brainard street and Tuscola avenue" (*DN* 9/12/1897).

Frederick J. Henning operated his drug store at 691 Third Avenue for 27 years. He was an avid collector of Chinese pottery and amassed an extensive collection. Frederick was born in Coldwater, Michigan to Anthony and Margaretta (née Specht) Henning on September 27, 1864. On December 19, 1889, Frederick married Miss Florence E. Hendershott, the couple had two children: John H. and Margaretta Henning. Besides overseeing his own drug store on Third Avenue, Frederick was a partner in the Standard Drug Store at 27 Monroe Avenue next to the Elks Hall, his associates were William DuPont and Andrew R. Cunningham. Most Detroiter's will remember Cunningham's Drug Stores founded by Andrew Cunningham in 1889. Even I can remember going to the store on the corner of Warren Avenue and Outer Drive in the early 1970s. Frederick J. Henning passed away at his home at 157 W Alexandrine Street on Tuesday, August 3, 1917.[141]

---

[141] See *DFP* 7/16/1905, *DFP* 3/18/1906, and *DFP* 7/4/1917.

GEORGE ST. JOHN HOME

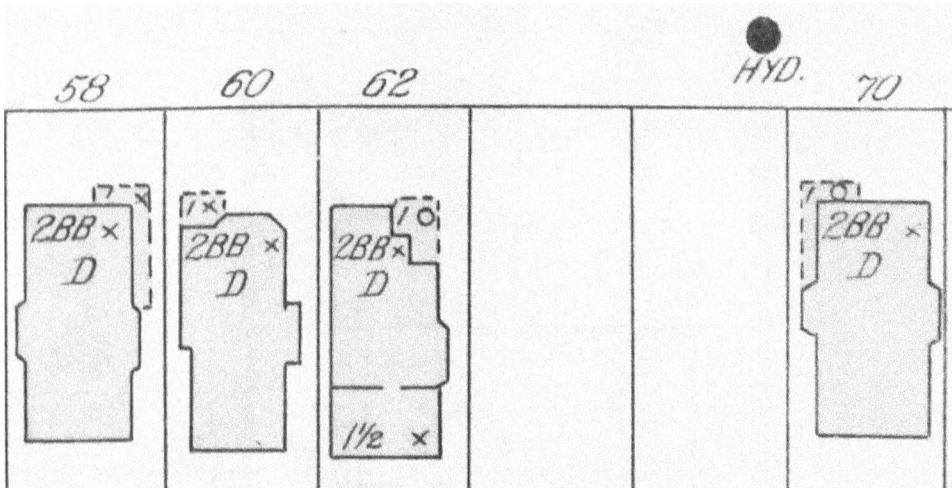

The 1897 Sanborn map of Horton Avenue in Detroit. Notice the two empty lots. The home for George St. John would have been built on the first open lot, or 64 Horton.

"Architect R. Arthur Bailey has prepared plans and let the contracts for the erection of a two-story frame residence for George St. John to be built on the south side of Horton avenue, between Woodward avenue and John R. street to cost $3,000" (*DN* 11/28/1897).

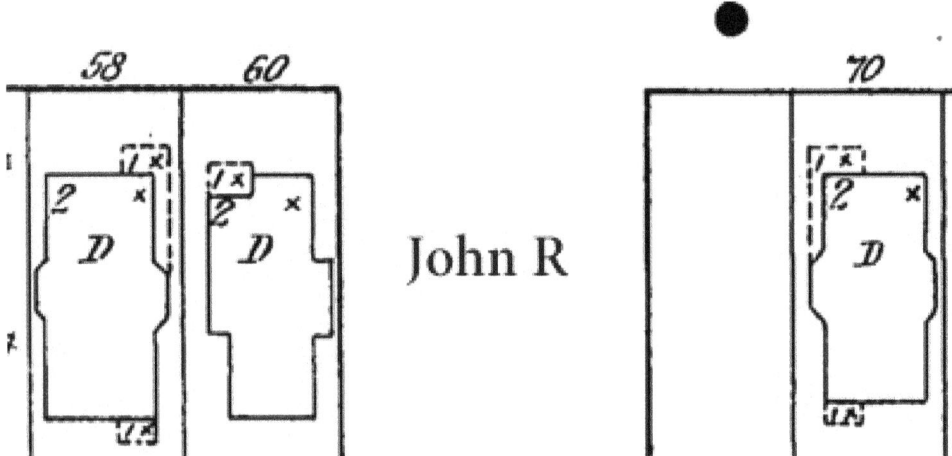

Notice how John R. Avenue now proceeds south of Horton Avenue, which is at the top of the image. In the previous image, John R. Avenue stopped south of Horton Avenue. Now look at the layout of the home at 60 Horton and 70 Horton Avenue, they are the same as in the 1897 Sanborn Map. The homes at 62 & 64 Horton was torn down with the expansion of John R. Avenue. From the 1915 Sanborn map of Detroit.

In 1900 George H. St. John lived at 685 Second Avenue and all indications are that this was a home which George built to be resold for his real estate business. Currently only one home is still standing on Horton Street between Woodward Avenue and John R.

Street and that home is located on the north side of the street. The *Detroit Free Press*, on November 28, 1897, recorded that John F. Shaening had obtained a building permit at 64 Horton Avenue. The 1898 *Detroit City Directory* listed 64 Horton Avenue as being on the south-east side of Horton and John R. Avenues and was vacant. The 1899 *Detroit City Directory* has the tenant at 64 Horton as William T. Nash, a bookkeeper at De Steiger, Fallon & Company. Between 1897 and 1898 the only new home built on the south-side of Horton Avenue between Woodward and John R. Avenues was 64 Horton Avenue and this is based upon the analysis of the Detroit City Directories. The problem is 64 Horton Avenue is not on the 1915 Sanborn Map and 64 Horton Avenue is listed in the 1906 *Detroit City Directory* but not the 1908 *Detroit City Directory*. It seems the home was torn down during the extension of John R. Avenue south of Horton Avenue in 1907-1908.[142] Of course, the home may have been moved but no record has been uncovered to substantiate this statement.

George H. St. John was born in Hulberton, New York in July 6, 1851 to Henry and Anne Eliza (née Brown) St. John. George came to Detroit where he first opened a confectionery shop with Henry Felter. The candy business did not suit George and he found employment with the Michigan Central Railroad as a mail clerk working on the Detroit to Mackinac line. George retired from that position in 1902 after 30 years of service and began his career as a contracting and real estate developer (*DFP* 4/22/1902). On March 3, 1887, George married Miss Carrie A. Wilson of Grosse Pointe Park, Michigan. The couple had one child, Clayton R. St. John, who passed away at a young age.

George made an impact on the growth of Detroit by developing the north side of Delaware Street, between Woodward and Second Avenues and on Chandler Street with the help of architect Clarence H. Bennett. It is odd that George did not employ Bailey as his architect for the development of Delaware and Chandler Streets. It may have been that Bailey's fees had become too expensive or his business interests were more important than his architectural work. Bennett was only 21 when he began his association with George St. John. Many of Bennett's designs were fairly conservative with the exception of the Moorish fantasque home that Bennett designed for George which was never built.[143]

---

[142] See the *DFP* 6/11/1907, the article mentions the extension of John R. Avenue. One needs to be aware that the suffix of a street changes over time, Horton Avenue and John R. Avenue changed from avenue to street seemingly at a whim, of whom I have not been able to determine.

[143] Clarence H. Bennett did not practice as an architect for an extended period in Detroit, but he designed numerous homes and buildings. See the *DFP* 2/10/1907 for a list of his works for 1907. He later worked for Detroit Edison and a construction engineer; his architectural work needs further examination.

Clarence Bennett designed this residence for George St. John to be built on Delaware Street in Detroit. There is no indication that this home was ever built, but it is a fascinating mixture of Moorish and Dutch design elements and in some sense, it was ahead of its time. (*DFP* 12/8/1901)

George's wife Carrie St. John passed away at the couple's home, 885 Nottingham Road in Grosse Pointe Park on June 27, 1929. George later resided with his sister Cora and her husband, Charles P. Niles at 34102 Jefferson Avenue in St. Clair Shores, Michigan until he was admitted to the Arnold Home for the Aged. George died on February 27, 1936 at the age of 84 and there was no obituary.[144]

---

[144] *DFP* 6/28/1929 and Death Certificate 207057

CHARLES JAMES MACLEOD RESIDENCE

509(179) Chandler, Detroit, MI.
The two-sided oriel window appears to be a later addition as well as the porch columns and the brick veneer on the front. Image from 2017.

"R. Arthur Bailey has had plans prepared for a two-story frame dwelling, to be erected on the corner of Chandler avenue and Beaubien street for James McLeod. Cost $3,000" (*DFP* 2/20/1898).

"He [R. Arthur Bailey] has also prepared plans for a two-story frame residence now being erected on the corner of Chandler avenue and John R. street for Jas. McLeod; cost $3,000" (*DFP* 3/27/1898). The 1901 *Detroit City Directory* has a James MacLeod living at 179 Chandler.

In many ways, this is an odd home. The multiple story oriel window, which begins on the second floor and extends to a dormer is an architectural feature that is rarely seen. Does it work? Or is it awkward, given the style of home? Basically, the MacLeod home is a traditional American foursquare, with the front dormer converted to a double story oriel. On the east and west side of the home there are the conventional dormers.

509(179) Chandler, Detroit, MI. (Walter)
The reader can observe the window on the side that is out of alignment with the other windows.
This usually indicates a stairway, which makes sense given the location of the entrance.

On the west side of the home is a two-sided oriel window on the first floor, which is odd given that both the east and west side of the house are essentially flat, with no other ornamentation. The two-sided oriel window may have been a later addition. The facade of the house is symmetrical with three over three, the slider windows were a later addition.

Charles James L. MacLeod was born just across the river from Detroit in Windsor, Ontario on October 13, 1856 to Charles and Jean (née Taylor) MacLeod. Charles found a position with Jewett Sherman S. & Company in 1875 as a clerk, by 1883 he was the assistant manager of the business. In 1884, Charles opened a hardware store, MacLeod & Company at 2236 (322) Woodward Avenue. If that address is familiar that is because the store was located directly across from Detroit's famous Fox Theater. On June 17, 1890 Charles married Miss Mary T. Brand in Detroit, the couple had one child, Charles Brand MacLeod. Charles James L. MacLeod passed away on Wednesday, December 7, 1938 all but forgotten by the citizens of Detroit for his role in helping to lay the foundation for a dynamic city (*DFP* 12/9/1938).

JOHN MOORE STORE

224 Columbus, Sandusky, OH.
The reader can observe the intricate brickwork on the facade.

"He [R. Arthur Bailey] also has the contract for the construction of two, two story brick stores to be erected in Sandusky, O., for John Moore, of this city, at a cost of $10,000" (*DFP* 2/20/1898).

SOME NEW BUSINESS BLOCKS

"At present Columbus avenue revels in the debris of the old frame structures opposite the postoffice which are being torn down to make room for two handsome brick business blocks to be erected by John Whitworth of the Sandusky Realty company and John L. Moore of Detroit.... The building to be erected by Mr. Moore will be a two-story brick with a handsome frontage on the avenue. There will be two store rooms, one which will be occupied by the dry goods and millinery establishment of James Doran. The other rooms have also been leased by a Columbus avenue merchant" (*Sandusky Star Journal* 3/8/1898).

"John L. Moore, representing the Stone estate, took out a permit for a two-story business block on Lot 10, Columbus avenue. The building will be 41 feet wide by 133 feet deep. It will cost $5,000 and will be completed about Dec. 1" (*Sandusky Star Journal* 4/2/1898).

The two buildings that Bailey designed for Moore were actually two business blocks but a better description would be two store fronts. This gets confusing, so it is best to provide a visual reference. In the above image, you can see one structure, which is two business blocks. A block was a separate business, or store front. The term block has no relationship to the term block or lot, used by city assessors. The two stores designed by Bailey for Moore were two business blocks, not two separate buildings. The blocks were later combined to form the Woolworth's store in Sandusky. The Moore building had a curious architectural design on the facade. The parapet has a diamond-work ornamentation at the top and above and below the diamond-work is a series of dentils. Just beneath is a decorated circle motif. The pattern between the second-floor windows is intriguing and the design seems to be an outline of a fortification which may have been a homage to Fort Sandoské, the first fortification built in the area.

The Moore building became the site of the Woolworth store in Sandusky in 1909. In 1949, the building expanded into the structure to the north to increase the square footage of the store (*Sandusky Register* 1/11/1949). At 6:30 am on Tuesday, January 5, 1960, Mrs. Francis Hoelzer called the Sandusky Fire Department to report smoke in the office of Dr. Edward I. Soltesz. When the fire department arrived, they observed a glow at the rear of the Woolworth store which they were unable to extinguish. Every available fireman and fire truck in the city was called to the blaze and the department also received support from the Perkins Township Fire Department. The cold and fierce winds that were blowing that day were a challenge to the fire fighters, who brought the fire under control six hours later. The financial loss from the fire was placed at over $400,000. (*Sandusky Register* 1/5/1960) In 1961 Mrs. Leah N. Siff was granted a permit to rebuild on the site, where the current structure now stands (*Sandusky Register* 3/17/1961).

John L. Moore 1846-1905

John L. Moore was born in August 1846 in Plattsburgh, New York. At the age of 15 his family moved to Sandusky, Ohio. John attended Williams College in Massachusetts, where he was a member of the baseball club, and graduated in 1867. After completion of his studies John accepted a position with the C.S. & C. Railroad, working in the Treasurer's office.[145] He remained with the railroad, becoming the Treasurer and then the General Manager. After the acquisition of the railroad by the 'Big Four' Railroad, John left the company.[146] John then raised the funds necessary to establish a short line railroad from Sandusky to Bellevue, Ohio. For a brief time, he engaged in the production of carriages and it is unclear if he was producing railroad carriages or horse carriages. He left that profession and moved to Detroit where he worked for the Merchant's and Manufacturing Exchanged Freight Bureau, a position he resigned from in 1899. It may have been during his time in Detroit that he met R. Arthur Bailey. After leaving Detroit, John and his family returned to Sandusky, spending time at their county home and their residence in Sandusky on West Washington Avenue. On October 27, 1879, John married Miss Mary Stone of Sandusky, the daughter of Judge Walter F. Stone, the couple had two children; Lawrence and Walter F. Moore. John passed away on Thursday morning, June 29, 1905 (*Sandusky Star Journal* 6/29/1905).

---

[145] The Cincinnati, Sandusky and Cleveland Railroad later became Cleveland, Columbus, Cincinnati and Indianapolis Railway. The history of railroad mergers is confusing; it may be likened to the acquisitions of Internet companies in today's world.

[146] The 'Big Four' Railroad was created in 1889 by the merger of the Cleveland, Columbus, Cincinnati & Indianapolis Railroad, the Cincinnati, Indianapolis, St. Louis & Chicago Railroad and the Indianapolis & St. Louis Railway. In 1890, the company purchased the Indiana, Bloomington & Western Railroad, commonly known as the CCC&StL.

JOHN B. THOMAS RESIDENCE

4428 (792) Second, Detroit, MI.
Note the steep mansard style roof on the side of the building. Image from 2017.

"Architect R. Arthur Bailey has prepared plans for the alterations to be made to dwelling owned by John B. Thomas, situated on Second avenue and Canfield. The alteration will cost $3,000" (*DFP* 3/27/1898).

"Architect R. Arthur Bailey is…Also preparing plans for enlarging and remodeling the residence of John B. Thomas on the east side of Second avenue between Canfield and Forest avenues, at a cost of $3,000" (*DN* 3/27/1898).

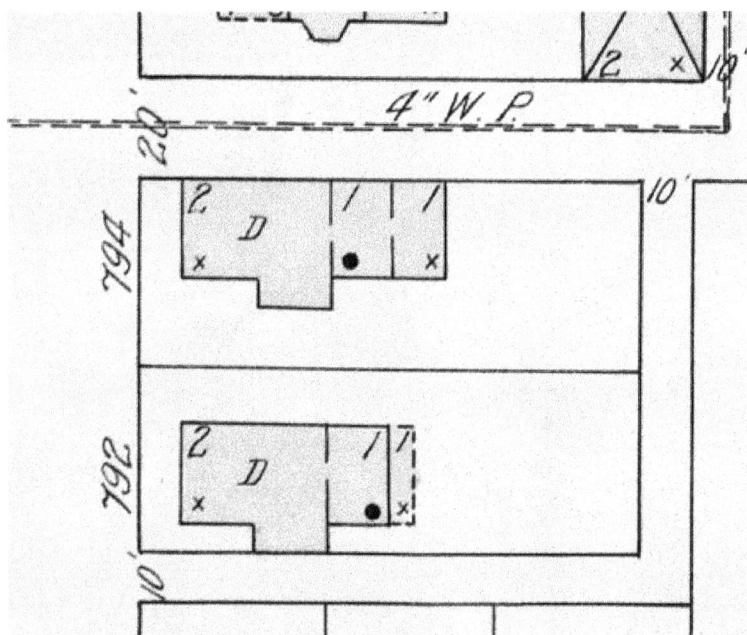

You can see that 792 Second Avenue has almost the same footprint as 794 Second Avenue which was torn down in favor of an apartment building constructed on the narrow lot. The image is from the 1897 Sanborn Map.

It is unknown what modifications Bailey performed on the Thomas residence, it may have been the addition of the third floor, however the 1897 Sanborn map does not show a third floor being present. In 1919 Thomas sold the building, which was then three apartments, to Dr. Earl A. Ranney for $17,500. The *Detroit Free Press* article on June 6, 1919 related that Thomas had owned the building for 40 years and built the residence (*DFP* 6/6/1919). Based upon this information Bailey's work may have been to modify the building into apartments, add a third floor and extend the structure to the rear. The building is a massive structure that is shoehorned onto the lot and there is very little open space on any side of the building. The third floor gives the appearance on the sides of being a mansard style roof that reverts near the front gable to a more traditional design. Notice the diamond motif brick work between the second and third floor, which extends around the home, a variation of what Bailey used on the Moore building in Sandusky, Ohio. The fine corbeling brick work under the windows of the two-story bay window is a nice feature. Like the diamond-work motif, these were inexpensive elements that helped contribute to the dignified appearance of the structure. There is also a small oriel window on the first floor that seems almost out of place given its location on the side of the structure. The large third floor dormer, which must be an addition with its four windows, is an attempt to add symmetry to the facade. Finally, the entrance porch and the second-floor porch may have been heavily modified as the shingle work on the second-floor porch does not fit with the style of the home. The building is still standing in 2019.

Notice how the window on the side gable interrupts the flow of the gable. An awkward design by the original architect, who was attempting to symmetrically stack the windows.

John Baldwyn Thomas was born on December 8, 1856 in Shrewsbury, England to John and Mary (née Davis) Thomas. The family immigrated to the United States in 1864 and settled in New York. As a young man, John moved to Chicago to work as a commercial artist and in 1887 he relocated to Detroit where he was employed by the Calvert Lithographing Company for 52 years. While working at that company, John was recognized for his work on the Ferry Seed Company's Catalog. In 1886, John married Miss Minnie McGrath, the couple had three children; Gladys M., Wilber J. B., Jean Andrew Thomas. John was an active member of Detroit's Methodist community; he was involved with the Central Methodist Church and was a founding member of the Cass Avenue Community Methodist Church. John passed away at Grace Hospital in Detroit on November 28, 1937, Minnie died ten years later, on November 20, 1947.[147]

---

[147] See *DFP* 11/21/1947, *DFP* 11/30/1937 and *DFP* 1/23/1991.

CHARLES E. SMITH RESIDENCE

66(34) Hazelwood, Detroit, MI.
The porch at the front of the house was a later addition. The reader can observe the remains of the original porch on the side of the structure, with its shed roof and ionic column. (Walter)

"He [R. Arthur Bailey] had prepared plans for a residence for C.E. Smith to be built on Hazelwood avenue, near Second. The building will be framed with brick foundation, two stories high, dimensions 36x44 feet, and will cost $3,300" (*DFP* 3/27/1898).

"Architect R. Arthur Bailey is…Also preparing plans for a two-story frame residence for Charles E. Smith, to be built on the north side of Hazelwood avenue, between Woodward and Second avenues. It will cost $3,000" (*DN* 3/27/1898).

"J.F. Shaening is building a two-story frame residence on the north side of Hazelwood avenue, west of Woodward, to cost $3.000. C.E. Smith is the owner" (*DFP* 4/24/1898).

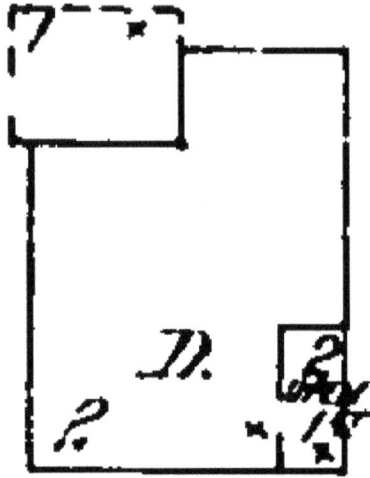

66(34) Hazelwood,
Image from the 1910 Sanborn Map, the front of the house is at the bottom of the image.

The home Bailey designed for Smith was a typical American foursquare with some embellishments. If you overlook the horrible faux brick siding, this is an attractive residence. The front bay window with its sloping roof merges into the home, while the second-floor oriel window over the front porch helps to balance the facade of the house. The 1910 Sanborn map shows the entrance porch as set back into the home and above it was a sleeping porch that was enclosed at a later date. Comparing the map image to the photograph, you can see that the front porch is a later addition, but that part of the porch is still recessed into the home, while the sleeping porch above the entrance has been enclosed.

Charles Edward Smith passed away at his son-in-law's home, near Fennville, Michigan on October 3, 1937 at 10:30 pm. As the obituary in the *Allegan Gazette* stated, "Death came as a relief to end the many months of illness during which time he [Charles] had [was] practically bed-ridden." Charles was born in Brooklyn, New York on October 14, 1856. On September 28, 1886 Charles married Miss Irene McCane in Detroit, Michigan, the couple had three children; Gertrude W., Muriel Elizabeth and Albert Knight Smith. Charles worked in the dry good business his entire life and he owned a store at 3953 (741) Woodward Avenue until 1913. After the sale of his business, Smith worked for the Newcomb-Endicott Company, a competitor to the J.L. Hudson Company. The Newcomb-Endicott Company was acquired by the J.L. Hudson Company in 1927. Charles retired to Fennville, Michigan shortly before the death of his wife Irene, who passed away on November 9, 1925.[148]

---

[148] See *Allegan Gazette* 10/8/1937 and *DFP* 10/5/1937. There is some confusion as to just when Charles retired to Fennville, the *Allegan Gazette* stated that he retired in 1926 prior to the death of

HENRY M. MARVIN HOME

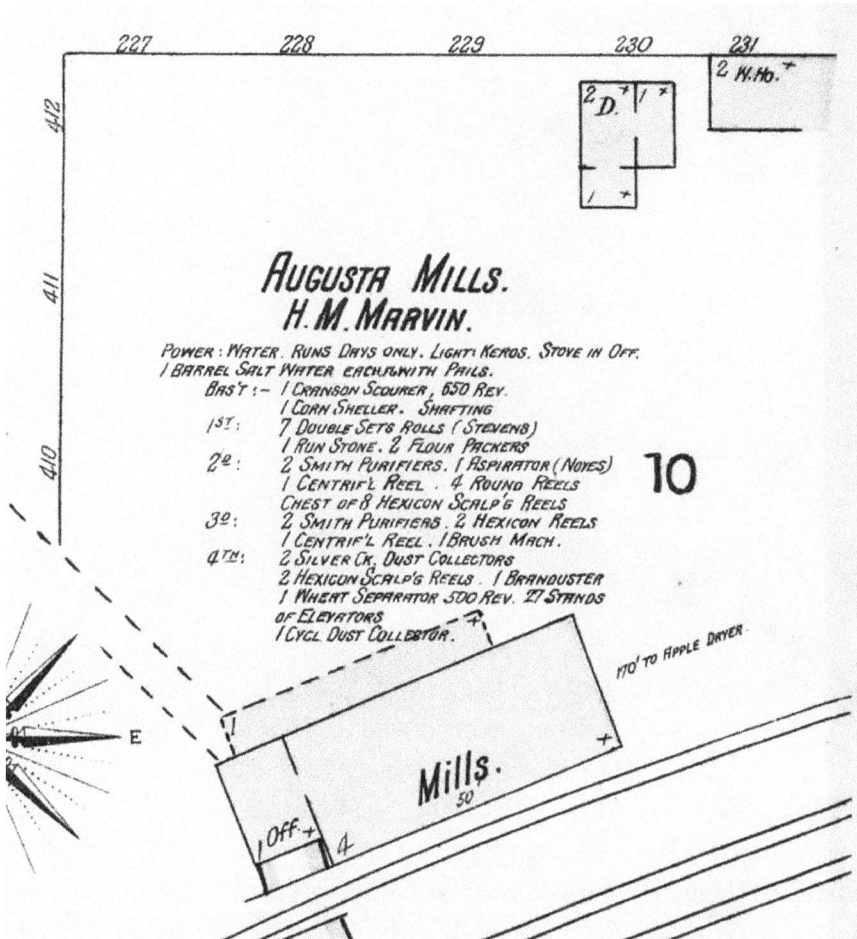

Marvin Home Augusta, MI.
The Marvin home was located just north of the mill. The house is visible on the above Sanborn map just to the left of the Warehouse (W.Ho.). The site is now an empty lot on the property of the Knappen Mill.

Architect R.A. Bailey is Busy

"Architect R. Arthur Bailey is preparing plans for a residence for M. H. Marvin, Augusta, Mich. It will be two and a half stories high. The walls to the top of the first story will be of stone. Above this line it will be frame covered with stained shingles in artistic design. It will cost $7,000" (DN 3/27/1898).

Irene, which is confusing because Irene died in 1925. The *Detroit Free Press* stated that Charles moved to Fennville in 1931. Irene McCane is also listed as Irene Goss McCaw or McCow. Charles and Irene's daughter Gertrude was born in 1884, two years before the couple married.

Henry's home was located at the corner of Fulton (Michigan) Avenue and Water Street right near the Knappen Mill in Augusta, Michigan. Alas the home is no longer standing, and no image of it has been discovered.

Henry M. Marvin 1859-1941

Henry M. Marvin was born in 1859 to Huntington M. and Lucinda (née Riley) Marvin in Bedford, Calhoun County, Michigan. Henry attend the local school in Olivet, Michigan and later Olivet College. After graduation, he learned the millers trade by his father, working first at the Bedford Flour Mill and then the Knappen Flour Mill in Augusta, Michigan. The family also owned a large lumber company. In 1902 Henry sold the Knappen Mill to Hubbard Food Company to concentrate on the lumber business and to establish a private bank. In 1906 Henry sold his business interests in Michigan and purchased a ranch in Manitoba, Canada which he operated until 1928, when he retired to Battle Creek, Michigan. In 1880 Henry married Miss Florence Cooper a native of Ohio, the couple had three children; Henry C., Bessie and Fred Marvin. Florence died on May 15, 1885 shortly after the birth of her son Fred. On February 6, 1895 Henry married Jennie (Virginia) C. Dodge; the couple had one child, Elizabeth. Jennie passed away July 11, 1914 of a perforated ulcer at Bronson Hospital in Kalamazoo. After Henry moved to Manitoba he married Gertrude Schwab on March 19, 1919 in Winnipeg. Henry Miller Marvin passed away on December 11, 1941 at his home in Battle Creek.[149]

---

[149] See Fisher 364, *Augusta Beacon* 12/18/1941 and Men 486.

EDWARD V. BRIGHAM HOME, DETROIT,MI

"Architect R. Arthur Bailey is…Also preparing plans for two story frame residence for E.V. Brigham, to be built on the south side of Hazelwood avenue, between Woodward and Second avenues, to cost $2,500" (*DN* 3/27/1898).

It is doubtful that this home was ever built and an analysis of the Detroit City Directories from 1896-1900 confirms this fact. There were no new homes built on Hazelwood between 1898-1899 and Edward V. Brigham lived at 1001 Trumbull in 1899 and 305 Farnsworth in 1900.

Edward Vickery Brigham was born on January 10, 1867 in Delhi, Michigan to Benjamin Franklin and Ann Martha (née Packard) Brigham. As a young man Edward attended schools in Delhi Township and Lansing, Michigan. He moved to Detroit in 1888 where he found employment with Edson, Moore & Company, a wholesale dry goods business. Edward was an initial investor in the Imperial Hat Company, a hat manufacturing business located In Detroit at 116 Jefferson Avenue. On January 19, 1902, the buildings on Jefferson Avenue where the Imperial Cap Company was located collapsed with a loss of $15,000 for the business. Three months later the Imperial Hat Company dissolved. After the failure of the company, Edward worked for the Kalamazoo Sanitary Manufacturing Company as vice president and business manager. It seems Edward was slowly acquiring interests in sanitary pottery companies, and in 1907 he purchased a controlling interest in the Columbia Pottery Company of Kokomo, Indiana. Edward was fined $5,000 in 1923, along with 23 other pottery manufacturing businessmen, for price fixing and restraint of trade. On December 10, 1890, Edward married Miss Elizabeth Rhonda Patton in Arapahoe, Cheyenne County, Colorado, there were no children. Edward and his wife retired to Pasadena, California where they lived at 1038 Prospect Boulevard. On September 30, 1937 Edward died in California having been forgotten for his role in the business history of Michigan.[150]

---

[150] See *DFP* 1/20/1902, *DFP* 3/4/1902, *LSJ* 4/18/1923.

MARY C. SPENCER HOME

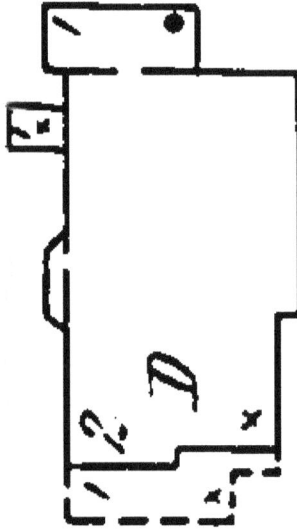

326 Seymour, Lansing, MI.
Image from the 1913 Sanborn Map, the front of the home is at the bottom of the sketch.

"Architect R. Arthur Bailey is…Also preparing plans for two story frame residence for Mrs. Mary C. Spencer, state librarian, to be built at Ypsilanti, Mich. It will cost $2,500" (*DN* 3/27/1898).

The above article is a bit of a surprise. Mrs. Mary Spencer maintained a residence in Lansing at 326 (314) Seymour Street from 1891 onward, so it would seem odd for her to build a home in Ypsilanti since she was the State Librarian. In 1898, Mary owned Lots 317 and 319 in the Norris & Cross Addition, which were 407 and 409 N. Huron in Ypsilanti, Michigan.[151] A review of the 1893 and the 1899 Sanborn Maps for Ypsilanti, Michigan show that the homes present on the 1893 Sanborn map had not changed on the 1899 Sanborn map. Usually on the Sanborn maps there would be a notation for new construction, but there was none on the 1899 map. The residences on Huron Street in Ypsilanti were torn down and it is now the site of the Michigan Firehouse Museum. The home at 326 Seymour in Lansing was torn down in 1948 to clear the site for a parking lot.

---

[151] From the Ypsilanti City, Michigan, Tax Assessment Rolls 3rd Ward 1898. A big thank you to Courtney Beattie, Ypsilanti Historical Society Archives.

Mary Clare Spencer 1842-1923

Mary Clare Wilson Spencer was born in Pontiac, Michigan, on May 2, 1842 to John A. and Olivia C. (née Edson) Wilson. Her family moved to Ypsilanti, Michigan where Mary married Captain Clinton Spencer in 1863. The couple had six children. Clinton served with the First Michigan Infantry and lost a leg at Gettysburg. After the war, Clinton was appointed postmaster for Ypsilanti. In 1885 he moved to Lansing with his family and became the Chief Clerk in the Secretary of State office. He died of a stroke in 1893 leaving Mary to raise the four surviving children. Mary became the State Librarian in 1893 after having worked in the state library since 1885. After becoming State Librarian, Mary expanded the library's book collection, established traveling libraries to serve rural communities, started the service of mailing books to students and researchers throughout the state, and also created an art collection. Mary's most important accomplishment was the realization that she needed to understand the political game and deal with politicians, using their own rules to exploit their weaknesses. She moved books out from behind locked doors so they could be read by the citizens. Mary demonstrated the best traits of a librarian, the ability to learn, adapt and create. Mary died at her home at 326 Seymour Street in Lansing on August 22, 1923.[152]

---

[152] *Marshall Statesman* 12/1/1893, *LSJ* 8/22/1923

JOHN MOHRMANN STORE

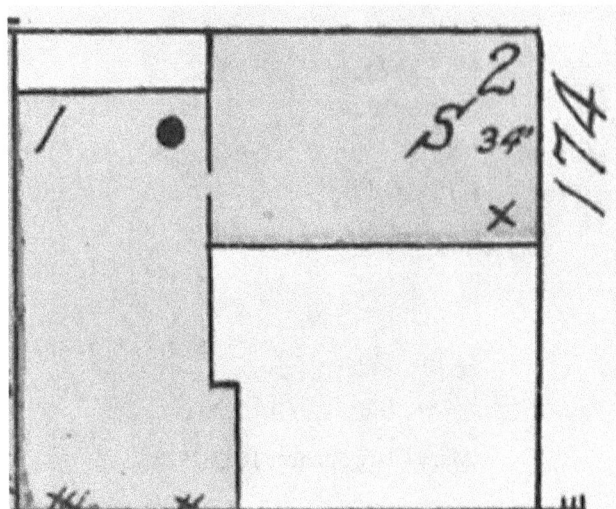

600 (174) Larned, Detroit, MI.
From the 1897 Sanborn Map.

"Architect R. Arthur Bailey is…Also preparing plans for a new store front for the store owned by John Mohrman on the north side of Jefferson avenue, between First and Second streets" (*DN* 3/27/1898).

John Mohrmann ran a saloon at 174 Larned and had his residence behind the saloon. No image has been located that verifies that this storefront was ever built. One interesting side note is that John's daughter Louise, worked for Bailey & Company in the early 1900s. John Herman Mohrmann was born in Hessen, Germany circa 1842 to Valentine and Barbara (née Greusbach) Mohrmann. In 1867 John opened a saloon at 174 W. Larned, near the corner of Second Avenue which he operated until prohibition. It was described as a first-class establishment that prohibited gambling, profanity and closed at 8pm. On September 7, 1869 John married Augusta Schevieger [Schweizer], the couple had six children; Pauline, Louise, Mina, Valentine G., Conrad W., and Herman J. Mohrmann. Augusta died on October 13, 1883 and John never remarried. John passed away at his home 16703 Burgess Street on December 19, 1929 and was buried beside Augusta at Elmwood Cemetery.[153]

---

[153] *DFP* 6/2/1914 and *DFP* 12/21/1929

THOMAS M. FORDYCE COTTAGE

Thomas N. Fordyce 1861-1927

"Architect R. Arthur Bailey is preparing plans for a two-story frame residence for Thomas N. Fordyce, to be built on the south side of Jefferson avenue, Grosse Pointe, at a cost of $3,600" (*DN* 4/17/1898).

It was originally thought that Bailey had designed a residence for Fordyce to occupy. That was not the case. As outlined below, Fordyce lived in a different area of Grosse Pointe. What is known is that Annie M. Fordyce platted a subdivision in 1893 along the east side of Notre Dame Avenue in Grosse Pointe, purchased from the estate of Archange Cadieux. It is possible that the cottage Bailey designed for Fordyce was in this subdivision. But given the financial difficulties that Fordyce found himself in 1898 it is doubtful this cottage was ever built. Because of the lack of tax assessment rolls or city directories for this area the location of this home designed by Bailey is unknown.[154] What follows is a description of the Fordyce residence in Grosse Pointe.

"Thomas N. Fordyce, whose beautiful Grosse Pointe residence, *The Pines* was burned to the ground." The home was originally built for Peter N. Dingemann [Dingeman] at a cost of $15,000, it was later sold to Bishop Borgess, who used it as his summer residence.

---

[154] The mystery is the location of the tax assessment rolls for Wayne County for 1898-1900. Inquiries of all the local archives, libraries, historical societies and governmental institutions have drawn a blank.

Fordyce acquired the property in 1893. "It was considered one of the finest frame buildings in Wayne County, and the double row of pines from the house to the water's edge planted many years ago, gave it the name of *The Pines*" (*DFP* 3/1/1899). The summer residence of Peter N. Dingeman, was located at the foot of Bishop Road, named in honor of Bishop Caspar Henry Borgess, the second Bishop of Detroit, who had acquired the Dingeman summer home.

Thomas N. Fordyce passed away at his home 218 W. Twelfth Street in Cincinnati, Ohio on June 3, 1927. Thomas was born in Wheeling, West Virginia on March 4, 1861, to Isaac and Sarah (née Miller) Fordyce.[155] Thomas moved to Detroit, Michigan in 1882 and worked as a salesman for James Nall & Company, which sold furniture and carpets. In 1884, Thomas began his association with William Y. Hamlin, a leading real estate developer in Detroit. Thomas used his sales skills to move the unsold vacant lots that Hamlin had left on the books, an exceptionally prized attribute for any real estate agent. In October 1886, Thomas became a partner with Hamlin, establishing the Hamlin & Fordyce Real Estate Company. In early 1895 the partnership ended, and Thomas started his own real estate company, Thomas N. Fordyce & Company. Just five years later Thomas filed for bankruptcy, with liabilities of $281,253 and assets of $13,625. Oddly, in 1890, he became President of the Upper Michigan Brewing Company which failed in 1893. After the collapse of his real estate business, Thomas became one of the officers of the Miami & Erie Canal Transportation Company, which seemed like a dodgy investment scheme. Thomas had a habit of sailing too close to the wind and seeking the next great investment deal no matter the risk or the danger. In 1884, Thomas married Annie M. Rogers, the couple had three children Evangeline, Lillias and Thomas N Fordyce Jr. Annie passed away 20 years after Thomas' death, on June 25, 1947.[156]

---

[155] Technically Virginia, West Virginia did not vote to separate from Virginia until October 1861.
[156] See Mitchell 70, *DFP* 12/15/1889, *DFP* 9/10/1895, *DFP* 1/19/1900, *Cincinnati Enquirer* 6/5/1927 and the *Cincinnati Enquirer* 6/27/1947.

GEORGE T. MARSHALL RESIDENCE

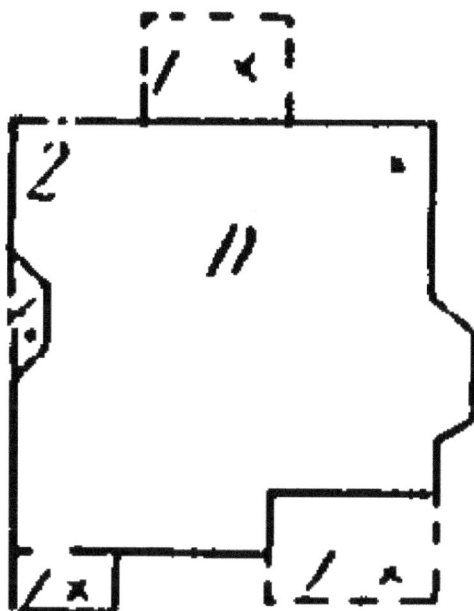

51(29) Seward, Detroit, MI.
The image is from the 1910 Sanborn map. The top of the image is the front of the home.

"Architect R. Arthur Bailey is preparing plans for a two and a half story frame residence to be built on Seward avenue, near Woodward for Geo. Marshall. It will cost about $4,000" (*DFP* 5/1/1898).

The 1901 *Detroit City Directory* listed George T. Marshall at 29 Seward Avenue; the address changed to 51 Seward in 1921. Essentially this is all that is known about the Marshall residence. The home was torn down in 1925 and on its site was built a massive apartment building named 'The Seward'. The apartment complex offered a main dining room with a la carte service at any hour, plus a barber and beauty shop, a valet store and a convenience store. The complex had studio, or two, three or four room apartments with kitchenette and cost $75-$200 a month rent. The apartments were later named the New Center Apartments and later the Wellington Place Apartments closing circa 1998. It is unknown if there are plans to renovate the abandoned apartment building.

The Marshall home is now the site of a derelict apartment building that, in its heyday, was known as 'The Seward Apartments', one of the finest apartments in Detroit.

George Tyler Marshall was born in Middletown, Ohio on August 24, 1864 to William S., and Elizabeth (née Miltonberger) Marshall. He moved to Detroit in 1881 and in 1890 he obtained a position with Alger, Smith & Company, a large lumber company. Twelve years later he became the secretary for the newly appointed Michigan Senator, Russell A. Alger. That same year George and his brother Luther established the firm Marshall Brothers Company, brokers of food products. One of the clients was the Michigan Condensed Milk Company. George was a charter member of the Cass Avenue Methodist Church and served on the church board. George married Alexandrina Bell on June 28, 1893 in Oakland, California, the couple had four children; Richard B., George T., John B., and Helen E. Marshall. George Tyler Marshall died at his home 291 E. Kirby on February 1, 1937. His wife Alexandrina Bell Marshall passed away on October 16, 1952.[157]

---

[157] *Oakland Tribune* 6/16/1893 *DFP* 2/3/1937 and *DFP* 10/18/1952.

THOMAS W. PARKER HOME

127 (63) Woodland, Detroit, MI.
Notice how the entrance is off-center, and the porch does not span the front of the house.

"Architect R. Arthur Bailey is preparing plans for a two-story frame residence for Thomas W. Parker, to be built on the north side of Woodland avenue, the first block east of Woodward avenue. It will cost $2,800" (*DN* 5/15/1898).

"Architect R. Arthur Bailey has prepared plans for a two-story frame dwelling to be built on Woodland avenue east of Woodward. It will have brick foundation, furnace and mantels. Cost about $3,000. Thos. W. Parker is the owner" (*DFP* 5/22/1898).

One can barely make out that the windows on the second-floor facade are original. (Walter)

The 1899 *Detroit City Directory* listed Thomas Parker as owning 127 (63) Woodland, with his son Thomas W. Parker as a resident. It is possible that Thomas W. Parker had the home built for his parents. Thomas Parker's death certificate is unusual in that he is listed as living at 356 (170) Woodland, a fact not corroborated by the Detroit City Directories. Did Bailey design 127 Woodland or 356 Woodland? The building permit for 356 (170) Woodland was not issued until August 1899, more than a year after the *Detroit Free Press* article. (*DFP* 8/13/1899) We may be getting too clever here, the *Detroit News* article from 1898, cited above, states that the home was built in the first block east of Woodward, that means 127 (63) Woodland is the likely candidate of a residence designed by Bailey. The Detroit City Directories record that after 1908 no Parkers lived on Woodland Avenue. The home at 127 (63) Woodland is your typical American foursquare house, a plain but practical dwelling, which can be found almost anywhere in the United States. All that is lacking in this foursquare is the extensive porch that would have spanned the façade, a characteristic usually found in this style of home.

Thomas W. Parker 1867-1942

Thomas Watts Parker was born in Michigan on March 1, 1867, to Thomas and Helen D. (née Watts) Parker. On September 30, 1916 Thomas married Grace M. Guirlinger, there were no children from the marriage. After touring the Far East, the couple settled in Highland Park, Michigan. The marriage was annulled on October 14, 1922 and the action was brought by Grace against Thomas with the allegation being a failure to consummate the marriage. Thomas had trained as a lawyer and spent the remainder of his life working in that capacity. He bounced around from apartment house to apartment house in Detroit. Thomas Watts Parker passed away on March 6, 1942 and his death notice in the *Detroit News* was barely two lines. No notice appeared in the *Detroit Free Press*. (*DN* 3/9/1942)

STERLING RESIDENCE

247 (85) King, Detroit, MI.
Notice the oriel window on the west side of the home and what seems to be a bay window
bracketed by the framing for the stairwell, mimicking the bay window on the east side.

"Architect R. Arthur Bailey is preparing plans for a two-story frame residence to be built
on the north side of King avenue between John R. and Brush streets. It will cost $2,500"
(*DN* 6/12/1898).

After evaluating the Detroit City Directories for this period and matching the findings
with a review of the Detroit newspapers, the best candidate for the house mentioned in
the above article is 247 (85) King. The home at 247 (85) King was offered for sale or to
rent in September 1898, which fits with the timeline for the house being completed. The
majority of the notices published in the Detroit newspapers mentioned the design
commissions an architect received but the *Detroit News* on June 12, 1898, listed no owner
or builder. It is possible the house was built as an investment for a developer to resell. The
first owner of the home was Ruluff R. Sterling.

Ruluff R. Sterling was born at Sterling Mill, Canton Center, Michigan on April 20, 1854 to Leander and Sarah (née Van Vlack) Sterling.[158] After attending the local public schools, Ruluff found employment with a clothing store in Ypsilanti, Michigan where he worked until 1879. He then moved to Escanaba, Michigan where he was employed at a shoe store for ten years. Ruluff moved to Detroit in 1892 where he found a position with the McRae & Roberts Company, a brass and metal working business.[159] The 1901 *Detroit City Directory* listed Ruluff as the President of the Cowles & Danziger Company, a manufacturer of metal barrels for the oil and gas industry. A year later along with Frederick G. Skinner, Ruluff founded the Sterling & Skinner Manufacturing Company which produced brass fittings for steam, water and gas plants as well as the automotive industry. On October 12, 1892 Ruluff married Miss Sarah A. Thomas in Buffalo, New York; the couple had one child, Ruth Sterling.[160] Ruluff was active in social affairs and he was a member of the Automobile Country Club, Detroit Athletic Club, Detroit Golf Club and the Detroit Automobile Club.[161] Ruluff lived an energetic life and it was unfortunate that he slipped into senility later in life. Ruluff R. Sterling passed away July 9, 1938 at Pontiac General Hospital, he was 84.[162]

---

[158] The information regarding Ruluff's date of birth comes from his Death Certificate, Item ID: 005240314_03453. Other sources list Ruluff's date of birth as April 20, 1858 and his mother's maiden name as Van Bleck.

[159] I have been unable to substantiate Ruluff's employment in Ypsilanti or Escanaba. In the 1880 Selected Federal Census, Ruluff is listed as owning a 95-acre farm in Van Buren, Michigan.

[160] *Buffalo Enquirer* 10/15/1892, Ruluff is listed as R.R. Strohling.

[161] The Automobile Country Club, was originally named the Detroit Automotive Club, but changed their name in 1917 to the Automobile Country Club. In 1921 the organization changed its name to the Pine Lake Country Club which still operates today.

[162] DFP 7/11/1938 and Burton 3: 631.

An image of the east side of the house at 247 (85) King, Detroit, MI. Notice the bay window on the side of the home and the curious lack of windows, which may be because it faced northeast.

Look beyond the stone veneer on the house at 247 (85) King Street and you see a well-designed home. The brick veneer was added later. It is possible to know because of how the veneer overlaps the aluminum awning of the porch. The two brackets underneath the second-floor oriel window are unusual because they are plain and not ornate. This may be a result of the transom on the first-floor window as there simply was not enough room to have any enhancement. It is almost as if Bailey was combining the oriel window with a dormer, a feature that he attempted with the Charles James L. MacLeod home. To the writer, neither were successful. All of the gables on the home are closed and the placement of the windows seems random with no sense of symmetry. A nice feature on the facade is the second-floor oriel window with the circular window at the pediment. Notice the battlement window on the facing of the gable above the porch. Bailey was trying to bring as much natural light as possible into the home.

CHARLES R. WHITMAN

1000 E. Ann, Ann Arbor, MI.
Observe the fieldstone base to the porch and the mass of wooden staircases, a later addition.

"Architect Harry J. Reif [Rill] is preparing plans for a three-story residence to be constructed of field stone and frame, for C.R. Whitman, Ann Arbor, Mich., to cost $3,000" (*DFP* 7/3/1898).

"Architect R. Arthur Bailey has prepared plans for a three-story residence for C.R. Whitman, Ann Arbor. It will be constructed of field stone and frame, with roof and gables covered with stained shingles. It will cost $3,000" (*DFP* 7/10/1898).

"Architect R. Arthur Bailey has prepared plans for a second residence for C.R. Whitman, Ann Arbor. The lower portion will be constructed of field stone; the upper part and roof will be covered with stained shingles. Cost $8,000" (*DFP* 7/24/1898).

It was odd to have two architects prepare plans for a structure within seven days, especially for a home with a cost of only $3,000. It may have been simply a case of Whitman's dislike of Rill's design. Given the dates on the articles it seems likely that

Bailey was the architect who designed the home.[163] The puzzle is the second home with a cost of $8,000. In 1892, Lansing architects Bowd & Mead designed a 3069 square foot home for William F. Sullivan for $3,000. The cost was a little less than $1 per square foot.[164] Nine years later, Bailey designed a home at 1000 E. Ann Street, which was 4,800 square feet in size. If $3,000 was spent on the construction of 1000 E. Ann Street, then the cost per square foot would have been 62¢, but if it was a $8,000 home then the cost per square foot was $1.66. It seems likely given the growth of Ann Arbor during this period that construction costs increased over those in Lansing from nine years previously, meaning that the home at 1000 E. Ann Street was an $8,000 residence. With no tax rolls for this period, it seems based upon a review of the Ann Arbor City Directories and the local newspaper that the $3000 home was never erected. It may be Bailey designed a set of plans for a $3,000 home and a $8,000 home and the $8,000 plans were accepted. Whitman left Ann Arbor for Chicago soon after the fiasco that was the construction of 1000 E. Ann Street.

In 1899, Edward Frohlich filed a lien on the Whitman property for material furnished for the building's completion. Whitman had engaged the services of John J. Sheldon and Christian Otto from the firm Sheldon & Otto to build the home on East Ann Street. He paid the firm $2,800 for its work. Sheldon & Otto did not complete construction of the home, in fact they abandoned the work and Whitman was forced to complete the construction using another contractor. The problem was that Frohlich supplied Sheldon & Otto with material to build the home and was not reimbursed by the contractors. Whitman was also sued by Adrian Hare over the cost of a furnace. It seems Hare had supplied the furnace to the contractors but was paid only half of the value of the furnace with the other portion to be paid upon the completion of the structure. Even though the furnace was installed in the home and fully functional, Hare removed the furnace. When informed of this development, Whitman claimed the furnace at the depot only to discover that the fire pot was cracked resulting in Whitman having to install a new furnace. Suit and counter suit resulted with both sides claiming victory and in fact no one won, and no money changed hands. Whitman was forced to buy a new furnace and Hare was out the cost of the original furnace. The fraternity, Kappa Sigma was the occupant of

---

[163] There is some confusion regarding the architect, Harry J. Rill. Born Heinrich J. Rill on April 30, 1854 in Germany, Heinrich immigrated to the United States in 1881-1883. When he Americanized his given name to Henry or Harry is unknown. He was married to Margarete W., the couple had one child Katherine A. Rill. Several of Rill's architectural designs are still intact. The Sacred Heart Catholic Church, in Hudson, Michigan, and an eight-residence terrace building at 201 Dougall Avenue in Windsor, Ontario and St. Paul's Church in Grosse Pointe, Michigan. Heinrich J. Rill died of pneumonia in Miami, Florida on January 17, 1923. Little of Rill's architectural work has survived and what does survive should be documented. Rill also submitted plans for the Conlisk residence that Bailey eventually designed. (*DFP* 6/18/1905, *DFP* 11/5/1905 and *DFP* 1/20/1923)
[164] See the State Republican 4/23/1892.

the home at 1000 E. Ann in 1899. Two of the articles clearly state that the home was being built for a fraternity. There was only one fraternity listed in the 1898-1900 Ann Arbor City Directories on Ann Street and that was the Kappa Sigma.[165]

1000 E. Ann, Ann Arbor, MI.
The property backs up to Whitman's previous residence on 1007 E. Huron Street.

Charles Rudolphus Whitman was born in South Bend, Indiana on October 4, 1847 to William Green and Laura Jane (née Finch) Whitman. He attended the University of Michigan where Charles completed a A.B., A.M., and a LL.B. He was admitted to the bar in Washtenaw County. He served as a Circuit Court Judge 1876-1878 and was a Regent of the University of Michigan from 1885-1893. In 1898 Charles and his family moved to Chicago where he practiced law until his death on April 2, 1921 at the Chicago Union Hospital. Charles married Miss Elvira Chase Joslyn on June 19, 1871, four children were born to the couple; Ross Chauncey, Lloyd Charles, Roland Dare, and Bayard Joslyn. Elvira sought a legal separation from Charles in 1910 when Lloyd Whitman, the couple's

---

[165] See the *Ann Arbor Argus-Democrat* 2/3/1899, 4/7/1899, 5/19/1899 and 10/20/1899.

son, filed a writ of ne exeat, for his mother to keep Charles from leaving the state. She alleged that her husband "reduced [her] to [wearing] rags, while her husband clothed himself in fine garments and maintained a separate residence". She also stated that in September 1905, Charles left Chicago for Mackinac Island with Alice Evans, where the couple registered as man and wife. The couple was granted a divorce in 1911 with Charles ordered to pay Elvira alimony in the amount of $15 a week for four years and $7,500 at the end of four years. After the divorce Charles married Alice Evans, on September 3, 1912, the couple had one child, Alice.[166]

Today, the home Bailey designed for Whitman is divided into separate apartments, but in its time this was an imposing structure. In many ways, this is a difficult structure to describe as it is a mixture of so many styles and elements. There is a Queen Anne style of architecture coupled with a German manor style residence. Because the home is built on a slight rise it presents a formable appearance. The tented roof tower with the knob at the top of the finial on the tower is a nice touch, although its presence today is surprising. Notice the canted bay window on the tower and the oriel window on the second-floor facade, coupled with the canted window on the third-floor gable. Quite an attractive facade is presented when viewed from the street. The timber framing on the facing of the home is reminiscent of the style of structure one would see in many of the half-timbered homes in renaissance Germany. The rear of the home is austere but functional. If you visit, the overgrown landscaping conceals the charm of the home. This is an odd but appealing structure, that in many ways seems out of place in Ann Arbor, but would not be in Germany.

---

[166] See *Chicago Tribune* 6/12/1910, *Chicago Tribune* 7/20/1911, Chicago 9, Carter 242, and Hinsdale 203. Elvira Whitman passed away on January 23, 1932.

WALLACE T. CONLISK HOME

550(202) King, Detroit, MI.
The drawing is from 1910 Sanborn, the top of the image faced the street

"Architect Harry J. Reif [Rill] is …Also, preparing plans for a two-story frame residence for Wallace T. Corlisk [Conlisk], to be built on the south side of King avenue, between John R. and Brush streets, to cost $2,500" (*DFP* 7/3/1898).

"Mr. Bailey has also prepared plans for a two-story framed residence for Wallace T. Conlisk, to be built on the south side of King avenue, between John R. and Brush Streets, to cost $2,500" (*DFP* 7/10/1898)

"John F. Shaenning has contracted to build a two-story frame residence for Wallace T. Coolick [Conlisk] on the south side of King avenue, between John R. and Brush streets. The plans were by Architect R. Arthur Bailey" (*DFP* 7/24/1898).

As with the Whitman residence in Ann Arbor it was odd to have two separate architects preparing plans for a home with such a small budget. Bailey was awarded the commission for the home and it would be interesting to find out why the Harry Rill design was rejected. [167] Unfortunately, given the lack of an image, it is impossible to describe the home. The site is now an empty lot and it is unknown when the home was torn down.

Wallace T. Conlisk was born in Adrian, Michigan in 1874 to Thomas and Nora E. (née Lauhiff) Conlisk. Thomas owned a cigar manufacturing company in Adrian, which was known for its 'Gentle Zephyr' cigar. Wallace moved to Detroit, circa 1895, to work as a clerk at the State Savings Bank. He may have worked in Buffalo, New York from 1891-

---

[167] For information on Harry J. Rill see the Whitman residence.

1894 as a clerk for the Courier Company, but this is unsubstantiated. In 1900-1904 Wallace is listed in the Detroit City Directories as living at 202 King Street with his mother Nora and his brothers and sisters. It seems he may have built the home as a residence for his mother. Wallace passed away at his home on King Street, on November 3, 1906 at the age of thirty-two from tuberculosis (*DFP* 11/4/1906).

JOHN T. WOODHOUSE STORE

The Woodhouse Cigar Store at 89 Woodward Avenue. The store is the third, four-story business block. Bailey remodeled the first floor of the store but did not design the building.

"Architect R. Arthur Bailey…Also prepared plans for a new front and remodeling the interior of the store on the west side of Woodward avenue north of Larned street, formerly occupied by Swan's restaurant. When the improvements are fully completed the store will be occupied by John T. Woodhouse & Co. for their cigar and tobacco business" (*DFP* 7/24/1898).

BEAUTIFUL CIGAR STORE

"The firm of John T. Woodhouse & Co opens its new store at 89 Woodward avenue to-day. The place is perfectly complete in all the latest ideas and fixtures known to the tobacco profession. Probably the most conspicuous thing about the whole store, aside from the decorations and appointments, which are in themselves beautiful and attractive, is the large refrigerator vault for keeping the box goods in condition. This vault is a two-story affair, capable of holding a million cigars. It is built the same as a refrigerator with double plated glass walls. It keeps the cigars in even condition, so that it is impossible for them to dry out. The store embodies many ideas which will be in the nature of revelations to the Detroit public" (*DFP* 10/15.1898).

John Thompson Woodhouse was born in Ontario, Canada on September 3, 1861 to William Thomas and Elizabeth (née Thompson) Woodhouse. The family moved to the United States in either 1867 or 1871. John took a job as a clerk for the Robert Wagner & Company, a wholesale tobacco and cigar company, and became a partner in the firm. He later acquired ownership of the company and changed the name to John T. Woodhouse & Company, which became one of the largest wholesale tobacco companies in the United States. On January 30, 1884 John married Miss Alice Matilda Goodyear and the couple had five children; Grace Alice, Elizabeth Irene, Susan Evelyn, Ruth Helen, John T. Jr. Woodhouse.[168] After Alice's death on March 4, 1911 John remained a widower for two years until he met Elizabeth E. Ewing, who he married on April 26, 1913, the couple did not have children. The pair later engaged in a sensational divorce trial in which John was accused of cruelty. John did not fight the charge and the divorce was granted on December 17, 1926. Nine months later, Elizabeth married Atlanta banker, Thomas Kearney Glenn. John married Clara S. Richardson in 1929, there were no children. John's body was found in the bathroom of his home at 337 Lake Shore Road, Grosse Pointe Farms, Michigan on Saturday January 25, 1930. He had placed a .38 caliber pistol to his right temple and fired the shot that ended his life. John was 66 years old. Family members stated that he was depressed over financial losses.[169]

---

[168] There may have been a sixth child, Jennie Rosemond Woodhouse who died in 1892, the records are unclear.
[169] See *DFP* 3/4/1911, *DFP* 1/24/1926, *DFP* 12/18/1926, *DFP* 8/21/1927, *DFP* 1/26/1930, and *DFP* 1/27/1930.

DOCTOR CHARLES GRAEFE REMODEL

631 Wayne, Sandusky, OH.
Known as the John Boalt House the property was acquired by Charles Graefe in late 1898.
Photograph by Nyttend ☺

"Mr. Bailey is also preparing plans for enlarging and remodeling the residence of Dr. Craeffe, at Sandusky, Ohio…" (*DFP* 7/24/1898)

There was no one by the name of Dr. Craeffe in Sandusky, Ohio; there was the Graefe family, who were physicians and one of the leading families in Sandusky. Philip, the father and his two sons, William and Charles, were doctors in Sandusky, Ohio as well as significant contributors to the development of the city. Mrs. Katherine Graefe, Charles' widow, stated in a 1958 article that in 1899, after purchasing the house from John M. Boalt, Charles and Katherine Graefe remodeled the structure. Among the renovations were the removal of the fireplace in the south parlor, the addition of a bay window and the addition of a side porch. The old laundry room was also enlarged with a bay window and the entire room was refinished in oak paneling and beams and converted to a dining room. The rear of the home was heightened with pine and cherry wood added to complete the remodel.[170] It seems that Bailey was responsible for the addition and

---

[170] *Sandusky Register* 9/6/1958. Mrs. Katherine Dorn Graefe, passed away at 631 Wayne Street on November 4, 1961 at the age of 96. *Sandusky Register* 11/6/1961.

remodeling the Graefe residence in late 1898.[171] Bailey's addition to the Graefe house blends well with the original structure. The curved porch with the small brackets under the eaves on the first floor, with the fine dentils and the slender Ionic columns make the entire addition very pleasing to the eye.

The addition on the rear of the Graefe home. Bailey did not mimic the brackets on the underside of the eaves on the second floor but used different lintels and sills on the windows instead.

Charles Graefe, was born June 10, 1859, in Sandusky, Ohio, to Dr. Philip and Dorothea (née Kranz) Graefe. Like his father and brother William, Charles pursued a career in medicine. Charles attended Oberlin College and later the University of Wooster where he graduated in 1880. He also attended Western Reserve College where he received his medical diploma then and studied in Europe for three years in Heidelberg, Leipzig and Vienna. He served for twelve years on the Sandusky Board of Education and in 1901 was the Democratic candidate for the state Senate. Charles was defeated by Charles A. Judson.[172] In 1891 Charles married Miss Katherine Dorn, the couple had three children, Carl F., Katherine and Elza Graefe. Charles passed away at his home at 631 Wayne Street on March 9, 1929.[173]

---

[171] The Italianate style home was built for John Boalt circa 1868. (Ohio 335)
[172] Charles A. Judson 13,491 votes to Charles Graefe 12,713 votes.
[173] See the *Sandusky Daily Register* 3/18/1890, *Sandusky Daily Register* 3/20/1890, *Sandusky Daily*

S.L. SCOFIELD STORE

Columbus Avenue in Sandusky, Ohio looking north. The Whitworth store was the three-story building to the left.

"Mr. Bailey is also preparing plans for enlarging and remodeling the residence of Dr. Craeffe, at Sandusky, Ohio; also, extensive improvements to a store for S.L. Scofield in the same city" (*DFP* 7/24/1898).

Just who S.L. Scofield is a bit of a mystery. No one by that name is listed in this period in either Detroit or Sandusky. Variants of the name were used in the course of the research, including Schofiled, Schoenfeld and Schoepfle. There was a S. L. Schoenfeld who married E. S. Cook in Sandusky, Ohio on October 7, 1879 but no other record was found. Based upon a *Sandusky Star-Journal* from March 8, 1898, which discussed the new buildings to be constructed in 1898, the most likely possibility was a business block for John Whitworth, which was built at 224 Columbus Avenue, directly across from the building Bailey designed for John L. Moore. No corroborating evidence has been found to substantiate this statement. The site is now a parking lot.

Star 8/24/1901 and *Sandusky Register* 9/6/1958.

WARREN G. VINTON HOME

521 Chandler, Detroit, MI.
Notice the bay window on the side and how it stacks with the window above and the flared gable end, a wonderful architectural element of the home.

"Architect R. Arthur Bailey has prepared plans for a two-story frame residence for Warren G. Vinton to be built on the north side of Chandler Avenue between Beaubien and St. Antoine streets. Cost $3,500" (*DFP* 8/6/1899).

Warren G. Vinton owned the Vinton Company, General Contractors & Builders. Vinton's residence was at 109 Charlotte Street in Detroit, so the home on Chandler was built as an investment. Vinton owned several lots on Chandler Avenue: 261 Chandler, 290 Chandler, 420 Chandler, 521 Chandler and 531 Chandler. Of all these lots on Chandler, there are only three options for this home based upon the lots Vinton owned in 1898: 420 Chandler, 521 Chandler and 531 Chandler. Only 521 Chandler was listed in the 1901 *Detroit City Directory*, the other two had yet to be built. The home is an interesting mix and the canted corner on the first floor is a feature not seen in many homes. The side gable with the flaring at the base and the arched window is the most appealing aspect of the home. These architectural features resemble those on the Robinson home, which Bailey designed. One odd aspect is the dormer on the facade. It seems out of place, almost an afterthought and one wonders if it should have been larger. It is doubtful that the door on the second floor over the porch is original to the home. It is off center and awkward.

Warren G. Vinton was born on January 3, 1830 to George and Lucy (née French) Vinton in Utica, New York. At the age of ten, Warren's father passed away leaving the family with limited financial support. The family moved to Fulton, New York, where Warren found work in the building trade. At the age of nineteen, Warren traveled to California to search for gold as a Forty-Niner. Finding no success he returned to New York. In December of 1853, he moved to Detroit and in 1855 Warren established a construction firm at the corner of Cass and Grand River Avenues, across from the Perkins Hotel. His business expanded in 1887 when he purchased an interest in the firm Nuppenau & Clark, buying out Ernst Nuppenau. Warren partnered with David C. Clark and the firm of Clark, Vinton & Company was established and operated until Clark's death in 1889. In July 1905, the Vinton Company was established, under the management of Warren's son Guy Jay Vinton. The business was responsible for the construction of many of Detroit's premier buildings: the Detroit Opera House, Masonic Temple on Fort Street, the First Congregational Church, the First Baptist Church, the Elks Club, the Detroit Athletic Club, Washington Arcade Building and many of the downtown theaters. Warren helped many young businessmen establish their businesses. Acting as a silent investor and mentor, he helped to found McClure Lumber Company, Fox Brothers, Kelsey, Herbert Company, the Bailey Company and many others.[174]

At the start of the Civil War, Warren raised a company of soldiers in Detroit at the Perkins Hotel. On July 26, 1862, the unit became Company H of the 24th Michigan Infantry, which was part of the Iron Brigade. Warren's health had always been precarious, and he was advised to resign his commission. Warren refused to do that until he commanded the troops in battle. On December 13, 1862 Warren led his company at the Battle of Fredericksburg where the unit helped to clear a Confederate artillery battery. After the battle, Warren resigned and was honorably discharged on December 29, 1862. In his personal life, Warren was a member of the Baptist Church, which he joined at the age of 12, and he never wavered in his faith. There is a story that when he was a boy he was taunted by wealthy children of the Baptist Church in Fulton because of his plain clothes. A fight ensued with quite a bit of profanity being tossed around by both parties. The local church deacons who were passing by observed the altercation and advised the church elders that Warren should be expelled from the church. After a hearing, Warren was dismissed from the church. Fifty years later the Fulton Baptist Church lifted Warren's expulsion and he was reinstated. On October 21, 1858 Warren married Miss Jane E.

---

[174] The Fox Brothers, Charles W. and Benjamin J. Fox built fireplace mantels; Kelsey, Herbert Company, Henry J. Herbert and John Kelsey, manufactured toilets; and the Bailey Company was owned by R. Arthur and Walter S. Bailey.

Putnam, the couple had six children; James, George (Guy) Jay, Clara Jennie, Grace E., Blanche, and Ralph Vinton.[175] Warren's wife, Jane, passed away in 1895. Warren was taken ill on December 27, 1906 with the grip (flu) that turned into bronchopneumonia. When informed of this, he planned for his own funeral. Warren G. Vinton passed away at his home on January 6, 1907 and his remarkable life had come to an end.[176]

WILLIAM F. METCALF RESIDENCE

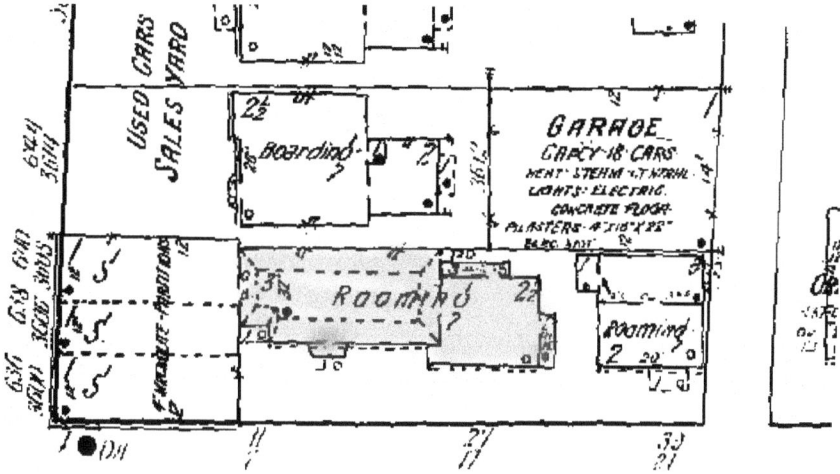

3600 [636] Woodward, Detroit, MI.
Metcalf's home is shaded in grey. It is possible that the brick stables were converted into a residence at the rear of the home. From 1921 Sanborn maps.

"The spacious brick residence at the north-east corner of Woodward avenue and Rowena street [Mack Avenue] has been purchased by Dr. W. F. Metcalf, for whom it is to be thoroughly remodeled and modernized for his office and residence. A suite of offices will be fitted up with mahogany with mosaic marble floors and an operating room in white enamel with white encaustic tile floor. The residence portion will also be treated in an elegant manner. The improvements were designed by Architect R. Arthur Bailey and will be made under his direction" (*DFP* 11/20/1898).

"Architect R. Arthur Bailey has prepared plans for a two-story Brick stable for Dr. W.F. Metcalf, to be built in the rear of his residence at the northeast corner of Woodward avenue and Rowena street. It will cost $3,000" (*DFP* 9/15/1901).

---

[175] There is the possibility that there was a seventh child Mary; see the 1870 Census.
[176] See *DFP* 1/7/1907, *DFP* 1/9/1907 and Burton 4: 74.

William F. Metcalf 1864-1935

Doctor William F. Metcalf passed away in Bayfield, Ontario on Thursday, October 17, 1935. William was born in Picton, Prince Edward County, Ontario in 1864 to Lawrence and Eliza (née Thompson) Metcalf. He attended school in Belleville, Ontario and later taught school in Providence, Ontario while preparing to attend the University of Michigan to study medicine. In 1888, he graduated from medical school and established a practice in Detroit, specializing in abdominal and pelvic surgery. William was on the staff of the old Detroit General Hospital which later became Henry Ford Hospital. After graduating from medical school, William married Miss Ella Venos in Sidney, Ontario on December 26, 1888.

William established his practice in the home of a former acquaintance, the late Dr. Frank L. Tiffany. William had been close with Belle M. Tiffany, Frank's widow, and the couple spent a great deal of time together. Ella Metcalf felt that William's affection for her was compromised and she filed to separate from William in 1891 and filed suit against Belle Tiffany as the reason for the loss of her husband's affections. She sought $10,000 in damages. Mrs. Ella Metcalf succeeded in obtaining a judgement against Belle Tiffany for $5,000 on May 5, 1893, but when the sheriff attempted to collect the levy it was discovered that Belle had deeded everything she owned to her brother-in-law, Burritt E. Tiffany at 1pm on May 5, 1893, in trust for Belle's daughter Lucile M. Tiffany. The judgement was eventually reversed by the Michigan Supreme Court, (Metcalf v. Tiffany 1895) and there is no indication that the suit was refiled. On June 29, 1897 William married Agnes M. Lovering, a school teacher, the couple had two children, Jessie and William. In 1928 William retired and moved to Bayfield where he lived until his death.[177]

---

[177] *St. Louis Post Dispatch* 10/4/1891 *DFP* 11/24/1891 *DFP* 6/23/1893, *DFP* 9/20/1893 and *DFP*

❧CHAPTER FOUR❧

FREDERICK J. THOMAN

Frederick (Fred) J. Thoman Jr. was born on September 13, 1869 to Frederick and Mary Elizabeth (née Reitz) Thoman.[178] The Thoman name was well known in Lansing; Fred's father, along with Frank A. Reitz, established the Oriental Milling Company in Lansing in 1868. Frederick sold his interest in the mill to his brother-in-law Frank Reitz; unfortunately, Frank passed away in 1870 and Frederick repurchased the business from his sister-in-law Mary L. Reitz in 1871. The business operated as the Oriental Milling Company until 1885 when Frederick's brother John P. Thoman joined the company and the name was changed to Thoman Mills. Fred's father was also a stakeholder in the Lansing Wheelbarrow Company, Lansing Wagon Works and Bement & Sons Company. Fred attended local schools and apprenticed as an architect with James Appleyard. Fred lived with the Appleyard's at their home in Lansing from 1896-1898. James Appleyard died in late June of 1896, so Fred's architectural education was undoubtedly influenced by Rufus Arthur Bailey and William Appleyard, but he may have apprenticed with James in the early 1890s. Although Fred's architectural output was brief, his designs demonstrated that he was a practical architect whose skill could only grow over time. Why he left the architectural profession is unknown. Fred was an up and coming architect whose decision to leave the vocation may have been influenced by the criticism he received in the press regarding the design of the Olds Motor Works in Detroit. After the fire at the plant, there was relentless disparagement in the newspapers concerning the structural strength of the buildings and speculation as to why the factory burned so quickly. Fred never designed another structure after the devastation of the Olds Motor Works plant and when required by law, never registered as an architect in Michigan.

Fred had relocated to Jackson, Michigan in 1900 and in the *Jackson City Directory* for that year, he is listed as an architect but there is no indication that he was engaged in any design work. The 1902 *Jackson City Directory* recorded Fred as working as a machinist for the Michigan Central Railroad where he remained until 1904. But in 1905 Fred changed professions and partnered with Stephen Avery to form the Avery-Thoman Plumbing Company of Jackson. The company quickly obtained the contracts to provide the furnace

---

10/19/1935.

[178] I have used Fred instead of Frederick in the biography to avoid confusion with Frederick Thoman, Frederick's father. In the survey of the architectural works I have not made this change.

for the Majestic Theater in Kalamazoo and the Ingham County Poorhouse. Fred continued to work as a heating contractor and obtained the contract in 1912 to install the furnace at the Franklin Avenue School in Lansing, Michigan. After the plumbing business closed, Fred briefly partnered with Charles R. Diehl and manufactured the Diehl Automatic Instantaneous Water Heater. The relationship was short lived and in 1915 Fred bought out his partner (*JCP* 3/27/1915). In 1915 Fred's father died and he left his son a considerable inheritance, $125,000 in property and investments (*JCP* 1/5/1916). He settled into a quiet life; Fred had no profession listed in the *Jackson City Directories* from 1915-1922, but he may have been managing his investments.

The only mention of Fred in the local newspapers, aside from social events, were two instances involving automobiles. In September of 1916, Fred engaged in a car chase with a 16-year-old speed demon who passed Fred at a high rate of speed on Fourth Street. Fred determined the young man's rate of speed by pulling even with him on the road; then the next day Fred swore out a complaint in police court. Some people questioned whether Fred should also have been charged for speeding (*JCP* 9/26/1916). The second instance was a bit more ominous. On July 23, 1921 Fred was brought to police headquarters for a parking violation. While at the station he was berated by Police Chief John Hudson, who Fred claims swore at him, threatened physical violence and finally warned him if he was any more trouble he would be tossed in the 'Bull Pen'. Hudson claimed that Fred was a 'old time trouble maker' who constantly annoyed his officers. No record has been discovered regarding the outcome of Fred's charges (*JCP* 7/26/1921).

Fred was an officer and investor in the Golden Age Junior Mining Company of Pioneerville, Idaho. The Golden Age Junior Mining Company was organized in 1915 by a syndicate of Michigan businessmen and the officers of the company were: Fred M. Sibley, President; Fred J. Thoman, Vice President; Morris Compton, Vice President; Frank B. LeClear, General Manager; and Fred W. Griswold, Secretary. The mine consisted of a vertical shaft and three tunnels; the No. 1 tunnel was 2000 feet in length, the No. 2 tunnel was 500 feet long and finally the No. 3 tunnel was 360 feet. The value of the gold, silver and lead in one ton of ore taken from the mine was said to be approximately $25 in 1924. The mill at the mine had the capacity to process over 150 tons of ore per day. The mining operation was quite extensive with investors building a new processing mill, and housing for the married and single workers. Production records are not available after 1915, but prior to that date the recovery of gold extracted from the ore had exceeded $200,000 (about $11,000,000 in today's dollars).

By all accounts the company created a model mining camp with family housing, bunkhouses for single men and a guesthouse for visitors. The two bunkhouses accommodated forty-four men with two men to a room, the guesthouse could house twelve individuals and had a private dining room. The mine closed in 1931 following a forest fire, which destroyed the mill and many of the surrounding buildings.[179]

By 1922 Fred worked for the George W. Rogers Company, which specialized in outdoor advertising; Fred was the Secretary of the company. An odd career change for Fred, it is unknown if he was a partner in the business. After the Stock Market Crash of 1929, Fred became an investment broker dealing in stocks and bonds. On February 22, 1899 Fred married Miss Nettie B. Avery in Jackson, Michigan; there were no children from the marriage. On Friday December 29, 1939 Fred J. Thoman died at his home at 1623 Fourth Street in Jackson Michigan. (*JCP* 12/29/1939) Nettie Avery Thoman passed away on March 5, 1955; Nettie was born in Jackson, Michigan on May 4, 1870 and was the daughter of Stephen Avery and Emma E. (née Potter) Avery. Stephen was a Civil War Veteran who served with the 22nd Michigan Infantry and saw service with Sherman on the March to the Sea. (*JCP* 3/6/1955)

---

[179] *Salt Lake Mining Review,* July 30, 1920, November 15, 1924 and *Golden Age Mine,* 2008.

ROBERT SMITH PRINTING

An artist rendering of the Robert Smith Printing Company and the State Republican Office 230-234 N. Washington, Lansing, MI.

"The new home into which the Republican and the entire establishment of the Robert Smith Printing Co. has just been moved, is a model one in every respect. It was built expressly for the big plant, which is regarded by well posted [known] men as the most complete printing establishment of its kind in the country. The building is 66 feet in width and 100 feet in depth, fronting on Washington avenue and Ottawa street, three stories and a basement, and is a monument to the builder, Frederick Thoman. The basement contains the boiler and engine room, dynamo, and 12 presses, paper cutters, folders, etc. It is lighted by immense windows in the front and on the north side and is equipped with every possible facility for turning out the work of so large of establishment.

"On the first floor are located the business offices, editorial rooms, linotype machines, the newspaper and job rooms. The second floor contains the bindery, which is one of the most complete in the west, and the book and proof rooms are located on the third floor. All have been arranged with the main idea of convenience, and it is safe to say there is no more thoroughly equipped printing plant in the country than that occupied by this concern.

The State Republican and Robert Smith Printing Company Office 230-234 N. Washington, Lansing, MI. Notice the corbeling on the parapet over the canted entrance. (CADL/FPLA)

"The building was designed by Frederick Thoman Jr., and erected by Frederick Thoman Sr., to the expressed order of the occupants, and it is only justice to Mr. Thoman to say that in every respect has his part of the work been satisfactory. This is the third business block he has erected for publishing houses. The Lansing Journal and Thompson & Van Buren occupying buildings erected for them by Mr. Thoman" (*SR* 12/12/1896).[180]

Robert Smith was born in Syracuse, New York on April 13, 1843, to Thomas and Judith (née Morton) Smith. Thomas moved his family to a farm outside of Syracuse in 1847 where Robert attended the local school. At the age of 13 Robert began his career in printing as an apprentice with the *Syracuse Standard*. Two years later Robert left the *Standard* and for a year traveled the country as a journeyman printer. After the year of travel, Robert obtained a position with the *Rochester Express* and in 1863 when the *Express* employees went on strike, Robert decided to move to Lansing, Michigan where he acquired a job with the John A. Kerr & Company, State Printers. In 1865 Robert, along

---

[180] It is unknown if Frederick Thoman Jr. designed the Lansing Journal and Thompson & Van Buren buildings, which were owned by his father. The Lansing Journal building was located at 119-121 E. Ottawa while the Thompson & Van Buren building was located at 122 E. Ottawa, both buildings were constructed between 1892-1894. It is possible that Frederick Thoman Jr. was involved in some capacity.

with Henry S. Hilton, purchased the *Clinton Republican*, and in 1866 the partners established the *Flint Globe*. The partners sold the *Globe* in 1869 to A.L. Aldrich, then they acquired a two thirds interest in the *Jackson Daily Citizen*. Just eight months later the partnership dissolved and Robert sold his interests back to James O'Donnell, the former owner of the *Jackson Daily Citizen* and moved to Taylors Falls, Minnesota, where he established a hardware store. Robert was not quite satisfied with the hardware business and less than two years later he purchased the *Gratiot Journal* in Ithaca, Michigan. Robert's typography and style was noticed by state officials and in 1890 he obtained the state of Michigan printing and binding contract. In 1896 D.D. Thorp & Sons, publishers of the *State Republican*, merged with the Robert Smith Printing Company with Robert Smith and his old partner Henry S. Hilton holding the controlling interest in the company. By 1911 the *State Republican* would acquire the *Lansing Journal* and the *Lansing State Journal* would be born.[181]

Robert Smith 1843-1916

On October 5, 1869 Robert married Miss Carrie H. Scattergood in St. Johns, Michigan; the couple had three children: Maude, Robert Jr., and Harry M. Smith. Carrie passed away in April 1887. Two years later, on October 2, 1889 Robert married Miss Henrietta Chapman, the daughter of Judge William H. Chapman of Lansing, the couple had a daughter, Frances.[182] Robert Smith passed away at his home on December 9, 1916. Robert was a self-made man. Through hard work, perseverance and an aptitude for commerce, he founded a business that controlled the printing contract for the state of Michigan and acquired the newspaper which eventually became the *Lansing State Journal*. My guess is he is rolling over in his grave observing what happened to his newspaper. (*Men* 488 and *LSJ* 12/9/1916)

---

[181] It was really called the *State Journal* but given the confused history of the paper it makes more sense to go with *LSJ*.

[182] Chapman was the mayor of Lansing 1861-1862.

With the fourth-floor addition to 230-234 N. Washington, the building's name block was moved from the top of the canted entrance to the fourth-floor front facing Washington Avenue. (CADL/FPLA)

The original Robert Smith building on North Washington, before its later additions, was a fantastic building. The canted entrance, coupled with the detailed corbeling that formed the arches over the second and third story windows on the facade, made this building an appealing structure to view from the street. Notice on the Ionia Street side the windows have far less detail. Observe the corbelling across the parapet coupled with the rusticated stones at the entrance which give the building the appearance of strength and stability, something all clients want. This is a remarkable first building for Thoman and one of the finest that he designed.

HOTEL WENTWORTH

201 E. Michigan, Lansing, MI.
The earliest image of the Hotel Wentworth from 1902.

A NEW HOSTELRY
LANDLORD WENTWORTH HAS ARRANGED TO BUILD ONE
At the Corner of Michigan Avenue and Grand Street Work Has Been Commenced

"The collection of one-story buildings at the northeast corner of Michigan avenue and Grand street, which has been an eyesore to the enterprising citizens of Lansing are now in the process of being torn down and a new hotel will be erected by Frank Wentworth, proprietor of the Chapman house. Mr. Wentworth's property is 60 by 100 feet in dimension and includes all the buildings on that corner except the frame structure upon the river bank occupied by Frank Hayes. The contract for removing the buildings was secured by John Carey, who expects to have the work completed Saturday night. The buildings were among the oldest in the city and have been on the property of Judge W.H. Pinckney since war times. He cleared the corner, which was covered with trees at that time. The building second from the river bank formerly stood on the lot north of Rouser's drug store and was used by Cannell and Edmonds as a harness shop. The corner structure was moved from the lot east of the federal building and the other buildings were erected by Judge Pinckney. The plans for the new hotel to be put up by Mr. Wentworth have been furnished by Fred Thoman Jr., and will necessitate an expenditure of from $7,500 to

$9,000. The structure will be three stories high and the third story will connect with the third story of the barn recently erected. It will be finished up in the latest and most modern style. The office will be located in the southwest corner of the building and the dining room behind that, opening on Grand street. The sample rooms will be located east of the office and the barber shop and bath rooms will be in the basement. The hotel will have about 40 rooms and it is Mr. Wentworth's intentions to have the building completed by the last of August at the latest" (*SR* 4/21/1897).

201 E. Michigan, Lansing, MI., picture circa 1906.
Notice the addition and front entrance designed by architect Thomas E. White.

A FINE HOSTELRY
Is the new Wentworth, which is Now Ready for Business.

"The doors of the new Hotel Wentworth on the corner of Michigan ave. and Grand st., were thrown open to the traveling public, Monday evening, and the house is doing business today. This finely appointed hotel will have an important place with the wayfaring public and be prominently identified with the hostelries in this city here after. The Hotel Wentworth is not large, but neat. Yet it has the capacity equal to a good-sized demand having 40 sleeping rooms. The Wentworth has 60 feet on Michigan ave. and 100 feet on Grand st., and was planned by Architect Fred Thoman Jr., and is well arranged. It is a three-story structure of red brick and substantial throughout. It was erected under the supervision of the proprietor, Mr. Frank Wentworth, who looked after all the details, and it has cost $12,000. The site is valued at a like amount. Its location between three of the depots and Washington ave., on the avenue leading up to the capitol is superb. It is only a block away from the leading thoroughfare of the city and overlooks Grand river and the Michigan ave. bridge. The office, dining room, halls and all of the rooms of the house are finely appointed. There is a harmonious finish of woodwork in natural colors and even fresh walls are attractive. It has the neatness of newness.

"Landlord Wentworth, wife and daughter, who presided over the Chapman House, on the opposite corner, for years, need no introduction to the traveling public and the people of this city.[183] They know how to keep a hotel. It is the universal verdict that they set one of the best tables in the city. With this reputation established in their old surroundings, their reputation will be much enhanced amid their splendid new place of operations. Early in the new year, the Hotel Wentworth will have an opening event, with a banquet and formal festivities, at which Landlord Wentworth and family will welcome their friends and they are legion" (SR 12/15/1897).

Frank Wentworth was born in Athens, Maine on June 1, 1849. Upon his arrival in Lansing in 1884, Frank became the landlord of the Chapman House on the southeast corner of Grand and Michigan Avenues. On December 24, 1885, Frank married Miss Ellen Mandley of Perry, Michigan; the couple had one child Elizabeth, who later married William G. Kerns. Tragically Frank Wentworth died at the age 54 from typhoid pneumonia on March 31, 1904 (SR 3/31/1904). On Sunday, February 15, 1931, Mrs. Ellen Wentworth, Frank's wife died in her suite of rooms at the Kerns Hotel at the age of 71 after an illness of five weeks. She had been one of Lansing's best-known hotel proprietors. Ellen was born in Perry, Michigan and came to Lansing in 1885 and after marrying Frank Wentworth, the couple managed the Chapman House for the Bailey brothers for several years until the couple built Wentworth Hotel. After Frank's death, the hotel continued under Ellen's supervision until it was sold to William G. Kerns in 1906.[184]

---

[183] The Chapman House one of the earliest hotels in Lansing was torn down in 1897. The building was in such poor state structurally that the City did not allow it to be repaired.
[184] LCN 2/16/1931 and the LSJ 2/16/1931

201 E. Michigan, Lansing, MI.
Just to the rear of the Hotel Wentworth structure is the infamous Kerns Hotel, which was designed by architect Judson Churchill. (CADL/FPLA)

An article appeared in the *State Republican* on November 11, 1892, which recounted the Wentworth's purchase of the property and his plans for a new hotel; it took Wentworth an additional five years to secure the finances to build the hotel. This was an important commission for Thoman. It is unknown if his father was one of the investors in the new hotel. In the above photographs the expansion of the building can be observed, notice the addition to the third floor on the east side of the building. In 1903 Architect Thomas E. White designed the new front entrance and porch, which became the iconic feature of the hotel, with decorative stained glass windows with the hotel's name as well as an elegant stop to sip cocktails. (*LJ* 3/4/1903) In 1909 Judson Churchill planned the new building to the rear of the Wentworth Hotel for William G. Kerns the owner of the Hotel Wentworth, the structure was known as the Kerns Hotel. (*SR* 4/16/1909)

Thoman's design for the Hotel Wentworth was workmanlike with the entrance being unadorned. The only ornamentation on the facade was the detailed corbelling and recessed panels along the parapet. The Wentworth Hotel survived the Kerns' fire in 1934, only to become a victim to downtown redevelopment; the building was torn down on September 17, 1966. The lot is now Wentworth Park and the site of the 9/11 Remembrance Memorial and the Rotary Steam Clock.

JAMES N. LEASIA BUILDING

100-120 E. Grand River, Williamston, MI.
Note the location of Leasia's store on the corner.

"In the case of Fred J. Thoman against James N. Leasia, an action brought to recover $400 for services in supervising the erection of a building at Williamston, the jury in the Circuit Court brought in a verdict in favor of the plaintiff of $94.27 and allowed a set-off [legal term] of $57.83, thus forcing the cost of the case upon the defendant" (*LJ* 4/1/1898). Thoman supervised the construction of the building, but it is unknown whether Thoman was responsible for the design of the building. In many cases the architect was engaged as the site-supervising architect. The building at 100-120 E. Grand River is an appealing structure. Notice the symmetry of the building, the cap on the parapet, which on the far left in the photograph, seems to have been removed. The corbelling on the upper facade and the recessed panels resemble those on the Wentworth Hotel before the additions. The building is still standing in 2019.

100-120 E. Grand River, Williamston, MI.
Compare the current image above of the corner to the postcard image prior, observe the change in windows and the loss of the parapet capstone.

James N. Leasia was born in Williamston, Michigan in 1859, the son of Doctor James A. and Martha (née Shaft) Leasia. James N. attended Williamston High School and worked in his father's drug store as a clerk and spent the remainder of his life in the drug store business. On Saturday night, August 21, 1897, the village of Williamston suffered a devastating fire in its central business district. Several structures were lost including James N. Leasia's business. In 1897, James rebuilt his drug store on the southeast corner of Grand River Avenue and Putnam Street and employed Fred Thoman to supervise the construction of his new brick building. After moving to Portland, Oregon, in 1906, James N. Leasia invested in the mining industry. He died at his home in Portland on Monday, January 31, 1916.[185]

---

[185] *ICN* 8/26/1897, *ICD* 8/26/1897, Cowles 136, *Morning Oregonian*; 2/01/1916; and *ICN* 2/10/1916

DR. CHARLES MARSHALL RESIDENCE

224 Michigan, East Lansing, MI.
The earliest image of 224 Michigan is from when it was the Hermian Society, image circa 1920.

"Morse & Moore of this city have secured the contract for a new $1,800 residence for Dr. Marshall, bacteriologist at the Agricultural College to be erected just north of the college grounds. Fred J. Thoman draughted [sic] the plans" (*LJ* 6/17/1898).

From the street, the facade of the residence is symmetrical; notice the stacking of the windows between the first and second floor even though the windows are not proportioned. When viewed from the side, the rear of the home, which has a gambrel roof, blends with the front section of the home; it is unknown if this addition was part of the original design. The front porch wraps around the home on the side and unfortunately the position of the street light in the second photograph obscures the column on the porch. After Dr. Marshall left the M.A.C. the residence became the home of the Hermian Society, a fraternity at the Michigan Agricultural College.[186] The home is no longer standing.

---

[186] The Michigan Agricultural College or M.A.C. is now Michigan State University.

224 Michigan, East Lansing, MI.

From the street, the facade of the residence is symmetrical; notice the stacking of the windows between the first and second floor even though the windows are not proportioned. When viewed from the side, the rear of the home, which has a gambrel roof, blends with the front section of the home; it is unknown if this addition was part of the original design. The front porch wraps around the home on the side and unfortunately the position of the street light in the second photograph obscures the column on the porch. After Dr. Marshall left the M.A.C. the residence became the home of the Hermian Society, a fraternity at the Michigan Agricultural College.[187] The home is no longer standing.

Charles E. Marshall was born in Port Clinton, Ohio on October 6, 1866 to Lavinas and Sarah Marshall. At the age of 18, Charles enrolled at Fredonia State Normal School in New York and graduated with a degree in the Classics in 1889. After commencement Charles served for two years as the principle of the Elliocottville Academy and then entered the University of Michigan to study medicine. After two years, he became interested in the study of bacteriology and transferred to that department. After completion of his degree he pursued graduate studies in bacteriology and hygiene. In 1896 Marshall accepted a position at Michigan State Experiment Station. Marshall received his Ph.D. from the University of Michigan in 1902 and became a professor at the

---

[187] The Michigan Agricultural College or M.A.C. is now Michigan State University.

Michigan Agricultural College. In 1902, he traveled to Europe and studied at the Pasteur Institute in Paris, Ostertag's Laboratory in Berlin and the Jorgensen's Laboratory of Fermentation in Copenhagen.

Doctor Marshall 1866-1927 (MSU Archives)

By 1908 Marshall had become the Vice Director of the Michigan State Experiment Station, a position he held for four years. In 1912 Marshall was recruited by the Massachusetts Agricultural College in Amherst to oversee the graduate school, which he helped to make one of the finest in the nation. Charles married Miss Maud Skidmore of Fredonia, New York in July of 1896, the couple had three children; Max F., Donald and Maud Alice. On March 22, 1927 Dr. Charles E. Marshall died at his home of a heart attack. At his funeral, the pallbearers were President of the College, Dr. Kenyon L. Butterfield, Fred C. Kenney Treasurer of the College, Dr. Nelson, Ray Standard Baker, Marshall's friend and Joseph Kuzmeski, the janitor at the Microbiology Laboratory, a trusted friend. Dr. Charles E. Marshall must have been an interesting person with whom to have coffee, something he did many times with Joseph Kuzmeski. In February 1935, the Microbiology Building at the college was renamed Marshall Hall in memory of Dr. Charles Edward Marshall. The building was torn down in 1996.[188]

---

[188] *Holyoke Times* 3/22/1927 and the *Massachusetts Collegian* 2/14/1935

PROFESSOR HERBERT W. MUMFORD HOME

235 Delta, East Lansing, MI.

"Architect Fred Thoman has let the contracts for two dwellings at the Agricultural college. The contract for a $1,800 house for Prof. Mumford was awarded to Morse & Moore and the job for a $2,000 house for Mrs. Olive Backus was taken by George W. Elliott. The architect has a small village in prospect out there, having four houses started and two under way" (*SR* 7/9/1898). Professor Herbert W. Mumford purchased Lot 7 in the College Delta Subdivision from the State Board of Agriculture in 1898 for $135 quite a bargain.[189]

The Mumford home in some ways resembled the Marshall residence; notice the design of the front dormer and the position of the windows. The front porch extends across the front of the home, unfortunately the bushes obscure the details of the porch. If you compare the side view of the Mumford residence and Marshall home (page 288), you can see the similarities. Notice the position and the style of the windows and how they are stacked symmetrically on the side of the home. Frankly this is a very plain home with a sterile appearance. Not one of Thoman's best designs. The home was torn down in the 1960s.

---

[189] *Ingham County Register of Deeds* Liber 130, Page 602

235 Delta, East Lansing, MI. (CADL/FPLA)

Herbert W. Mumford was born in Moscow, Hillsdale County, Michigan on February 26, 1871, the son of Elisha Charles Lindsley and Julia Ann (née Camburn) Mumford. Herbert attended Hillsdale schools and graduated from Hanover High School in 1887. He enrolled at Albion College where he stayed for two years and then taught school in central Michigan. In 1890 Herbert registered as a student at the Michigan Agricultural College and graduated in 1891. Four years later, in August of 1895 he was appointed to a position at the Michigan Agricultural College and later became head of the Department of Practical Agriculture. On July 5, 1898, Herbert married Miss Lena Crosby of Lansing; the couple had five children. In 1901, the family moved to the University of Illinois where he was employed for twenty-one years as professor of Animal Husbandry. Herbert retired in 1922, as Dean and Director of the University of Illinois, College of Agriculture, Agricultural Experiment Station and the Extension Service. On May 14, 1938 Herbert was involved in an automobile accident where he sustained head and chest injuries. Mumford rallied from his injuries, but on Sunday May 29, pneumonia developed in his lungs and he was placed on oxygen. Herbert Windsor Mumford died on May 31, 1938 in Champaign, Illinois.[190]

---

[190] *Chicago Daily Tribune* 5/15/1938, *Pantagraph* 5/31/1938, *Educators* 183. *American Journal* 740.

OLIVE BACKUS HOME

214 Michigan, East Lansing, MI.
It has been very difficult to locate images of the homes that were built in the College Delta
Subdivision in East Lansing. Many are culled from other photographs resulting in the poor image
quality. Note the interesting street light.

"Architect Fred Thoman has let the contracts for two dwellings at the Agricultural college. The contract for a $1,800 house for Prof. Mumford was awarded to Morse & Moore and the job for a $2,000 house for Mrs. Olive Backus was taken by George W. Elliott. The architect has a small village in prospect out there, having four houses started and two under way" (*SR* 7/9/1898).

Mrs. Olive Backus owned Lot 1 of College Delta Subdivision, which she purchased in 1898 from the State Board of Agriculture for the sum of $150.[191] The house was located at the apex of the Delta Subdivision, formed by Grand River and Michigan Avenues. Unfortunately, the Backus home has been lost to history. The Backus home resembled the residence designed for Professor Herbert W. Mumford. The large front dormer extended out over the porch, an element that was also present on the Mumford home. Notice the extent of the rear dormer; it is similar in appearance to the rear of the Doctor Charles E. Marshall home. These are the only images that have been located regarding this residence and provide few clues regarding the structure.

---

[191] *Ingham County Register of Deeds Liber* 130 Page 491.

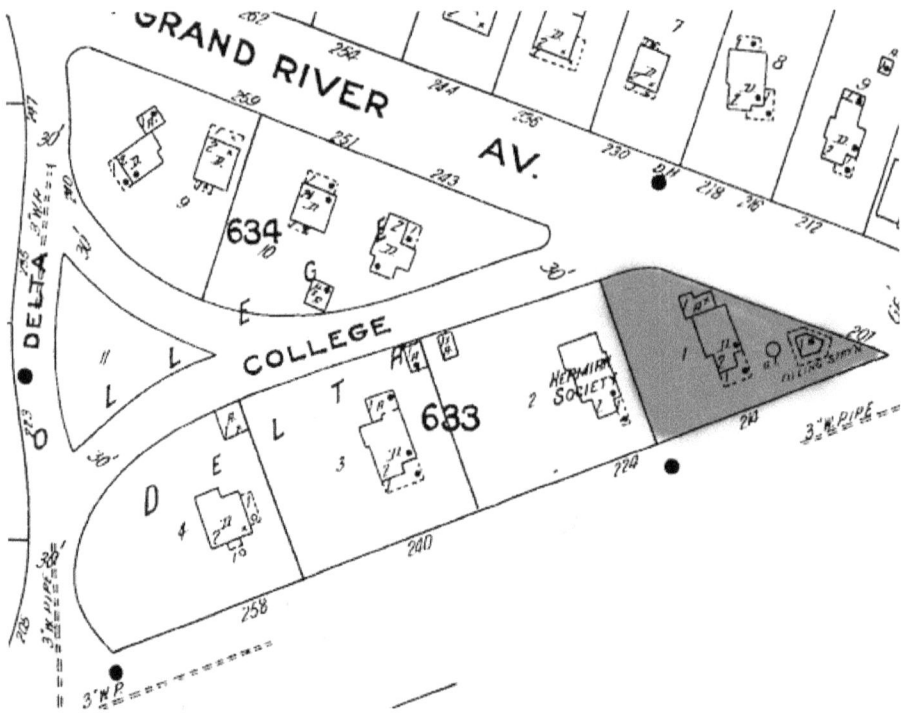

214 Michigan is shaded in grey, notice the home and the gas station at the point of the lot.
(Sanborn Map 1926)

Backus Cottage

"The cottage that Mrs. Backus has built on the east end of the Delta is a model student's home for ten young women who live there. It was planned for students, and in building everything possible has been done to make it comfortable and attractive. On the first floor is a well-lighted reception room finished in oak and Georgia pine, with a fireplace in one corner. This room opens into a parlor on the south; a library and study, used at present for a bedroom, on the west; and a dining room on [to] the north, all finished in the same woods. A well-appointed kitchen connects with the dining room on the west.

"Going from the reception room to the second floor we find five rooms for students, one room for servants, and a bathroom. These rooms and the halls are finished throughout in Georgia pine. Mrs. Backus has furnished each student room with bedstead, springs, mattress, pillows, three chairs, study table, dresser, commode and shades. The whole house is heated with hot water, lighted by electricity, and has water from the college water works accessible in convenient places. Finally, Mrs. Backus has had experience with students that will enable her to make life pleasant for the young women entrusted to her care" (*M.A.C. Record* 9/20/1898).

"Mrs. Olive Backus who owns the corner lot on the Delta has informed me that she intends to erect a building on the "point" of the Delta for the purpose of erecting a store on same. I [Arthur C. Bird] have examined the record fully and although it is evident that the intent of the Board was that nothing of this kind should ever be done, yet Mrs. Backus' deed from the Board does not mention the fact that her legal right to use this property as she sees fit seems to be unquestionable; on the other hand, Mrs. Backus is receiving from the College certain accommodations in the nature of water supply and sewerage for which there has been no written agreement entered into. I would suggest that if the Board so wills it might be possible to present [prevent] the erection of this building by suggesting to Mrs. Backus that in the event of her persisting in her present intention, water supply at least would be cut off from her premises."[192]

"Mrs. O. Backus has sold her cottage at the M.A.C. and has moved to her farm here [Dansville]" (*ICN* 10/5/1899). No one is certain why Mrs. Backus sold her home, but it may have been a result of pressure from the College.

Oddly enough, despite the college's objections, within ten years there was a gas station on the apex of the Delta. On the 1926 Sanborn map you can observe a small filling station that was built at the apex of Lot 1. Eventually the station was enlarged and the home was torn down. The house stood at the peak of the Delta, but the property worth far exceeded the purchase price and was suitable for a commercial development, a factor the trustees of M.A.C. did not consider. It is nice to know that things never change; it took an outsider to demonstrate the failings of the Board of Trustees.

Born Olive Bygraves on September 25, 1855 to Richard and Cynthia (née Aseltine) Bygraves, she grew up in the Dansville, Michigan area.[193] In September of 1876 Olive married Robert Thomson, the couple had two children; Elmer and Eber. On March 5, 1883 Robert died of inflammation of the lungs at the age of 32.[194] After living as a widow for several years, Olive married Chancey R. Backus, a widower, on July 2, 1887. Just three years later, on October 15, 1890, Chancey died of heart disease at his home in Wheatfield Township.[195] Then on October 24, 1901 Olive married Jacob Dakin, who was 20 years her senior, the newlyweds honeymooned at the Pan American Fair in Buffalo. (*ICD* 10/24/1901) The couple divorced in January 1921 and Olive moved to Los Angles in the 1930s to live with her son Elmer and his family. On December 29, 1940 Olive died at the home of her son in Lansing, Michigan. It is interesting that Olive kept the name of Dakin but was buried at the Fairview Cemetery in Dansville, Michigan next to her first husband Robert Thomson.[196]

---

[192] Offices of Board of Trustees and President MAC, Meeting Minutes, 8/29/1899
[193] Some records list Olive's date of birth as 1858.
[194] *ICN* 3/8/1883 and *ICD* 3/8/1883.
[195] *ICN* 7/7/1887 and *ICN* 10/16/1890.
[196] *ICN* 1/4/1940. Jacob Dakin passed away at the age of 85 on April 10, 1923.

THE DELTA SUBDIVISION

The residences located in the west part of the Delta subdivision in 1900. From left to right, Burton O. Longyear, Fred C. Kenney, Professor Mumford, Jenison, Snyder homes.

"Architect Fred Thoman has let the contracts for two dwellings at the Agricultural college. The contract for a $1,800 house for Prof. Mumford was awarded to Morse & Moore and the job for a $2,000 house for Mrs. Olive Backus was taken by George W. Elliott. The architect has a small village in prospect out there, having four houses started and two under way" (*SR* 7/9/1898).

The residences located in the east part of the Delta subdivision in 1900. From left to right you see the Newman, Marshall and Backus homes. In the background, you can see the land rising and forming a ridge. This natural feature no longer exists, it is amazing how we reshape our cities.

From the July 1898 article in the *State Republican* we know that Thoman had six homes under construction on the Delta in Collegeville, but it is difficult to know for sure which homes he designed. It is possible to determine from previous *State Republican* articles that Thoman designed the residences of Olive Backus, Herbert Mumford and Charles E. Marshall. The other homes Thoman may have designed are those for Chace Newman, Burton Longyear, Fred Kenney, Jonathan Snyder and Luther Jenison. Given the limited number of lots on the College Delta Subdivision Plat these are the only possible options and each one of these candidates will be examined in detail.

BURTON O. LONGYEAR HOME

205 Delta, East Lansing, MI.
This is the only image that has been located of the home.

The first to be examined is the Longyear residence. Burton Orange Longyear was born in Leslie, Michigan on July 16, 1868 to William D. and Ann E. (née Barlow) Longyear, where he spent his childhood on a farm. After high school the brothers Henry and Burton Longyear worked part-time at the Mead & Merritt drug store. In 1888 the brothers passed the state pharmacy board exam and opened their own business. On December 29, 1897, Burton married Miss Jessie L. Bond in Onondaga, Michigan. The couple had three children: Lawrence L., Leslie S. and Florence L. Longyear. With his brother, Henry B. Longyear, Burton opened Longyear Brother's Drug Store in Mason, Michigan in 1888. In 1898, Burton changed careers and enrolled at the Michigan Agricultural College to study botany under the Dean of American Botanists, William James Beal, a distant cousin of Burton's. After obtaining his B.S. in 1903, Burton accepted a position as a Professor of Forestry at Colorado Agricultural College [Colorado State University] where he remained until retirement. Burton wrote several books on botany and forestry including *Michigan Mushrooms* (1903), *Rocky Mountain Wild Flower Studies* (1909), *Evergreens of Colorado* (1914), *Some Colorado Mushrooms* (1914), *Trees and Shrubs of the Rocky Mountain Region* (1924) and several other titles. On April 3, 1953, Jessie Louise Longyear passed away in Fort Collins, Colorado. Burton spent the remainder of his years living in Phoenix during the winter and returned to Fort Collins for the summers. After the death of his wife, Burton married Mrs. Addie R. Harris, who passed away on January 4, 1974. Burton Orange Longyear died in Phoenix on April 10, 1969 at the age of 100.[197]

Burton Orange Longyear 1868-1869
Courtesy of the Colorado State University Archives

The home for Burton Longyear was built before the July 1898 *State Republican* article. *The M.A.C. Record* stated that the Longyear home was the first house built on the Delta and was occupied by the Longyear family on January 1, 1898.[198] "The Hall Lumber Co. has been awarded the contract for building a $1,200 residence for Bert Longyear at M.A.C., E. H. Mead is the architect" (*LSJ* 9/12/1922). The article is from a *Lansing State Journal* feature on what occurred in Lansing history 25 years earlier. So, it seems Earl H. Mead designed the Longyear residence and not Thoman. In 1904, the home was sold to Luther H. Baker when Burton moved to Fort Collins. Towar, in his *History of the City of East Lansing*, records that 205 Delta was the first home built on the College Delta plat (Towar 43). The home was torn down in 1957.

---

[197] *Arizona Republic* 4/13/1969 and *ICN* 4/16/1969
[198] *The M.A.C. Record*, 9/13/1898.

KENNEY RESIDENCE

223 Delta, East Lansing, MI. (CADL/FPLA)

Fred Chester Kenney was born in Lapeer, Michigan on December 20, 1869 to Joel D. and Elizabeth S. (née Woodhouse) Kenney.[199] Joel Kenney was involved in the lumber trade and in 1876 he moved his family to Port Huron, Michigan. Fred attended the local schools and became a teacher in the Port Huron area. After working as a teacher for several years, Fred saved enough money to attend college and enrolled in the Ferris Institute, today Ferris State University; he graduated in 1892. From 1892 to 1895 he worked for the Manistee & Northwestern Railroad.

In 1895 Fred obtained a position at the Michigan Agricultural College as Assistant Secretary and later Cashier of the college. At the MAC, he met several men that he later was associated with at the Massachusetts Agricultural College, Kenyon L. Butterfield, Roscoe W. Thatcher and Hugh P. Baker. Fred left the Michigan Agricultural College in 1907 and accepted a position as treasurer with the Massachusetts Agricultural College where he worked until his retirement in 1940.[200] On February 12, 1896 Fred married Miss

---

[199] Some accounts record Fred's birth as December 30, 1869.
[200] Massachusetts State College *Alumni Bulletin* 3 and the *Massachusetts Collegian*, December 7, 1939.

Cora Shan in Batavia, Michigan. The couple had three children: Irene E., Chester D. and George D. Kenney. After a long career at Massachusetts Agricultural College, Fred retired in 1939 and spent his retirement engaged in his favorite pursuit, hiking with the Metawampe Club. Fred Chester Kenney passed away on February 1, 1951 in Amherst, Massachusetts.

An image of the Dorian Literary Society after the fraternity acquired the home in 1920.

The Kenney residence was eventually sold to the Dorian Literary Society in 1920. In 1923, the Dorian Literary Society applied for a charter with Phi Kappa Tau, which was granted in 1924. The home was of a pretty standard design except for the third-floor dormer with the ornate scrollwork at the pediment. Because of the placement of the dormer the entire house seems off center, however it does have some wonderful ornamentation at the peak of the dormer. The porch, is an interesting design with the delicate three column corners and the double column support. The porch is also the strongest feature of the home. In 1898 Fred Kenney built his home between the Longyear home and the Mumford residence. "This season Mr. Kenney and Prof. Mumford have built houses north of Mr. Longyear's facing the east on the same street."[201] This assures that Thoman designed the Kenney residence. The home was torn down between 1966-1967.

---

[201] *The M.A.C. Record,* 9/13/1898.

CHACE NEWMAN HOME

240 Michigan, East Lansing, MI., image from 1944. (CADL/FPLA)

"Mr. Chas Newman, instructor of drawing; and Miss Emma A. Young of Portland were married there on Dec 28. They will be home after Mar. 1 in Mr. Newman's new house on the Delta." (*ICN* 1/5/1899).

Chace Newman 1872-1953 (MSU Archives)

Chace Newman was born in Portland, Michigan in 1872 to Frederick M. and Emma L. (née Chase) Newman. Little is known concerning Chace's childhood in Portland, but the Newman family were prominent citizens in Ionia County. Frederick for a time operated a gristmill in Portland. Chace attended the Michigan Agricultural College but never completed his studies and began working for the college in 1891. By 1897 Chace was the Assistant Foreman of the Wood Shop and was paid $500 per year, plus housing. In 1898, he was promoted to the position of Instructor in Mechanical Drawing and Assistant in Wood Work. The following year he married Miss Emma A. Young on December 28, 1898; the couple had three children: Harold, Phyllis J. and Ruth M. Newman. Three years later, in 1901 Chace was appointed Instructor in Mechanical Drawing. Chace spent his entire working life at the Michigan State College and in September of 1939 he retired and was named the Professor Emeritus of Engineering Drawing. For local historians, Chace Newman is remembered for his map of East Lansing, which he produced in 1913 and was included in William J. Beal's book on the *History of the Michigan Agricultural College*. Why is this map so important? It helped to unravel the street numbering system that was employed in East Lansing prior to 1920, oddly enough a system developed by Newman. Chace was active in politics and civic affairs; he served on East Lansing's first city council in 1907 and helped to establish the People's Church. Chace Newman passed away in a Lansing hospital on November 2, 1953 (*LSJ* 11/3/1953).

240 W. Michigan, East Lansing, MI., image from 1955. (CADL/FPLA)

One of the confusing factors of the Chace Newman home is that it resembles the Longyear residence, designed by Earl Mead. There is a pattern: both homes have a large and small dormer on the facade. The difference is the ornamentation of the dormers which were dissimilar. The Newman home has open gables on the large gable and the dormer while the Longyear home has partially closed gables. The fact that the *Ingham County News* from January 5, 1899 stating that Newman and his bride were moving into their new home assures that it was built in 1898 and therefore a Thoman designed home. The house was torn down in 1961.

JONATHAN SNYDER HOME

258 Michigan, East Lansing, MI. (CADL/FPLA)

"At the east end of the Delta Mrs. Backus has built a neat dwelling in which she can accommodate ten young women with board and rooms. Dr. Marshall's house is just west of this, and west of him Mr. Newman and President Snyder are building, the latter for Dr. Waterman."[202] This means the Snyder home was the last home that Thoman designed on the Delta in East Lansing.

---

[202] *The M.A.C. Record*, 9/13/1898.

Jonathan L. Snyder 1859-1919

Jonathan LeMoyne Snyder was born on a farm near Slippery Rock, Butler County, Pennsylvania on October 29, 1859. He spent his childhood on the family farm with his eleven brothers and sisters where he attended the rural school and completed his secondary school work at Grove City College. Jonathan completed his undergraduate degree at Westminster College in 1886 and five years later he was awarded a PhD in Philosophy from the same institution. After graduation Jonathan served two years as superintendent of the Butler County Schools, where he worked with the community to establish the Slippery Rock State Normal School. Later in 1889 as principal of the 5th Ward School in Alleghany, Pennsylvania, he established free kindergarten classes and established a manual training school. On June 15, 1892 Jonathan married Miss Clara M. Mifflin of North Washington, Pennsylvania and the couple had three children: Robert, LeMoyne and Plummer all of who attended the M.A.C. When Doctor Snyder was appointed President of the Michigan Agricultural College in 1896 it came as a shock to many. Snyder was just 37 years old, had no experience in College administration and was relatively unknown in Michigan. But under Snyder's guidance many changes took place at the M.A.C.; coursework for women was adopted, dormitories were established, enrollment grew from 300 students to over 2000 students under his leadership. He was a master at building partnerships and working with the legislative branch to gain the funding needed to grow and improve the college. After his resignation from the college in 1915 Snyder devoted himself to his family and helped to establish the People's Church. On October 22, 1919 Dr. Jonathan LeMoyne Snyder passed away at his home in East Lansing. His body laid in state at the college armory and funeral services were held on Friday, October 24, 1919. All classes were canceled Friday afternoon at the college and business in East Lansing closed out of respect for Dr. Snyder.[203]

---

[203] *M.A.C Record* 10/24/1919, *LSJ* 10/23/1919, *M.A.C Record* 10/31/1919, *The Wolverine* 1915.

258 Michigan, East Lansing, MI.
Note the large Widow's Walk on the roof. (East Lansing Public Library)

The Snyder home was an interesting design. It appears to be a typical American foursquare home, but if you look at the image closely it seems to be a hybrid of the French Second Empire and the standard American foursquare home. Notice how the shape of the roofline changes based upon the perspective. You can see a steep pitch to the roof, reminiscent of a Mansard roof, with a Widow's Walk plus the surrounding railings. The facade of the home and the stacking of the windows follows the traditional style and is rather plain. Except for the Widow's Walk there is little to set this home apart from its neighbors. The home was torn down in 1974-1975.

JENISON RESIDENCE

247 Delta, East Lansing, MI. (CADL/FPLA)

"A New residence is being erected on the Delta by Mrs. Mary Jenison" *ICN* 6/22/1899.

As will be outlined later, the Jenison home could not have been a happy house. Luther F. Jenison and Mary E. Burridge married in Lansing on October 28, 1891. This was not the first marriage for Luther. On August 22, 1883, Luther married Miss Helena E. Clark of Lansing, Michigan. Helena was the daughter of William M. Clark a local newspaper editor. It is unknown when the marriage between Luther and Helena was dissolved and the couple granted a divorce, because on November 3, 1890 Helena married Richard T. Kelley in Butte, Montana. One year later Luther married Miss Mamie (Mary) E. Burridge, a clerk at Horatio H. Larned's crockery store in Lansing. Mamie lived with her father George L. Burridge at 520 S. Capitol.[204]

---

[204] Mary's mother Annie E. (née Reed) Burridge was deceased.

Mary E. Burridge Jenison circa 1903. (CADL/FPLA)

The wedding of Luther and Mary was a large affair held at the home of Horatio Larned and the Reverend Charles H. Beale of Plymouth Congregational Church performed the wedding ceremony. Luther and Mary had two children, an infant daughter who died at birth in 1892 and a son, Larned Jenison who died in 1901 from complications after surgery to remove his appendix. Luther worked as a bookkeeper at several businesses in Lansing until accepting a position with the Michigan Agricultural College in 1896 as a bookkeeper.

In April of 1899, Luther purchased Lot 8 in the Delta Subdivision from the MAC Board of Trustees. Soon after the couple moved into their new home on the Delta their world came crashing down around them with the death of their son Larned. The couple remained together until 1910 when Luther and Mary divorced; Mary obtained a judgment against Luther for extreme cruelty. Luther moved to 350 E. Grand River and boarded with the Wyse family while Mary retained ownership of the home at 247 Delta. There was another troubling incident which occurred in Luther's life. Late in the afternoon of July 26, 1911, Jacob Schepers, Treasurer at the college, asked Luther about a $1,000 error in the footing of Jenison's "daily balance sheet".[205] Luther at first gave several evasive answers but Schepers kept up the pressure and reviewed Luther's other financial work. At that point, Luther admitted to Schepers that he had been embezzling funds and $3,580 had been taken (about $100,000 on today's money). Oddly enough, Luther was allowed to leave the office, while Schepers tried to locate Addison M. Brown, the Secretary of the College. When Brown met Schepers at 10:00 p.m. that evening they went in search of Luther but were unable to locate him. Mrs. Wyse, Luther's landlady, testified that Luther had been out most of the night and left the house again at 6:30 a.m. returning at 7:00 a.m. Mrs. Wyse heard Luther praying and reading chapters from the bible, then silence. A few moments later Mrs. Wyse was startled by a gunshot. Luther had shot himself in the heart with a .32-caliber revolver. A review of the accounts by Charles M. Turner revealed that

---

[205] The footing is the final balance when adding the debits and credits together.

the embezzlement began in early July of 1911 just after Luther had been informed that his contract as bookkeeper would not be renewed. Just why Luther began misappropriating funds is unexplained. Nor was it ever established where Luther went the night before the suicide. Did he seek Dutch courage? Or did he visit his ex-wife Mary? All that is known is that the funeral for Luther was held at his former home at 247 Delta and he was interred at Mt. Hope Cemetery. The lost funds became the responsibility of Jacob Schepers and Addison M. Brown who employed Luther without requiring a bond.[206] Mary Jenison lived for 43 years at her home at 247 Delta, renting rooms to students and professors as her main source of support. Mary Jenison was active in religious affairs; she was a member Plymouth Congregational Church and was the Secretary of the first Sunday school in East Lansing at the Peoples Church. On April 2, 1942 Mary E. Jenison passed away at her home, she was survived by two nephews Robert Y. and Edward S. Larned and one niece Mrs. Kate L. Runnels (*LSJ* 4/3/1942).

247 Delta, East Lansing, MI. (CADL/FPLA)

The saga of the Jenison family made for tragic but interesting reading. Essentially, the Jenison home could not be the third home designed on the Delta by Thoman simply because the lot was purchased by Luther in April of 1899, while the article describing Thoman's work on the Delta was published in July of 1898. The home was torn down sometime between 1956-1957.

---

[206] See the *LSJ* 7/27/1911 and the *Offices of Board of Trustees and President MAC, Meeting Minutes*, August 16, 1911.

CHISHOLM HOME

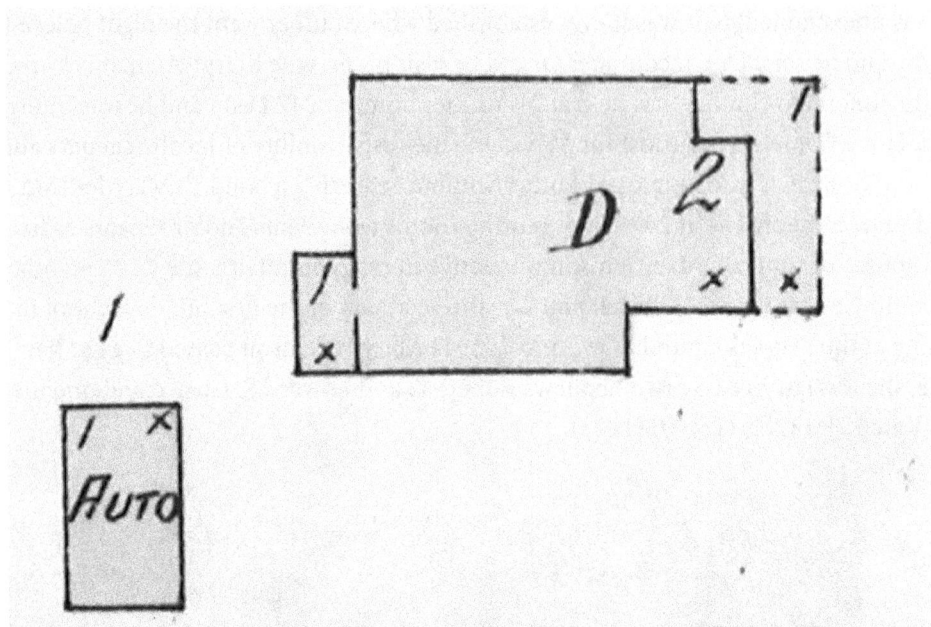

The Sanborn map drawing of 1700 S. Washington from 1913.

"Architect F.J. Thoman has let the contract for a $2,000 dwelling for D. Hewitt Chisholm on Sparrow ave. to Morse & Moore" (*SR* 8/25/1898).

If the information provided in the *State Republican* article from August 25, 1898 was correct then the Chisholm home was located at 1602 S. Washington Avenue. However, D. Hewitt Chisholm did not own the home at that address, he owned no property on Sparrow Avenue between 1896-1900. His wife Minnie, owned land in Lansing's old 6th Ward; the property that Minnie Chisholm held was located at Lot 1 Block 17 Park Place Subdivision or 1700 S. Washington Avenue, which she purchased in 1896 from Frederick W. Bertch for $600.[207] No image survives of 1700 S. Washington; the home was torn down circa 1928.

---

[207] *Ingham County Register of Deeds Liber 125 Page 136.*

1602 S. Washington, Lansing, MI. (CADL/FPLA)

However, 1602 S. Washington was a beautiful home, notice the half-moon stacked porch on the front of the residence and the small second floor porch. One of the striking elements of the home is the gradual increase in size of the dormers, they increase in size from left to right, characteristics I have not seen before in a home. The city of Lansing is much poorer because of the loss of 1602 S. Washington which was torn down circa 1962.

Dwight Hewitt Chisholm was born in Marshall, Michigan on July 31, 1856 to Thomas and Mary (née Hewitt) Chisholm. Dwight's early life was spent as a farmer in Marengo Township, Calhoun County, Michigan. On April 25, 1877, Dwight married Miss Minnie Rice in Marshall, Michigan, the couple had three sons; Earl H., Homer D., and Donald R. Chisholm. After the death of his mother, Dwight moved to Lansing where he worked in a variety of professions including traveling salesman and insurance agent. In 1900, he moved his family to Chicago where Dwight found employment with an iron manufacturer, and later in his life as a salesman. Dwight Hewitt Chisholm died in Chicago on November 23, 1924.

OLDS MOTOR WORKS PLANT

Olds Motor Company, 1808-1818 Jefferson Avenue, Detroit, MI., 1899. *DFP*

"The buildings plans for which are prepared and upon which work will begin at once will consist of a machine shop of two stories, 70 by 300 feet; a foundry 70 by 140 feet; a blacksmith shop 31 by 100 feet; and a double building, standing 400 feet back from the avenue, with a frontage of 179 feet, one-half of which will be used for the show room and the other half for offices. Space will be left on the riverfront for the erection, in the near future, of a plant devoted to the manufacture of marine engines. It is intended to have the works in operation by August 15, with a force of 150 men, which will soon be increased to 300. Within two years it is expected the output will reach $400,000 annually" (*DFP* 5/14/1899).

"Fred Thoman Jr., is making plans for three buildings in Detroit for the Olds Motor Co. The machinery building will be 300x70 feet, the finishing department 300x32 feet, and the show room and offices 170x50 feet. Work on these buildings will begin at once, and it is expected that the factory will be in full operation Aug. 15 employing from 100 to 150 men" (*SR* 5/15/1899).

"R.E. Olds took plans prepared by Architect Thoman for the building for the Detroit plant of the Olds' Motor Vehicle Co, to that city today. He will let the contract for its erection before he returns. Mr. Olds will be in Cleveland tomorrow" (*SR* 6/10/1899).

Olds Motor Company, Detroit, Michigan in 1899.
The factory to the right, at the back, was not part of the Olds plant. Notice that the *Detroit Free Press* drawing shows a two-story administrative structure at the front while the postcard image above, shows a three-story building. The structure ended up being three-stories.

The plant that Thoman designed for the Olds Motor Company in Detroit was, at the time, the culmination of factory design in the United States. It was the first factory specifically designed to produce automobiles. The buildings were long to maximize the production of the Curved Dash Olds in an economical manner, using a rudimentary assembly line. "The company will erect six large two-story buildings with a floor space of two and a half acres. The largest will be 70x330 feet, the next 50x170 feet, another 35x280 feet. Others are respectively 70x140, 50x65, 65x65. A number of others are smaller. They will be completed in 90 days" (*SR* 6/17/1899). The factory was rectangular with the administrative building facing Jefferson Avenue while the two wings each of two stories extended toward the Detroit River; a one-story building that connected both wings closed the rectangle. Because of the contours of the building site, the second floor of the two wings was level with the first floor of the administrative building, which explains why the 1901 fire was so destructive. Thoman used steel supports throughout the construction and tried to increase the amount of natural light that entered the production area using arched windows and skylights. From all the surviving images, the facade of the administrative building was quite plain, in fact it was sterile, and the entrance to the plant somewhat resembled an entrance to a prison.

The factory was located at the corner of Concord Street and Jefferson Avenue, which placed the plant in the 6600 Block of East Jefferson using today's address system. For Detroit residents, the plant was located near the old Uniroyal Tire Plant, just southwest of the Belle Isle Bridge. The address of the Olds plant kept changing because the city of Detroit expanded and modified its postal address street numbering system.[208]

---

[208] The original street numbering system in Detroit was built upon the one used in New York City; in January 1921 it changed to one based upon the Chicago system of numbering addresses. For example the address for the Olds Motor Works plant in 1899 was 1908 Jefferson Avenue, in 1901

Smoldering ruins of the Olds Motor Company in 1901, the image is of the entrance facing Jefferson Avenue. (CADL/FPLA)

THE OLDS WORKS WAS BURNED UP
Little Will Be Saved from the Wreck of the Extensive Concern
LANSING CONCERN ONCE
And Several from This City Were Employed in the Establishment
Special to the *State Republican*

Fire which broke out about 1:30 this afternoon in the rear of the Olds Motor works destroyed the big building razing the walls and burning out the floors and fixtures within a short time. Three men are badly injured and are now in the hospital. All the rest of the 150 to 200 employees who were in the building escaped in safety.

"The Olds Motor works 1308 Jefferson ave Detroit was entirely destroyed by fire shortly after noon today. Word was immediately received of the occurrence at the *State Republican*, the message giving little hope that anything will be saved from the extensive building of the famous manufacturing company. The Olds Co. began business on River st. in this city in 1880 in a frame building 18x26 feet, with one iron planer, one engine lathe and an old drill. In 1885, their first gasoline engine was put out, and a year so increased the demand that a new building, 24x110 feet was erected. Five years later another building was built, and since that time each year's trade has demanded from one to three new buildings. The Detroit plant, destroyed today, was completed over a year

---

the plant's address was 1808-1818 Jefferson Avenue.

ago, and covered four and a half acres of ground. The combined floor space of the Detroit and Lansing factories is 200,000 square feet. These factories are filled with modern machinery and equipment for producing the Olds patented stationary and marine gas engines, and motor carriages and trucks. The factory is one of the largest in the world for the manufacture of such products, and has offices in Philadelphia, Chicago, Omaha, Minneapolis and Los Angeles. Ransom Olds is the manager of the Detroit factory, and moved to that city from Lansing about a year ago. Horace Loomis, Roy Chapin, Harry Case, Edsel Brown, S.S. Olds Jr., Harry Cronkite, Jacob Siegist, Charles Ward, and other Lansing boys worked in the factory, which burned today. No one was injured, though several of the workmen narrowly escaped" (*SR* 3/9/1901).

The *Detroit Free Press* published a lengthy article in March of 1901 detailing the fire at the Olds Motor Works; portions of the article are reproduced below.

$72,700 Loss by Quick Fire at Olds Motor Factory Yesterday Afternoon

"Rush for your lives, the building is all on fire!" yelled one of the employees at the plant of the Olds Motor Works 1308-1318 Jefferson avenue, about 1:35 o'clock yesterday afternoon. Then followed a scene of the wildest excitement. Men dashed for every exit. Ten of the most nervous of them threw up the windows on the second and third floors and the crowd held its breath as the frantic employees climbed out and deliberately jumped or dropped to the ground. Only one was seriously injured, but four were removed to hospitals in ambulances. Fire department history recalls few such rapid fires in Detroit in a factory of this kind. The structure was in two sections and of brick. One had a frontage toward Jefferson avenue of 100 feet and this section extends back about 70 feet. The rear section was 50 feet wide and about 230 feet in depth, a court 50 feet wide being between the narrow section and the plant of the Detroit Stove Works. The front section was three stories high while the remaining portion of the building was but two stories. It was near the wash room on the west side and towards the rear of the main building that the fire originated. The cause? Several theories are advanced. Some say natural gas exploded; others talk of electricity, but an investigation seems to satisfy most of the firemen that an explosion of gasoline was the real cause. In fact, at least three explosions were certainly heard, according to statements of persons who were in the neighborhood at the time. The flames seem to have first swept towards the north and then taken a course towards the river. The conductor on an east bound Jefferson avenue line car was passing the scene when the fire broke out. Sixteen minutes later when he returned on his trip westward the walls had crumbled. To show the fierceness of the tongues of fire and the excessive heat, truck company No. 6 drove directly to the vacant lot in front of the building shortly after the alarm was turned in, and it was impossible to get closer to the structures than sixty feet. The necessary fleetness of those in the building can be easily appreciated when these facts are taken into consideration.

Building Not Strong

Apparently, the building was weak. The walls of the first story appeared to be about fourteen inches thick, but the upper walls were considerably narrower. Of course, the explosion may have had something to do with the great destruction, for a big portion of a manufacturing building to be ruined by fire in such a remarkably short space of time is a surprise to men whose business it is to save burning property. The Olds Motor Works employ in the neighborhood of 300 men, but fortunately, from a standpoint of life and death, not more than two dozen persons were in the building at the time, owing to the fact that the shop closed down at noon on Saturday. The loss to the draughtsmen, machinists and other mechanics will probably reach as high as $1,500, with very little insurance. Groups of these sufferers gathered about the doomed building and bewailed their losses yet congratulated one another on the fact that their lives had been spared. The Olds Motor Co. manufactured patent gas and gasoline launches and automobiles. The firm's damage is estimated at $65,000, which includes the damage on stock, very costly machinery and the building. Aside from the actual loss occasioned by the fire, the business of the company will be in such shape that the loss cannot be figured in dollars and cents. However, the Lansing branch will assist the local plant in meeting urgent orders. The narrower section of the main building was the machinery shop and the flames certainly played havoc there. Adjoining this part of the plant at the south end and to the east is the forging department and strange enough the water seems to have caused the principal damage here. The powerful streams from the fireboat stopped the flames in their angry efforts to cross the railroad tracks and reach the foundry and that building was not damaged. The wide court between the Olds building and that of the stove concern tended to prevent the flames from making any headway in the latter structure. The water, however, caused no little amount of damage in the mounting rooms, where there is a large quantity of stove plate as well as stoves ready to be made or already mounted. The damage may reach $5,000. The building was only slightly burned. The wind was blowing towards the south and west. The plant of the Peninsular Iron Co. is in this direction from the doomed building and the roof of the boiler house and the top house of the iron company was damaged to the probable extent of $1,000. The long brick barn, owned by the United Railway Co., to the west was visited by the flames, but the roof alone was burned, and the damage will not exceed $200. It is understood that, with the exception of the personal losses of the workmen, the total damage is about $72,000 and is fully covered by insurance.

Ruins of the Olds Motor Company in Detroit after the fire in 1901. Notice the bent steel girders and floor ties and the side walls. There is no indication of a concrete floor being in place. (CADL/FPLA)

Four Severely Injured

Out of the number of men who jumped to escape the fury of the flames four were less fortunate than their co-workers receiving injuries which while not necessarily dangerous are extremely painful. Robert T. Prong, who lives at 56 Division street, is probably the most seriously hurt. He was at work in the finishing department on the third floor of the structure but was delayed in getting to the front. When he reached the open window, the flames were licking up everything back of him in furious style, and there was nothing for him to do but leap. In jumping he seemed to lose control of himself and fell on the frozen ground with great force. At St. Mary's Hospital, it was found that his left arm was broken, and his hip dislocated. He was resting easy last night and unless injuries of an internal nature develop he will recover.[209] Andrew W. Peterson, who lives at 485 Plummer avenue, was also in the finishing room, when the alarm was given. He was obliged to jump through the window and landed heavily on his feet in such a manner that both ankles were broken. He was taken to St. Mary's Hospital. Herbert S. Smith, foreman of the finishing department was among the last to leave the burning building, and almost before

---

[209] Robert T. Prong survived his injuries and is listed in the1910 Census as well as the 1910 and 1912 *Detroit City Directories* as a plant foreman.

he was carried away the walls were falling. He was taken to Harper hospital where he now lies with a badly sprained back and right ankle. His home is at 445 Hubbard avenue. William Van Every, of Birmingham, 23 years of age, in jumping from the third story, broke the instep of his right foot, and was taken to Harper hospital. There were several others shaken up, and bruised slightly, but all were able to get home unassisted.

Detroit Fire Boat James Battle ☺

The first alarm was received at 1:37 o'clock, and James J. Brady, a young employee in the office, turned in by phone. Battalion Chief Kelly, who was the first officer in charge, sent in a second and third alarm at 1:45 o'clock. The fireboat James Battle made an excellent run, and the businessmen in the community were enthusiastic over the boat's good work. In fact, for such a quick fire, the department did excellent service in protecting the adjoining property. In all there were eight engines and three trucks at the fire.

Electrical Autos Were Ready

W.G. Murray, manager of the automobile department was in the building at the time the fire started and he was able to give the clearest idea of the number of men in the building at the time. He could not assign any cause for the fire, but did not deny that a gasoline explosion might have occurred. 'We do not run at all on Saturday afternoon,' he said, 'although there were a few men in my department getting out work that was imperative'. They, with a few in the finishing department and the regular office force constitute all that were in the building, and I believe all got out safely. My department will no doubt suffer the greatest loss, as there were any number of machines nearly completed. We have been experimenting with electrical automobiles for the past two years and this year we were getting ready to put them on the market. We had orders for several months ahead, many of which were started and other nearing completion. The automobile department was stocked with all parts of the machine, and we were running a full force of men assembling them. But one machine was saved, and that is one that the company has been running. In one portion of the building there were twenty of more machines almost ready for the market that are totally destroyed" (*DFP* 3/10/1901).

Olds Factory to be Constructed After Former Plans

"The buildings of the Olds Motor Co. at the corner of Jefferson and Concord avenues in Detroit, which were destroyed by fire a few days ago, will be rebuilt at once, in accordance with the original plans, which were prepared by Architect E.A. Bowd.[210] The buildings will cost about $40,000" (*LJ* 3/18/1901).

The Olds plant in Detroit was never rebuilt, the business was moved to Lansing where Darius Moon designed the new plant buildings. Frederick Thoman's career as an architect ended with the destruction of the Olds Motor Works. There is no record of Thoman designing another structure after the fire. Just why Thoman gave up his career as an architect may never be known. The Detroit newspapers' criticisms of the plant's design may have been a factor, or it may have been a personal reaction by Thoman to the injuries suffered to the men who worked at the plant, although there were no fatalities. Thoman's design of the Olds Plant was criticized in the *Detroit Free Press*, which felt that the building was not strong given that the walls narrowed on the second story. Based upon the information in the two photographs published above, the *Detroit Free Press's* statement that the building was not strong was incorrect. It was quite common in the method of factory architecture employed at that time to have a wider wall on the lower level to support the load of the second floor, that is why the wall narrows as the wall rises. Albert and Julius Kahn revolutionized factory design with the use of reinforced concrete with the construction of Building 10 at the Detroit Packard Plant in 1905 and later employed the same method at the Ford's Highland Park plant and in countless other factories. The Olds Plant in Detroit did employ steel columns and trusses to support the flooring on the second story. The use of steel in this manner was innovative at that time, but if done incorrectly may have contributed to the destruction of the plant. Because of the nature of the steel manufactured in the later 19th Century, the steel needed to be shielded from heat, either by bricks or concrete. When unshielded steel was exposed to the heat from a fire, the steel would twist and fail. You can see the twisted steel and the bent support columns in the image labeled Ruins of the Olds Motor Company. The other factor was the manner in which the floor was constructed. There was no indication that concrete was employed in the construction of the flooring on the second story, which indicated that wood was used, and this posed a problem. Thoman must have used a slow burning wood floor, as opposed to joisted floor. A slow burning wood floor was built with

---

[210] In 1904, Bowd designed the REO Plant for R.E. Olds in Lansing.

a tongue and groove subflooring with wood boards laid in the opposite direction as the surface. This prevented fire from quickly spreading in a building unless there was an accelerant like gasoline, that would increase the intensity of the fire. The structured also contained many ramps and doors for moving equipment and vehicles between workshops and floors which allowed the flames to move rapidly between the levels. With unshielded steel supports, wood flooring and a gasoline fire the building was doomed. So, in a sense Thoman's attempt to use modern building materials resulted in, given the right set of circumstances, the potential for failure.[211]

Was Frederick Thoman a significant architect in Michigan History? The answer is simple, no, his career ended too soon. Thoman's plans for homes were workman like and fairly plain, but in the area of commercial and industrial buildings Thoman demonstrated an ability for growth. Compare the design of the Wentworth Hotel to that of the Leasia building in Williamston and you will see an improvement in the design from one building to the next. With the Olds Motor Works plant in Detroit, Thoman worked closely with Ransom Olds to develop a manufacturing plant that implemented Olds' ideas on creating a movable assembly line, which was improved upon and perfected by Henry Ford.[212] Throughout his career as an architect, Thoman demonstrated an ability to learn and improve his architectural plans; it is unfortunate that Frederick J. Thoman chose to end his career as an architect; based upon his work, he had a remarkable talent for improving his architectural vision.

---

[211] See Gordon, 297 for an outline on the different methods of factory construction.

[212] Henry Ford and Ransom E. Olds were rivals and competitors in the early years of the automobile business, but they also were good friends and remained so throughout their lives. The bond between the two was formed early in their careers when Ford and Olds met in Detroit. Ford used to visit the Olds Motor Company plant in Detroit where the two pioneers certainly spoke about automobile production but also their views on their workers lives. Henry Ford created the Sociological Department at Ford Motor Company to monitor his workers' lives while Ransom later built the REO Clubhouse, a place where his employees and their families could go for good clean entertainment. Undoubtedly when Ford visited the Olds Motor Company plant he observed the crude production line that was employed at the factory. Did Olds create the automobile assembly line? Yes, but not in the efficient manner that Ford later implemented. Did Olds care that Ford received the credit? No. Why? Because they were friends. The automobile industry was in its early stages and not unlike the early development of the Internet it was more about the exchange of ideas rather than the profit driven companies that resulted.

❧APPENDIX A❧

APPLEYARD AND GLAISTER HOMES

Richard Glaister's home at 402 S. Walnut, Lansing, MI.

There has always been some question as to who the architect of the Richard Glaister residence was. I believe that the architect of the Glaister residence was James Appleyard. Richard Glaister was a master stonemason who served as the Superintendent of Stone Work on the new Michigan State Capitol, while James Appleyard served as the Supervisor of Construction for the Capitol. Essentially James was Richard's supervisor. The two men were friends, and both men decided to remain in Lansing after the construction of the state Capitol. In 1876, both men began to build their homes while the Capitol was still under construction. James Appleyard's home was located at 123 N. Walnut while the Glaister's residence was situated at 402 S. Walnut. James Appleyard undoubtedly designed his own home; he had the experience and skills to successfully plan and build the house, there always was a rumor, unsubstantiated, that both Appleyard and Glaister used rejected materials from the state capitol building site in the construction of their homes. It needs to be mentioned that no clear image of James Appleyard's home survives.

An aerial view of James Appleyard's home at 123 N. Walnut.

You can observe in the above image that the Appleyard home was in the rough shape of a cross, notice the short end of the cross to the right, the placement of three windows on the second story on the front gable roof end and the location of the chimneys, one to the left, two on center and one to the front right.

The Glaister home, 402 S. Walnut, notice the lack of windows on the south gable end.

There is another factor that needs to be mentioned; in both the Glaister and Appleyard homes there were no windows on the south gable end, first and second floors. This is a similarity to obvious too be ignored.

A view of Appleyard's home, 123 N. Walnut, there are no clear images of the home. Notice the lack of windows on the south gable.

In the above image, you can clearly make out the three windows on the second floor as well as the Oculus [round] window at the base of the gable. There was also an extensive wrap around porch on the first floor.

An aerial view of Richard Glaister's home at 402 S. Walnut.

In the above aerial photograph, you can observe the same chimney pattern as the Appleyard house except that the rear chimney is off-center. It is significant that the home has the same short cross layout as the Appleyard home. Also, if you compare the porch layouts in the images of both homes you can observe the wrap around porch on both structures. In the next you can see that the porch was removed from Glaister's home, you can just make out the former outline of the porch along the brickwork. In the first image of Glaister's home at the beginning of Appendix A you can see the full extent of the porch.

Richard Glaister's home at 402 S. Walnut, notice how the porch has changed but the marking on the brickwork provide an outline of where the wrap around porch was.

In the above image of the Glaister's home in the 1940s, you still could distinguish the markings where the wrap around porch was removed. So, what does this all mean? The aerial footprints of the homes are almost identical, they both displayed a similar window, chimney and porch placement, together with the absence of windows on the south gable are all factors that point to the same architect designing both homes. If you accept the premise that James Appleyard was an experienced builder and designer, then James designed the Glaister residence. In the early 1870s in Lansing the only practicing architect was Israel Gillett, there is a possibility that Israel planned both homes, but no information has been discovered to substantiate that he was the architect for the structures.

It is conceivable that Elijah E. Myers designed both homes, but that is doubtful given Myers' ego and James refusal to work with Myers on later projects. One of the enduring myths in Lansing is that Darius Moon was the architect for both the Appleyard and Glaister residences. This is high questionable; Moon was still working as contractor during this period and was a relatively unknown. The only homes Moon had built in Lansing prior to 1880 was his own double house on Logan Street (now Martin Luther King Jr. Blvd) and a residence for Charles J. Olin on River Street and it is unclear if he designed the Olin home, or just acted as the contractor.

320

An image of the north side of the Appleyard home. Notice the side entrance is located after the bay window, while on the Glaister home the side entrance was before the bay window. See the earlier images of the Glaister home. (CADL/FPLA)

It is conceivable that Elijah E. Myers designed both homes, but that is doubtful given Myers' ego and James refusal to work with Myers on later projects. One of the enduring myths in Lansing is that Darius Moon was the architect for both the Appleyard and Glaister residences. This is highly questionable; Moon was still working as a contractor during this period and was a relatively unknown. The only homes Moon had built in Lansing prior to 1880 was his own double house on Logan Street (now Martin Luther King Jr. Blvd) and a residence for Charles J. Olin on River Street and it is unclear if he designed the Olin home, or just acted as the contractor.

Both the Appleyard and Glaister residences were built traditional and in a well-known architectural style, one that James was familiar with, based upon James' years of work in the construction field. One other factor: frankly it was expensive to employ an architect, when you consider James' and Richard's salary in the 1870s, the cost of engaging an architect may have been prohibitive. Likely, James Appleyard was the architect for both houses given their traditional design, his experience as a builder and the cost both men would have incurred if they employed an architect. The Appleyard home was torn down in May of 1956. (*LSJ* 4/30/1956)

❧APPENDIX B❧

GEORGE APPLEYARD

The Strand Theater in Alma, Michigan, originally the Idlehour Theater designed by
George T. Appleyard.

Although the book has a focus on William Appleyard, James Appleyard had another son,
George, who followed him into the contracting business and eventually became an
architect. George T. Appleyard was a distinguished building contractor for many years in
Grand Rapids, Michigan. What has never been recognized is that George was the

323

uncredited architect on many of the buildings where he is listed as the contractor. George was born in New York, on February 12, 1861 to James and Johanna Appleyard. In 1871, James moved his family to Detroit and then relocated to Lansing in 1872 where he supervised the construction of the Michigan State Capitol. George attended the Michigan Agricultural College and later Sandwich College in Canada.[213] On September 16, 1891, George married Miss Bertha Patterson; the couple had two sons George T. and John J. Appleyard.

George as well as his brother William worked with their father in the role of construction supervisor in the building of the Union Trust Building and the Fort Street Union Passenger Station, both buildings were in Detroit, Michigan. George and his wife moved to Grand Rapids in 1893-1894 where George appeared in the 1894 *Grand Rapids City Directory* as George Applegard, architect. Eventually George partnered with William J. Hayden and the construction firm of Hayden, Appleyard & Company General Contractors was formed. Charles T. Johnson was also a member of the firm, later George and Charles purchased William's share of the business and the Appleyard, Johnson Company was established. Part of the terms of the sale was that the new company absorb the $10,000 debt of the old company. Appleyard and Johnson could never overcome this debt and declared bankruptcy in 1913. (*GRP* 10/20/1920) After the bankruptcy, George hung up his shingle as an architect, he is known to have designed in Grand Rapids the addition to the Hespolsheimer's Department Store, the Globe Knitting Company, the Johnson Furniture Factory, the Idlehour Theater in Alma, Michigan and at least fifty other buildings in the Grand Rapids area along with several more throughout the state. George's architectural/contracting work would make a noteworthy book. What is not recognized is that George was also responsible for the design of several buildings he served as the general contractor. The W.S. Winegar Storage Warehouse, the Grand Rapids Underwear Company and the Grand Rapids Cigar Company factory are just a few of the examples of his work. George T. Appleyard died at his home in Grand Rapids on April 18, 1920.[214]

---

[213] Sandwich College was likely Assumption College, later Assumption University which became part of the University of Windsor in 1963.
[214] *GRH* 11/1/1914, *GRP* 4/19/1920 and *GRH* 4/20/1920

❧BIBLIOGRAPHY❧

PRINT WORKS

Aldinger, Frederick C., *The History and Growth of the Lansing School District*. Vol. 1. Lansing: Board of Education, n.d. Print.

American architect and building news. Vol. 18. Boston: James R. Osgood, 1885. Print.

American Journal of Agricultural Economics 20.3 (1938). Print.

Baker, Henry B. *Thirteenth Annual Report of the Secretary of the State Board of Health of the State of Michigan: ... for the fiscal year ending Sept. 30, 1885*. Lansing: Thorp & Godfrey, 1886. Print.

Barnard, F. A. *American Biographical History of Eminent and Self-made Men ... Michigan Volume*. Vol. 2. Cincinnati,: Western Biographical, 1878. Print.

Beal, W. J. *History of the Michigan Agricultural College and Biographical Sketches of Trustees and Professors*. East Lansing: Agricultural College, 1915.

Biennial Report of the Board of Commissioners of the Michigan School for the Blind.: By Authority. Vol. 2. Lansing : W.S. George &, State Printers and Binders., 1885. Print.

Brief History of the Industrial School for Boys, Lansing, Michigan, 1902. Lansing, Mich.: [Press of the Industrial School for Boys], 1902. Print.

Brooks, John A., ed. *Michigan Reports: Cases Decided in the Supreme Court of Michigan*. 1st ed. Vol. 119. Chicago: Callaghan &, 1900. Print.

Burton, Clarence Monroe, William Stocking, and Gordon K. Miller. *The City of Detroit, Michigan, 1701-1922*. 5 vols. Detroit-Chicago: S.J. Clarke Pub., 1922. Print.

Carpenter, Rolla C., and Herman Diederichs. *Internal Combustion Engines, Their Theory, Construction and Operation*. New York: Van Nostrand, 1908. Print.

Carpenter, Rolla C. *Heating and Ventilating Buildings. A Manual for Heating Engineers and Architects*. New York: J. Wiley and Sons, 1895. Print.

Carter, Charles Simeon, 1846-. *History of the Class of '70: Department of Literature, Science and the Arts,* University of Michigan. Supplement, 1903-1921. Milwaukee, Wis.: Published by authority of the Class, 1921.

Carter, Frank, ed. *The Michigan Manufacturer*. 26th ed. Vol. 5. Detroit: Pick Publications, 1910. Print.

Chicago Bar Association Record. Vol. 4. Chicago, IL: Chicago Bar Association, 1921. Print.

Ching, Frank. *A Visual Dictionary of Architecture*. Van Nostrand Reinhold, 1997.

Cowles, Albert E. *Past and Present of the City of Lansing and Ingham County, Michigan: Together with Biographical Sketches of Many of Its Leading and Prominent Citizens and Illustrious Dead*. N.p.: Michigan Historical Pub. Association, 1905.

Creecy, John. *A Century at Harbor Point, 1878-1978*. Grosse Pointe Farms, MI: Madrus, 1978. Print.

Detroit City Council. Historic Designation Advisory Board. "*Proposed New Center Area Historic District.*" City of Detroit, pp. 1–17. Print.

Detroit City Directories, various years.

Documents of the Assembly of the State of New York: One Hundred and Twelfth Session, 1889. Vol. 2. Albany: Troy, Printers, 1889. Print.

Donnelly, Walter A., et al. *The University of Michigan: an Encyclopedic Survey: The Libraries; The Press, The Museums and Collections, The School of Public Health, The Institutes; Television and Broadcasting, The Buildings and Lands*. Vol. 8, The University of Michigan Press, 1956.

Educators of Michigan Biographical. Chicago, IL: J.H. Beers, 1900. Print.

Emery, Sarah EV. *Seven Financial Conspiracies Which Have Enslaved the American People*. Lansing: Launt Thompson, 1887. Print.

Fisher, Ernest B., ed. *Grand Rapids and Kent County, Michigan: Historical Account of Their Progress from First Settlement to the Present Time*. Vol. 2. Chicago: Robert O. Law, 1918. Print.

Fisher, David, and Frank Little. *Compendium of History and Biography of Kalamazoo County, Mich*. Chicago: A.W. Bowen, 1906. Print.

Forty-Sixth Annual Report of the Superintendent of Public Instruction of the State of Michigan. N.p.: W.S. George, 1883. Print.

Golden Age Mine: Preliminary Assessment Report. Boise: Idaho Department of Environmental Quality, 2008. Print.

Gordon, Robert B., and Patrick M. Malone. *The Texture of Industry an Archaeological View of the Industrialization of North America*. New York: Oxford UP, 1994. Print.

Grand Rapids City Directories, various years.

Harold, Steve. *Know Your Schools*. Manistee: League of Women Voters of Manistee County, 1979. Print. Manistee Area Public Schools

Hinsdale, B. A. *History of the University of Michigan 1837-1900*. Ann Arbor: Published by the University, 1906.

Ingham County Register of Deeds, Deed Books various years.

Iron Age. Vol. 103. New York: David Williams, 1919. Print.

Jackson City Directories, various years.

Lansing City Directories, various years.

Lansing Improvement Association. *Lansing, the capital of Michigan: its advantages, natural and acquired, as a center of trade and manufactures, showing how it is to become the commercial and financial, as well as the political capital of a great state*. Lansing, MI , W. S. George, 1873.

Leach, Josiah Granville. *Chronicles of the Bement Family in America for Clarence Sweet Bement.* Philadelphia: Publisher Not Identified, 1928. Print.

Lowery, David Thomas. *Perry Michigan: It's History in Pictures 1850-1913.* Williamston: Fletcher Printing, 1998. Print.

Lowrey, David Thomas. *Perry, Michigan: It's History in Pictures: 1914-1950.* Perry, MI: D. T. Lowrey, 2001. Print.

MAC Record. Lansing, Mich: Agricultural College. Print.

Maclean, James V. *Darius B. Moon: The History of a Michigan Architect 1880-1910.* Lansing, MI. SoloVerso, 2015. Print.

MacLean, James, V. "Re: Question." Message to Mark Frost, Dover Museum. 14 May 2009. E-mail.

Men of Progress: Embracing Biographical Sketches of Representative Michigan Men; with an Outline History of the State. Detroit, MI: Published by the Evening News Association, 1900. Print.

Massachusetts State College Alumni Bulletin XXII.4 (1940): n. pag. Print.

Michigan Historical Collections. Vol. 13. Lansing: W.S. George, 1877. Print.

Michigan Historical Collections. Vol. 29. Lansing: W.S. George, 1877. Print.

Mitchell, James J. *Detroit in History and Commerce a Careful Compilation of the History, Mercantile and Manufacturing Interests of Detroit: Illustrated with Views of the City's Principal Streets, Points of Interest, Prominent Buildings and Portraits of Its Noted Business Men.* Detroit, MI: Rogers & Thorpe, 1891. Print.

National Archives and Records Administration, Records of Public Building Service, Record Group 121.

Notre Dame Scholastic VII. 10 (1873): 75-80. Print

Offices of Board of Trustees and President MAC, Meeting Minutes.

Ohio historic places dictionary. Vol. 2. Hamburg, MI: State History Publications, 2008. Print.

Old and New House Numbers: New House Numbers Effective January 1st, 1921. Detroit: Dept. of Public Works, 1920. Print.

Peeke, Hewson L. *A Standard History of Erie County, Ohio: An Authentic Narrative of the Past, with Particular Attention to the Modern Era in the Commercial, Industrial, Civic, and Social Development. A Chronicle of the People, with Family Lineage and Memoirs.* Vol. 2. Chicago: Lewis Pub., 1916. Print.

Portrait and Biographical Album of Ingham and Livingston Counties, Michigan,. Chicago: Chapman Bros., 1891. Print.

Prince, Benjamin F., ed. *A Standard History of Springfield and Clark County, Ohio; an Authentic Narrative of the Past, with Particular Attention to the Modern Era in the Commercial, Industrial, Educational, Civic and Social Development.* Vol. 2. Chicago and New York: American Historical Society, 1922. Print.

Record of Deeds: Land Transactions of the Lansing School District from 1843 to 1980. Lansing: Lansing School District, 1980. Print.

Stanford, Linda Oliphant, and C. Kurt Dewhurst. *MSU Campus-- Buildings, Places, Spaces: Architecture and the Campus Park of Michigan State University.* East Lansing: Michigan State UP, 2002. Print.

"Synopsis of Building News." *Inland Architect and News* 29.5 (1897): 50. Print.

Towar, James DeLoss. *History of the City of East Lansing.* East Lansing, MI: East Lansing Public Library, 1933. Print.

Transactions of the State agricultural society of Michigan: with reports of county agricultural societies, for the year 1849-59. Vol. 5. Lansing, MI: Michigan State Agricultural Society, 1853. Print.

Turner, Frank N., and George N. Fuller. *An Account of Ingham County from Its Organization.* [Dayton, Ohio]: National Historical Association, 1924. Print.

Twenty-Fifth Annual Report of the Secretary of the State Board of Agriculture of the State of Michigan. Vol. 25. Lansing: Thorp & Godfrey, 1896. Print.

Universalist Church Meeting Minutes. Lansing Universalist Society.

Wineberg, Susan, and Patrick McCauley. *Historic Ann Arbor: an Architectural Guide.* Ann Arbor Historical Foundation, 2014.

Wolverine. East Lansing: Michigan State College of Agriculture, 1915. Print.

Youngstrand, Charles Oscar. *A gallery of pen sketches in black and white of our Michigan friends "as we see 'em,".* Detroit: W. Graham Printing Co., 1905. Print.

Ypsilanti City, Michigan, Tax Assessment Rolls 3rd Ward 1898

NEWSPAPERS

Allegan Gazette, Michigan
Alpena Argus, Michigan
Ann Arbor Argus-Democrat, Michigan
Arizona Republic, Arizona
Augusta Beacon, Michigan
Buffalo Enquirer, New York
Charlotte Tribune, Michigan
Chicago Daily Tribune, Illinois
Cincinnati Enquirer, Ohio
City Pulse, Michigan (LCP)
Daily Democrat, Indiana
Detroit Evening News, Michigan
Detroit Free Press, Michigan (DFP)
Detroit News, Michigan (DN)
Detroit News Tribune, Michigan (DNT)

Fremont Journal, Ohio
Grand Rapids Herald, Michigan (GRH)
Grand Rapids Press, Michigan (GRP)
Grosse Pointe Review, Michigan
Hawke's Bay Herald, New Zealand
Holyoke Times, Massachusetts
Ingham County Democrat, Michigan (ICD)
Ingham County News Michigan (ICN)
Jackson Citizen Patriot, Michigan (JCP)
Lansing Capital News, Michigan (LCN)
Lansing Evening Press, Michigan (LEP)
Lansing Journal, Michigan (LJ)
Lansing Republican, Michigan (LR)
Lansing Republican Weekly, Michigan (LRW)
Lansing Republican Semi-Weekly, Michigan (LRSW)
Lansing State Journal, Michigan (LSJ)
Leslie Local Republican, Michigan
Manistee Advocate, Michigan
Manistee Democrat, Michigan
Manistee Sentinel, Michigan
Manistee Weekly Times, Michigan
Manistee Advocate, Michigan
Marshall Statesman, Michigan
Massachusetts Collegian
Morning Oregonian, Oregon
Nevada State Journal (NSJ)
New York Times (NYT)
Niles Daily Star, Michigan
Oakland Tribune, California)
Owosso Times, Michigan
Pantagraph, Bloomington, Illinois
Post Standard, Syracuse, New York
Prescott Journal-Miner, Arizona
Saginaw News, Michigan (SN)
Salt Lake Mining Review, Utah
Sandusky Daily Star, Ohio
Sandusky Daily Register, Ohio
Sandusky Register, Ohio
Sandusky Star Journal, Ohio
South Bend Tribune, Indiana
State Republican, Michigan (SR)
St. Louis Post Dispatch, Missouri (SLPD)
Times-Picayune, New Orleans, Louisiana

ELECTRONIC RESOURCES

Ancestry Library Edition. http://www.ancestry.com/

Death Certificate for George H. St. John, 27 February 1936, State Office No., 207057, Michigan Department of Health.

Edwards, Elaine. "A Cool Place Named Oxley. Yeah, O-x-l-e-y." *Windsor Then Windsor Now*. N.p., 27 July 2012. Web. 25 Mar. 2015.

Family Search. http://www.familysearch.org/

Find a Grave. http://www.findagrave.com/

HathiTrust. http://www.hathitrust.org/

Interment.net. http://www.interment.net/

Kissane, Joseph A. William Kissane Rogers – A Forgotten Anti-Hero from Another Time. https://temelec.files.wordpress.com/2014/10/william-kissane-rogers-journal-version.pdf

Measuring Worth. http://measuringworth.com

Michigan County Histories and Atlases. http://quod.lib.umich.edu/m/micounty/

Michigan Department of Community Health, Genealogical Death Indexing System http://www.mdch.state.mi.us/gendisx/search2.htm

Sanborn Maps Library Edition. http://www.sanborn.com/

Seeking Michigan. http://seekingmichigan.org/

Transactions of the State Agricultural Society, with…, Volume 5; 1853/ Hathi Trust. https://babel.hathitrust.org/cgi/pt?id=miun.ajq5427.0005.001.

❧INDEX❧

Case, Daniel L., 72
Chaney, Louise B., 184
Chapin, Charles H., 117-118
Charlotte, MI.
    416 Lawrence, 174
Chicago, IL.
    Post Office, 1
Chisholm, Dwight Hewitt, 304-305
Chittenden & Clark Contractor, 151
Chittenden, Charles M., 18, 27
Christopher, Edith M., 173
Churchill, Judson, 279
City National Bank,
    Lansing, MI., 198
Clark School, 517 W. Kalamazoo, 36
Clark, Helena E., 301
Cleveland & Ward Contractors, 115
Clute, Oscar, 115
Compton, Morris, 270
Conlisk, Wallace T., 259-260
Coolidge, Elisha, 145
Coolidge, Emily M., 118
Crane, Isaac M., 189
Crosby, Lena, 286
Crotty, John F., 9
Cumback Motor Company, 131
Cumback, O.R., 131

❧ D ❧

Dakin, Jacob, 289
Davis, Charles Hurd, 30
Davis, Charles J., 37-40
DeGroff, Inez, 175
Denison, Rolin C., 166
Derby, James D., 152
Detroit Commercial Car Company, 130-131
Detroit Package Wagon, 130-131
Detroit, MI.,
    116 Delaware, 201
    121 Hazelwood, 220
    127 Woodland, 250
    135 Delaware, 212
    220 Chandler, 215
    2417 Pennsylvania, 223
    247 King, 252
    3600 Woodward, 267
    3661 Third, 225
    4428 Second, 234
    4605 Cass, 203
    509 Chandler, 229

    51 Seward, 247
    521 Chandler, 265
    550 King, 269
    600 Larned, 244
    628 Pingree, 204
    64 Horton, 226
    650 Van Dyke, 210
    655 Hazelwood, 219
    66 Hazelwood, 237
    748 Seminole, 207
    82 Hazelwood, 218
    89 Woodward, 260
    City Hall, 4
    Union Depot, 3
Dewey, Marian, 81
Diehl, Charles R., 270
Dorian Literary Society, 294
Dorr, Adam Lansing, 8-9, 126
Doty, Sarah A., 85
Downey, Charles P., 181-182
Durant, William C., 182

❧ E ❧

East Lansing, MI.,
    205 Delta, 291
    214 Michigan, 287
    223 Delta, 293
    224 Michigan, 282
    235 Delta, 285
    240 Michigan, 295
    247 Delta, 301
    258 Michigan, 298
Eaton, Orsmus, 166
Edbrooke, Willoughby James, 141
Edmonds, James P., 9, 144-145, 165
Edmonds, John W., 6, 144-145
Ellair, Archie G., 218
Elliott, George W., 285
Emery, Sara Vandervoort, 29
Emery, Wesley, 29, 102
Ennis, William, 73-74

❧ F ❧

Fallis, Edward Oscar, 52
Farwell, James V., 3
Fields, Eleanor P. Smith , 155
Finsthwait, Rillie, 162
First Presbyterian Church
    Lansing, MI., 104

✣ABOUT THE AUTHOR✣

James MacLean is Head of Community Outreach at the Capital Area District Libraries and a graduate of the University of Detroit. He holds a Masters in Library Science and an MA in History, both from Wayne State University. James is the co-author of *Lansing: City on the Grand 1836-1939* and the author of *Darius B. Moon: The History of a Michigan Architect 1880-1910*.

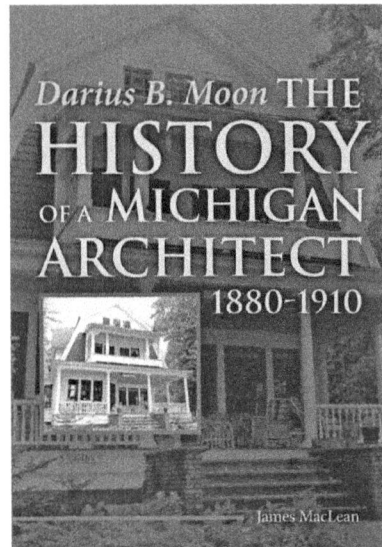

Titles available on Amazon.com

www.ingramcontent.com/pod-product-compliance
Lightning Source LLC
Chambersburg PA
CBHW062033090426
42740CB00016B/2898